# Modeling and Analysis of Dependable Systems

## A Probabilistic Graphical Model Perspective

# Modeling and Analysis of Dependable Systems

## A Probabilistic Graphical Model Perspective

**Luigi Portinale**
**Daniele Codetta Raiteri**
University of Piemonte Orientale, Italy

 World Scientific

NEW JERSEY · LONDON · SINGAPORE · BEIJING · SHANGHAI · HONG KONG · TAIPEI · CHENNAI

*Published by*

World Scientific Publishing Co. Pte. Ltd.

5 Toh Tuck Link, Singapore 596224

*USA office:* 27 Warren Street, Suite 401-402, Hackensack, NJ 07601

*UK office:* 57 Shelton Street, Covent Garden, London WC2H 9HE

**British Library Cataloguing-in-Publication Data**
A catalogue record for this book is available from the British Library.

ISBN 978-981-4612-03-6

Printed in Singapore

*To my father Domenico, who did not have the possibility of viewing this book.*
*To Maura, Lorenzo and Gaia, who are definitely more important than any book or paper: you have patiently tolerated my busy time during the writing of this book. I owe you a debt of gratitude.*

Luigi Portinale


*To my family.*

Daniele Codetta Raiteri

# Preface

For many physical systems (e.g., computer systems, computer networks, industrial plants, etc.) one of the most important property is definitely the *system dependability*. Dependability is a property involving several different aspects concerning the behavior of a system, such as reliability, availability, safety and security among the others. The main perception when thinking about a dependable system is to consider a system that does not fail during its regular activity. From the point of view of a system user, it reflects the extent of his/her confidence that the system will operate as the user expects, and thus that it will not fail during normal use.

In fact, system failures are often unavoidable and they may have widespread effects, by affecting other systems, as well as people somewhat related to the system itself; this includes system operators, system users, but also people indirectly involved in the system environment (we can think for instance to the population living around a potentially dangerous plant). Systems that are not dependable are in fact unreliable, unavailable when needed, unsafe or insecure, and because of that, they may be rejected by their users. Moreover, cost issues must also be taken into account; if a failure leads to economic losses or physical damage, both direct failure impacts, as well as recovery costs have to be seriously considered.

If one wants to reason about all the above mentioned aspects, it is clear that formal models must be introduced. Such models have to be properly defined with respect to a system specification, since a failure (and all the consequences of that) is a deviation from a specification. However specifications can rarely be complete, as well as deterministic; thus a problem arising in building dependability models is the problem of uncertainty. It follows that some of the most relevant problems related to system dependability concern the representation and modeling of the system, the quantification of system model parameters and the representation, propagation and quantification of the uncertainty in the system behavior.

Moreover, in order to address a concrete dependability problem, other important issues to be considered are: the temporal dimension, with particular attention to the modeling and analysis of temporal dependencies that can arise among system components, the multi-state nature of several components (that cannot be constrained in the standard dichotomy *working/failed*), the risk/utility analysis, often related to the definition of suitable control or recovery policies on the system under examination.

Classical approaches to dependability modeling and analysis show several limitations with respect to the above mentioned issues: combinatorial approaches (such as Fault Trees or Reliability Block Diagrams) are simple to use and analyze, but they are limited in modeling power; on the other hand, state-space approaches (such as Markov models) pay their augmented representational power, with more complex or less efficient analysis techniques (and with the state space explosion problem, typical of such models).

The main problem is then to define an approach where important dependencies among system components can be captured, while keeping the analysis task manageable at the same time. In the Artificial Intelligence (AI) field, similar problems have been addressed and solved by the adoption of Probabilistic Graphical Models. Model languages belonging to such a class are Bayesian Network and Decision Network formalisms. The former is a graphical and compact representation of a joint probability distribution, allowing to localize dependencies among modeled entities (system components or sub-systems in the case of a dependability application), and exploiting such dependencies, in order to reduce the number of probabilistic parameters to be specified. This results in a sound probabilistic model, relying on local specifications, where different kinds of probabilistic queries can be asked (in particular, posterior probability queries, after the gathering of specific information). Several important tasks for dependability analysis can be naturally framed in the setting of such probabilistic queries. Temporal aspects and dynamic dependencies can be addressed with dynamic versions of Bayesian Networks, having the advantage, with respect to standard Markov models, of considering a factored state space. Decision Networks are finally extensions to Bayesian Networks, where also external actions, as well as the utility of specific system conditions can be modeled. This allows the analyst to exploit a decision theoretic framework to perform risk/utility analysis, which is very important in the dependability field (as noticed above).

The aim of the book is to present approaches to the dependability (reliability, availability, risk and safety, security) of systems, using the Artificial Intelligence framework of Probabilistic Graphical Models. This framework (and in particular the Bayesian Network formalism) has been extensively employed in several sub-fields of AI which are strictly related to dependability and reliability issues, like diagnostic problem solving, intelligent monitoring and recovery planning.

After a survey on the main concepts and methodologies adopted in dependability analysis, the book discusses the main features of Probabilistic Graphical Models, by considering Bayesian Networks, Dynamic Bayesian Networks and Decision Networks. The advantages, both in terms of modeling and analysis, with respect to classical dependability formalisms are deeply discussed. Methodologies for deriving Probabilistic Graphical Models from standard dependability languages (such as Fault Tree or Dynamic Fault Tree) are introduced, by pointing out tools able to support such a process.

Several case studies are presented and analyzed in the book, in order to support the claim concerning the suitability of the use of Probabilistic Graphical Models in the study of dependable systems. Such case studies concentrates on different facets of the dependability concept, like standard reliability, dynamic reliability, selection of optimal repair policies, cascading failures, fault detection, identification and recovery, safety and security assessment. Some of such examples refer to real-world case studies, where the approach based on Probabilistic Graphical Models has proven to be very successful.

This book would not have come into existence without the direct or indirect contribution of several people, many of them part of the PROGRAM research lab at UPO[1]. First of all, we are very indebted to *Andrea Bobbio*, who introduced us to the world of reliability and dependability; with his unique open mind, he pursued with us the vision that Probabilistic Graphical Models could have been a breakthrough for reliability and dependability engineers. Most of the work described in the present book is the result of a strict research collaboration with him.

We would also like to thank the various people who contributed to different parts of the work presented in the book, and in particular (in alphabetical order): *Ester Ciancamerla, Stefano Di Nolfo, Andrea Guiotto,*

---

[1]PROGRAM: Probabilistic Graphical Models Research Group and Lab at the University of Piemonte Orientale, Alessandria, Italy (http://www.di.unipmn.it/program)

*Helge Langseth, Michele Minichino, Stefania Montani, Roberta Terruggia, Marco Varesio, Yury Yusthein.*
Last but not least, we are very grateful to *Steven Patt*, who has been our official interface at World Scientific Publishing. His help and support has been really appreciated.

*L. Portinale and D. Codetta Raiteri*
*Alessandria, April, 2015*

**Luigi Portinale** received a Ph.D. and a M.Sc. in Computer Science from the University of Torino (Italy). He is Full Professor of Computer Science and Head of the Computer Science Institute at the University of Piemonte Orientale (Italy). His main research interests are in the Artificial Intelligence field, with particular attention to case-based reasoning and probabilistic uncertain reasoning for dependability and reliability applications. He's author of more than 120 pubblications on the above topics. He's member of IEEE Computer Society, of the Italian Association for AI (AI\*IA) and of the Association for the Advancement of AI (AAAI).

**Daniele Codetta Raiteri** received the Ph.D. in Computer Science from the University of Torino (Italy) in 2006. He is currently an assistant professor at the University of Piemonte Orientale (Italy). He works on probabilistic models for reliability analysis, with a particular experience in fault trees, Petri nets, Bayesian networks.

# Contents

*Preface*                                                                       vii

*Acronym List*                                                                   xv

1. Dependability and Reliability                                                  1

   1.1   System Dependability: Basic Notions . . . . . . . . . . . .   1
          1.1.1   Dependability evaluation . . . . . . . . . . . . . .   4
          1.1.2   Measures of dependability . . . . . . . . . . . .   5
          1.1.3   The probabilistic approach . . . . . . . . . . . .   6
   1.2   Combinatorial Models . . . . . . . . . . . . . . . . . . .  10
          1.2.1   Fault Tree . . . . . . . . . . . . . . . . . . . . .  10
          1.2.2   Dynamic Fault Tree . . . . . . . . . . . . . . . .  23
   1.3   State Space Models . . . . . . . . . . . . . . . . . . . .  28
          1.3.1   Markov Chains . . . . . . . . . . . . . . . . . . .  28
          1.3.2   Petri Nets . . . . . . . . . . . . . . . . . . . . .  29

2. Probabilistic Graphical Models                                                37

   2.1   Bayesian Belief Networks . . . . . . . . . . . . . . . . .  39
          2.1.1   Conditional independence and factorization . . . .  42
          2.1.2   Causal independence . . . . . . . . . . . . . . . .  44
          2.1.3   Inference . . . . . . . . . . . . . . . . . . . . . .  45
   2.2   Decision Networks . . . . . . . . . . . . . . . . . . . .  49
          2.2.1   Policies and strategies . . . . . . . . . . . . . . .  52
   2.3   Dynamic Models . . . . . . . . . . . . . . . . . . . . .  58
          2.3.1   Inference in Dynamic Bayesian Networks . . . . .  61

3. From Fault Trees to Bayesian Networks                                         69

3.1    Mapping Fault Trees to Bayesian Networks . . . . . . . .    70
3.2    Common Cause Failures . . . . . . . . . . . . . . . . . . .    74
3.3    Noisy Gates . . . . . . . . . . . . . . . . . . . . . . . . .    76
3.4    Coverage Factors . . . . . . . . . . . . . . . . . . . . . .    78
3.5    Multi-state Variables . . . . . . . . . . . . . . . . . . . .    78
3.6    Sequentially Dependent Failures . . . . . . . . . . . . . .    79
3.7    Dependability Analysis through BN Inference . . . . . . .    81

4.  From Dynamic Fault Tree to Dynamic Bayesian Networks        87

4.1    Translating Dynamic Gates . . . . . . . . . . . . . . . . .    88
       4.1.1    Warm spare gate . . . . . . . . . . . . . . . . . .    88
       4.1.2    Probabilistic dependency gate . . . . . . . . . . .    92
       4.1.3    Priority AND . . . . . . . . . . . . . . . . . . . .    95
4.2    Combining the Modules into a Single DBN . . . . . . . .    96
4.3    Modelling Repair . . . . . . . . . . . . . . . . . . . . . .    104
4.4    A Case-study Example . . . . . . . . . . . . . . . . . . .    114

5.  Decision Theoretic Dependability                            123

5.1    Decision Networks for Repairable Systems . . . . . . . . .    124
5.2    A Repairable System . . . . . . . . . . . . . . . . . . . .    125
       5.2.1    The Decision Network model . . . . . . . . . . . .    127
       5.2.2    System unreliability and expected cost . . . . . .    129
       5.2.3    Importance measures of components under given
                strategies . . . . . . . . . . . . . . . . . . . . . .    130
       5.2.4    Computation of the best repair strategy . . . . . .    132

6.  The RADYBAN Tool: Supporting Dependability
    Engineers to Exploit Probabilistic Graphical Models         137

6.1    Tool Architecture . . . . . . . . . . . . . . . . . . . . . .    138
6.2    Editing a DFT . . . . . . . . . . . . . . . . . . . . . . . .    139
6.3    Editing a DBN . . . . . . . . . . . . . . . . . . . . . . . .    141
6.4    Compilation of a DFT into a DBN . . . . . . . . . . . . .    142
6.5    Analyzing a DBN . . . . . . . . . . . . . . . . . . . . . .    142

7.  Case Study 1: Cascading Failures                            145

7.1    Problem Introduction . . . . . . . . . . . . . . . . . . . .    145
7.2    Modeling Cascading Failures by Means of DBN . . . . .    147
       7.2.1    Building the DBN model . . . . . . . . . . . . . .    149

7.2.2     The cascading failure scenario . . . . . . . . . . . 152

7.3    Quantitative Results . . . . . . . . . . . . . . . . . . . . . 153

8.   Case Study 2: Autonomous Fault Detection,
Identification and Recovery      157

8.1    Problem Introduction . . . . . . . . . . . . . . . . . . . . 157

8.2    The Testing Environment . . . . . . . . . . . . . . . . . 159

8.3    Off-board Process . . . . . . . . . . . . . . . . . . . . . . . 161

     8.3.1     DFT model of the case study . . . . . . . . . . . 162

     8.3.2     DBN model of the case study . . . . . . . . . . 163

8.4    On-board Process . . . . . . . . . . . . . . . . . . . . . . . 166

8.5    Testing ARPHA . . . . . . . . . . . . . . . . . . . . . . . 169

9.   Case Study 3: Security Assessment in Critical Infrastructures    175

9.1    Problem Introduction . . . . . . . . . . . . . . . . . . . . 175

9.2    Attack Tree Based Formalisms . . . . . . . . . . . . . . 176

9.3    Decision Networks for Attack/Defense Scenarios . . . . . 177

     9.3.1     From Attack Countermeasure Trees to Decision
Networks . . . . . . . . . . . . . . . . . . . . . . . 178

     9.3.2     Quantitative analysis . . . . . . . . . . . . . . . 183

10.   Case Study 4: Dynamic Reliability      191

10.1    Problem Introduction . . . . . . . . . . . . . . . . . . . . 191

10.2    The Benchmark . . . . . . . . . . . . . . . . . . . . . . . . 192

     10.2.1    Version 1: basic system . . . . . . . . . . . . . . 192

     10.2.2    Version 2: state dependent failure rates . . . . . 193

     10.2.3    Version 3: controller failure on demand . . . . . 194

     10.2.4    Version 4: repairable components . . . . . . . . 194

10.3    Related Work . . . . . . . . . . . . . . . . . . . . . . . . . 195

10.4    DBN Models of the Benchmark . . . . . . . . . . . . . . 196

     10.4.1    Modelling Version 1 . . . . . . . . . . . . . . . . 196

     10.4.2    Modelling Versions 2 and 3 . . . . . . . . . . . . 202

     10.4.3    Modelling Version 4 . . . . . . . . . . . . . . . . 202

10.5    DBN Analysis Results . . . . . . . . . . . . . . . . . . . . 205

     10.5.1    Predictive analysis . . . . . . . . . . . . . . . . . 205

     10.5.2    Diagnostic analysis . . . . . . . . . . . . . . . . 206

Appendix A    The Junction Tree Algorithms      219

A.1   JT Algorithm for Static Bayesian Networks . . . . . . . . 219

    A.1.1   Constructing the Junction/Join Tree . . . . . . . 219

    A.1.2   Belief Propagation on Junction Tree . . . . . . . . 223

A.2   JT Algorithm for Dynamic Bayesian Networks . . . . . . 226

    A.2.1   The 1.5JT algorithm . . . . . . . . . . . . . . . 227

    A.2.2   The Boyen-Koller algorithm . . . . . . . . . . . 232

*Bibliography*                                                   235

*Index*                                                            247

# Acronym List

| | |
|---|---|
| 2-TBN | 2 time-slice Temporal Bayesian Network |
| ABB | Autonomy Building Block |
| ACT | Attack Countermeasure Tree |
| ADT | Attack Defence Tree |
| ARPHA | Anomaly Resolution and Prognostic Health management for Autonomy |
| AT | Attack Tree |
| BDD | Binary Decision Diagram |
| BE | Basic Event |
| BGP | Border Gateway Protocol |
| BI | Birnbaum Index |
| BK | Boyen-Koller algorithm |
| BN | Bayesian Network |
| BP | Belief Propagation |
| CAS | Cardiac Assist System |
| cdf | cumulative distribution function |
| CCF | Common Cause Failure |
| CFR | Constant Failure Rate |
| CI | Causal Independence |
| CIF | Critical Importance Factor |
| Cov | Coverage set |
| CPT | Conditional Probability Table |
| CR | Component Repair |
| CSM | Combinatorial Solution Module |
| CSP | Cold SPare gate |
| CTMC | Continuous Time Markov Chain |

| DAG | Direct Acyclic Graph |
|-----|---------------------|
| DBN | Dynamic Bayesian Networks |
| DDN | Dynamic Decision Network |
| DDP | Defect, Detection and Prevention |
| DFR | Decreasing Failure Rate |
| DFT | Dynamic Fault Tree |
| DIF | Diagnostic Impact Factor |
| DN | Decision Network |
| DRBD | Dynamic Reliability Block Diagram |
| DTMC | Discrete Time Markov Chain |
| EDFT | Extended Dynamic Fault Tree |
| ET | Event Tree |
| EU | Expected Utility |
| FDEP | Functional DEPendency gate |
| FDIR | Failure Detection, Identification and Recovery |
| FMEA | Failure Mode Effect Analysis |
| FSPN | Fluid Stochastic Petri Net |
| FT | Fault Tree |
| FTA | Fault Tree Analysis |
| FVI | Fussell-Vesely Index |
| GSPN | Generalized Stochastic Petri Net |
| GUI | Graphical User Interface |
| HBN | Hybrid Bayesian Network |
| HMM | Hidden Markov Model |
| HSP | Hot SPare gate |
| ID | Influence Diagram |
| IDPF | Inter-Domain Packet Filter |
| IE | Intermediate Event |
| IFR | Increasing Failure Rate |
| JT | Junction Tree |
| k:n | k out of n |
| LBP | Loopy Belief Propagation |
| LIMID | LImited Memory Influence Diagram |
| MAP | Maximum A Posteriori |
| MC | Markov Chain |
| MCMC | Markov Chain Monte Carlo |
| MCS | Minimal Cut Set |
| MCSeq | Minimal Cut Sequence |

| | |
|---|---|
| MDP | Markov Decision Process |
| MEC | Minimum Expected Cost |
| MEU | Maximum Expected Utility |
| MIF | Marginal Impact Factor |
| MPE | Most Probable Explanation |
| MPS | Minimal Path Set |
| MRF | Markov Random Field |
| MSP | Most Severe Prevailing |
| MTE | Mixture of Truncated Exponentials |
| MTTF | Mean Time to Failure |
| OD | Optical Depth |
| PAND | Priority AND gate |
| PDEP | Probabilistic DEPendency gate |
| PGM | Probabilistic Graphical Model |
| pdf | probability density function |
| PF | Particle Filtering |
| PN | Petri Net |
| PNL | Probabilistic Networks Library |
| POMPD | Partially Observable Markov Decision Process |
| PPTC | Probability Propagation in Trees of Clusters |
| PRA | Probabilistic Risk Analysis |
| PSS | Power Supply Subsystem |
| RAW | Risk Achievement Worth |
| RB | Repair Box |
| RBD | Reliability Block Diagram |
| RBPF | Rao-Blackwellised Particle Filtering |
| ROI | Return On Investment index |
| RRW | Risk Reduction Worth |
| SA | Solar Array |
| SAA | Sun Aspect Angle |
| SAN | Stochastic Activity Network |
| SEQ | SEQuence enforcing gate |
| SGR | Subsystem Global Repair |
| SLR | Subsystem Local Repair |
| SIS | Sequential Importance Sampling |
| SPU | Single Policy Updating |
| SSM | State-space solution Module |
| TCP | Transfer Control Protocol |

| TE | Top Event |
|---|---|
| UML | Unified Modelling Language |
| VE | Variable Elimination |
| WSP | Warm SPare gate |
| XML | eXtensible Markup Language |
| XOR | eXclusive OR |

# Chapter 1

# Dependability and Reliability

## 1.1 System Dependability: Basic Notions

We talk about safety critical systems when their incorrect behavior may cause undesirable consequences to the system itself, the operators, the population, or the environment. This definition fits categories of systems such as industrial production plants, electric power plants, and transportation systems. In these cases, *Dependability* is a crucial point in the design of the systems. The dependability is the property of a system to be dependable in time: we can say that the dependability level of a system is as high as we are confident that the system will correctly provide its service during its life cycle. Thus the notion concerns the ability of a system to deliver a service that can justifiably be trusted.

Dependability is an integrated concept that can be best described following the scheme by Laprie [Laprie (1985)] (see Figure 1.1). First of all, it encompasses various attributes, and in particular:

- *Reliability*, the property representing the continuity of correct service.
- *Availability*, the property representing the readiness for correct service.
- *Maintainability*, the property representing the ability to undergo modifications and repairs.
- *Safety*, the property concerning the absence of catastrophic consequences.
- *Confidentiality*, the property concerning the absence of unauthorized disclosure of information.
- *Integrity*, the property concerning the absence of improper system state alterations.

1

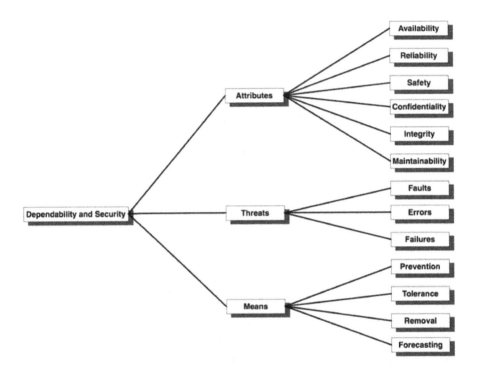

Fig. 1.1   Concept and terminology diagram for dependability [Laprie (1985)].

In the present book we will concentrate on the first four attributes of the list, since they are the most typical from the point of view of the dependability applications (see [Avizienis *et al.* (2001)] for a more detailed discussion on the relationships among such attributes).

The Laprie's scheme also involve other aspects for the dependability notion, namely *Threats* and *Means*. The incorrect behavior of a system may be caused by faults, failures or errors involving its components; these are actually called *threats* and can be defined as follows:

- *Failure*: a system deviation from the correct/expected service; we talk about *failure modes* to characterize the potential different ways on which such a deviation takes place.
- *Fault*: a cause of a failure, that is a defect in the system; this notion can often be identified with a particular abnormal/faulty state of a system component (e.g., a stuck-on valve), in contrast with the nominal/normal state (e.g., a working valve).

- *Error:* a discrepancy between the intended behavior of a system component and its actual behavior; errors can be detected through observations on the system or on specific components.

All threats are related through the so called *Fault-Error-Failure chain*: a fault, when activated, can lead to an error (which is an invalid state) and the invalid state generated by an error may lead to another error or a failure (which is an observable deviation from the specified behavior at the system boundary)[1].

Finally, the *means* of dependability are the tools on which the design and development of a dependable systems has to rely; following Laprie, they are:

- *Fault Prevention*, concerning how to prevent the occurrence of faults.
- *Fault Tolerance*, concerning how to deliver correct service in the presence of faults.
- *Fault Removal*, concerning how to reduce the number or severity of faults.
- *Fault Forecasting*, concerning how to estimate the current number, the future incidence, and the likely consequences of faults.

These are all aspects aimed at improving the dependability of a system; for instance a system providing a service is *fault tolerant* when the system is characterized by the capacity of assuring the service, although a failure has involved a part of the system. The fault tolerance is typically achieved by replicating the critical components in the system. Fault prevention and forecasting are clearly related to diagnostic (*fault identification and localization*) and prognostic procedures; fault removal and prevention are related to monitoring (*fault detection*) and maintenance strategies. In particular, in order to minimize the maintenance cost, two maintenance policies are possible: the *proactive maintenance* and the *reactive maintenance*; in the first case, the maintenance action tries to prevent the component or system failure; in the second case, the maintenance action is triggered by the failure of the system.

Furthermore, we can notice that the notion of dependability does not concern only safety, risk and design specifications of the system, but it influ-

---

[1]The chain can actually be a loop (having faults causing failures, causing other faults, causing other failures, etc.).

ences other aspects as well, such as the technical assistance and maintenance of the system, and the market competition. For instance, the technical assistance can be planned in terms of time, cost and logistic, according to the dependability evaluation of the system. Another example concerns the decision of the warranty period of a technological item, which is linked to the dependability of the item itself. Moreover, the repair or replacement of failed components by a maintenance crew is an aspect to take into account when forecasting the cost of maintenance of the system; this cost is the sum of the cost of spare components, the cost of personnel dedicated to the system repair, and the economic loss due to the production suspension during the repair time.

Finally, the dependability may influence customers' choices: advertisement messages stress the dependability and the image of a brand may depend on the dependability of its products or services. Recently, we assisted at the wide diffusion of computing and information technologies in several industrial and economic areas; when computing or networking systems are adopted to support activities with associated relevant risks, the concept of dependability becomes relevant for this class of systems as well.

### 1.1.1 *Dependability evaluation*

There are two main methods to evaluate the dependability of a system:

(1) the *Measurement-based* method;
(2) the *Model-based* method.

The first method requires the observation of the behavior in the operational environment, of the physical objects composing the system. In this way, dependability measurements are obtained and concern items such as component prototypes or effective components of the system; in the second case, the component may be evaluated by means of accelerated life tests [Nelson (1980); Donahoe *et al.* (2008)].

The measurement-based method is the most believable, but it may be unpractical or too expensive; in these cases, the model-based method is preferable and consists of the construction of a model representing the behavior of the system in terms of primitives defined in the formalism associated with the model. The model of the system must be a convenient abstraction of the system; this means that a model may not completely capture the behavior of the system, but the level of accuracy of the model must be high enough to correctly represent the aspects of the behavior which are relevant to the dependability evaluation of the system. The degree of accuracy of a model depends on the capacity of the associated formalism to extrapolate the system features.

With respect to the measurement-based method, the model-based method is less believable, but less expensive. Models can undergo analysis or simulation, and can be mainly classified into two main categories:

- *combinatorial models*
- *state space based models.*

The models in the first category represent the structure of the system in terms of logical connection of failed (working) components in order to obtain the system failure (success). State space based models instead, represent the behavior of the system in terms of reachable states and possible state transitions. In the following, we will present the details about the main features of such approaches.

### 1.1.2 *Measures of dependability*

The concept of dependability is quite general; in order to evaluate the dependability of an item, we need some measures to numerically characterize the dependability. The mechanisms that lead a technological item to failure are very complex and depend on many factors, such as physical, technical, human and environmental factors. These factors may not obey deterministic laws, so we can consider the time to failure of an item as a random variable. For this reason, the dependability evaluation in quantitative terms, is based on the probabilistic approach, and consists of the computation of several numerical measures characterizing the dependability. Let us formally define the most relevant ones.

**Definition 1.1.** The *Reliability* of an item (component or system) at time $t$, denoted by $R(t)$, is the probability that the item performs the required function in the time interval $(0, t)$ given the stress and environmental conditions in which it operates.

**Definition 1.2.** The *Unreliability* of an item at time $t$, denoted as $U(t)$, is the probability that the item has failed during the time interval $(0, t)$. The unreliability is given by $U(t) = 1 - R(t)$.

Repairable systems are characterized by the alternating up and down states (i.e., working and failed respectively), due to the alternating occurrences of failures and repairs of the system. In these cases, we talk about availability instead of reliability.

**Definition 1.3.** The *Availability* of an item at time $t$, denoted as $A(t)$, is the probability that the item is correctly working at time $t$.

**Definition 1.4.** The *Unavailability* of an item at time $t$ is the probability that the item is not performing the required function at time $t$. The unavailability is given by $1 - A(t)$.

Given in the above terms, in case of non repairable systems, reliability and availability refers to the same quantity.

Finally, in case of repairable systems, another relevant notion is that of maintainability

**Definition 1.5.** *Maintainability* is defined as the probability that a failed component or system will be restored or repaired to a specified condition, within a specified period of time, when maintenance is performed according to prescribed procedures.

The maintenance procedures have to be defined as specific policies, taking also into account the impact of component repair or replacement on the other components (e.g. the repair of a failed component without removing the cause of failure, will produce the same failure again).

### 1.1.3   *The probabilistic approach*

Considering the model-based method to dependability, the main approach that is usually adopted is the probabilistic one. Let $X$ be a continuous random variable representing the time to failure of a non repairable item. The *cumulative distribution function* (cdf) of $X$ is indicated by $F(t)$ and provides the unreliability of the item at time $t$:

$$F(t) = Pr\{X \le t\} \tag{1.1}$$

The following properties hold for $F(t)$:

- $F(0) = 0$
- $lim_{t \to +\infty} F(t) = 1$
- $F(t)$ is non decreasing.

The reliability of the item at time $t$ is given by the *survivor function*:

$$R(t) = Pr\{X > t\} = 1 - F(t) \tag{1.2}$$

The following properties hold for $R(t)$:

- $R(0) = 1$
- $lim_{t \to +\infty} R(t) = 0$
- $R(t)$ is non increasing.

Given a derivable cdf $F(t)$, the *probability density function* (pdf) $f(t)$ of $X$, is defined as

$$f(t) = \frac{dF(t)}{dt} \qquad (1.3)$$

$$f(t)dt = Pr\{t \leq X < t + dt\} \qquad (1.4)$$

The *Mean Time To Failure* (MTTF) of the item is given by

$$MTTF = E[X] = \int_0^{+\infty} t f(t)dt = \int_0^{+\infty} R(t)dt \qquad (1.5)$$

The *hazard (failure)* rate $h(t)$ of an item is defined as:

$$h(t) = \frac{f(t)}{R(t)} = \frac{f(t)}{1 - F(t)} \qquad (1.6)$$

In particular, we have that $h(t)\Delta t$ is the conditional probability that the item will fail in the interval $(t, t + \Delta t)$, given that it is functioning at time $t$. On the other hand, $f(t)\Delta t$ is the unconditional probability that the unit will fail in the interval $(t, t + \Delta t)$.

Figure 1.2 shows the classical bathtub shape of the $h(t)$ function curve, in the standard life cycle of a given item. In fact, the typical life cycle of an item consists of the sequence of the following phases.

- *Decreasing Failure Rate* (DFR) phase: the failure rate decreases with time. This phase is due to undetected defects of the item.
- *Constant Failure Rate* (CFR) phase: the failure rate is *age independent*; this means that the failure rate remains constant in time. Moreover, the failure rate value is much lower than in the early-life period. In this phase, the failure is caused by random effects. The CFR phase is the useful life period of the item.
- *Increasing Failure Rate* (IFR) phase: the failure rate increases with age. This phase is due to deterioration (wear-out) of the item.

The last phase does not concern all the classes of item; for instance, mechanical components can undergo deterioration, while the IFR phase is not present in the life cycle of several electronic components and in software systems. In the second case, the reason is that software is not a physical item, so it does not physically deteriorate.

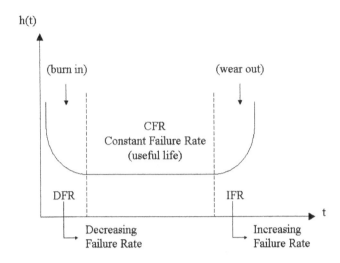

Fig. 1.2    The bathtub shape of the hazard (failure) rate function ($h(t)$) curve.

An important distribution often adopted in reliability is the *negative exponential distribution*.

**Definition 1.6.** A continuous random variable $X$ with cdf given by $F(t : \lambda) = Pr\{X \le t\} = 1 - e^{-\lambda t}$ is said to have a *negative exponential distribution* with parameter $\lambda$.

If the random variable $X$ representing the time to failure of an item, is ruled by the negative exponential distribution, the failure rate, represented by parameter $\lambda$, is constant and age independent along the complete life cycle of the item; in other words, the DFR phase and IFR phase are not present in the life cycle of the item.

The unreliability function $F(t : \lambda)$ (cdf), the reliability function $R(t : \lambda)$ and the density function (pdf) according to this distribution are reported in Table 1.1. Figure 1.3.a and Figure 1.3.b show the $F(t : \lambda)$ curve and the $R(t : \lambda)$ curve, respectively, for $\lambda = 1$.

The negative exponential distribution is characterized by the *memoryless property*. If we suppose that an item has been operating (has not failed) until time $t_1$, then the remaining (residual) lifetime of the item is given by $Y = X - t_1$; in this case (i.e., with the negative exponential distribution) the distribution of $Y$ does not depend on $t_1$. In other words, the distribution of the residual lifetime of the item does not depend on how long the item

Table 1.1   The negative exponential distribution.

| | |
|---|---|
| Unreliability (cdf) | $F(t) = 1 - e^{-\lambda t}$ |
| Reliability | $R(t) = e^{-\lambda t}$ |
| Density function (pdf) | $f(t) = \lambda e^{-\lambda t}$ |
| Failure rate | $h(t) = f(t)/R(t) = \lambda$ |
| Mean Time To Failure | $MTTF = 1/\lambda$ |

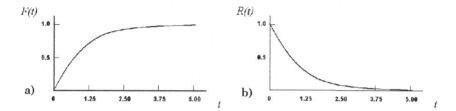

Fig. 1.3   a) The cdf (unreliability) function curve for $\lambda = 1$. b) The reliability function curve for $\lambda = 1$.

has been operating. If the distribution of $Y$ is indicated by $G_{t_1}(t)$, the memory-less property can be proved in this way (for the sake of clarity we omit here the parametrization on $\lambda$ on the cdf specification):

$$
\begin{aligned}
G_{t_1}(t) &= Pr\{Y \leq t | X > t_1\} \\
&= Pr\{X \leq t_1 + t | X > t_1\} \\
&= \frac{Pr\{t_1 < X \leq t_1 + t\}}{Pr\{X > t_1\}} \\
&= \frac{F(t_1 + t) - F(t_1)}{1 - F(t_1)} \\
&= \frac{1 - e^{-\lambda(t_1+t)} - \left(1 - e^{-\lambda t_1}\right)}{1 - \left(1 - e^{-\lambda t_1}\right)} \\
&= \frac{e^{-\lambda t_1} - e^{-\lambda(t_1+t)}}{e^{-\lambda t_1}} \\
&= \frac{e^{-\lambda t_1} - e^{-\lambda t_1} \cdot e^{-\lambda t}}{e^{-\lambda t_1}} \\
&= \frac{e^{-\lambda t_1}\left(1 - e^{-\lambda t}\right)}{e^{-\lambda t_1}} \\
&= 1 - e^{-\lambda t} = F(t) \qquad (1.7)
\end{aligned}
$$

Thus $G_{t_1}(t)$ is independent of $t_1$ and is identical to $F(t)$ which is the original exponential distribution of $X$. This means that, in this model, the failure of the item is not due to its gradual deterioration, but it is a failure suddenly appearing.

## 1.2 Combinatorial Models

As mentioned in Sec. 1.1.1, combinatorial models represent the structure of the system in terms of logical connection of working (or failed) components in order to obtain the system success (or failure). Models like *Reliability Block Diagrams* (RBD) [Sahner *et al.* (1996)], *Event Trees* (ET) [Contini and Poucet (1990)] and *Fault Trees* (FT) [Schneeweiss (1999)] belong to this category. Combinatorial models have an intuitive notation, they are easy to be designed and manipulated, and they can be efficiently analyzed by means of combinatorial methods. Despite of these advantages, combinatorial models suffer from a very limited modeling power, mainly due to the assumption of the statistical independence of the events.

In the present book, we focus our attention on FT; this kind of model is widespread in the reliability field and several evolutions have been proposed in the literature [Dugan *et al.* (1992); Bobbio *et al.* (2003b); Codetta-Raiteri *et al.* (2004)]. However, similar considerations can be done for both RBD [Torres-Toledano and Sucar (1998)] and ET [Bearfield and Marsh (2005)].

### 1.2.1 *Fault Tree*

The *Fault Tree* (FT) [Schneeweiss (1999)] is a widespread model for the reliability analysis of complex systems, because it provides an intuitive representation of the system failure modes, it is easy to manipulate and it is currently supported by several software tools. A FT models how combinations of component failure events can cause the failure of the system. An example of FT is shown in Figure 1.6. Despite its name, a FT is in general a *directed acyclic graph* (DAG) characterized by two categories of nodes: *events* and *gates*[2]. Events concern the failure of components, of subsystems, or of the whole system. An event is a Boolean variable: it is initially *false* (F) and it becomes *true* (T) when the failure occurs.

More in depth, the set of primitives elements in a FT are the following.

---

[2]A FT is structurally a tree in two different cases: either each event node is connected to at most one gate node or nodes representing events connected to more than one gate are replicated.

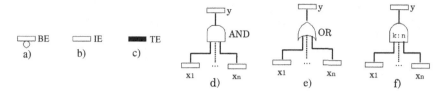

Fig. 1.4 The nodes of a fault tree (FT): a) basic event (BE); b) Intermediate Event (IE); c) Top Event (TE); d) AND; e) OR; f) k:n.

**Basic Events** (BE) (Figure 1.4.a) model the failure of the elementary components of the system; the occurrence time of such events is a random variable ruled by a probability distribution, typically the negative exponential one. In this case, the distribution parameter is the component failure rate $\lambda$ equal to the inverse of the mean life time of the component (Table 1.1). BE are statistically independent and are the terminal nodes of the FT.

**Intermediate Events** (IE) (Figure 1.4.b) represent the failure of subsystems. Their occurrence is not ruled by a probability distribution, but it is modeled through a Boolean function instead; they are the output of a gate defining such a function.

**Gates** are the other category of nodes that a FT can contain. Gates are connected by means of arcs to several input events and to a unique output event; the effect of a gate is the propagation of the failure to its output event, if a particular combination of its input events occurs. The occurrence of an IE is immediate, as soon as the particular combination of input events required by the gate is verified. Considering that the *true* value of an event indicates the fact that the event has occurred, the output event of the AND gate (Figure 1.4.d) is *true* if all the input events are *true*, otherwise the output event is *false*. The output event of an OR gate (Figure 1.4.e) is *false* if all the input events are *false*, otherwise the output event is *true*. Another gate is called and "k out of n" ($k : n$): it returns *true* if at least $k$ of the $n$ input variables are *true*; otherwise it returns *false* (Figure 1.4.f). This gate is also referred as voting gate, and can be expressed by means of the functions AND, OR.

**Top Event** (TE) (Figure 1.4.c) is a unique event modelling the failure of the system; the TE is the output of a gate, and is the root of the FT.

**Arcs.** A FT is a directed graph and arcs respect a logic circuit orientation: from the input events to the gate, and from the gate to the output event. Any gate has at least two input events and only one output event. A BE or an IE must be the input of at least one gate. A FT is also an acyclic graph, so the connection of events with gates (and vice-versa) by means of arcs, must not determine the presence of cyclic paths in the FT. In particular, a BE cannot be the output of any gate, while the TE can not be the input of any gate.

**Coherent FT.** A FT encodes a Boolean formula expressing the failure of the system (TE); the Boolean variables of such formula are the BE of the FT and are combined through Boolean operators corresponding to the gates present in the FT. FT containing the three types of gate mentioned above, are referred as *coherent* FT [Schneeweiss (1999)]. In a coherent FT, the failure of the system is only possible with the failure of its components (i.e., it is not possible that by changing the state of a failed component to working, it causes the system to fail); this means that in the Boolean formula equivalent to a FT model, the negation operator is not present [Xing and Amari (2008)]. The negation of events (Boolean variables) is possible in FT models, if other two types of gate are used: NOT and XOR. The NOT gate corresponds to the negation operator, and has only one input event, and the Boolean value of its output event is the negation of the value of its input event. The XOR gate represents the *exclusive OR* operator: the output event is *true* if only one of the input events is *true*. In the following sections, we limit our attention to coherent FTs.

### 1.2.1.1 *A Fault Tree Modeling Example*

This section provides an example of FT concerning the case study of a multiprocessor computing system (referred in the next sections as "Multiproc"), inspired from [Bobbio *et al.* (2003b)]). Figure 1.5 shows the scheme of the system which is mainly composed by three processing units ($PU1$, $PU2$, $PU3$), two shared memories ($R1$, $R2$) and two hard disks ($D1$, $D2$) containing the software and the data respectively. Each processing unit is composed by one processor and three internal memories; they are $P1$, $M11$, $M12$, $M13$, respectively, in the case of $PU1$. $PU1$, $PU2$, $PU3$ are connected to $R1$ and $R2$ by means of the buses $B1$ and $B2$, respectively. Any processing unit can use $R1$ or $R2$ to perform computations when its internal memories are failed. The connection of $PU1$, $PU2$, $PU3$ with $D1$, $D2$ is established by the bus $DBUS$.

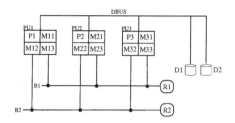

Fig. 1.5 The scheme of the Multiproc system.

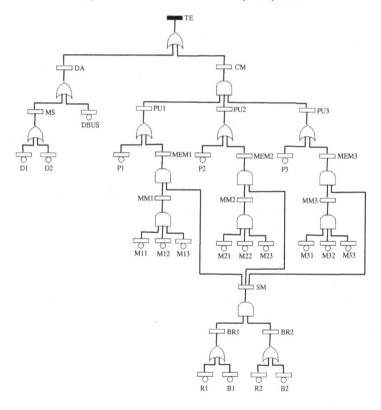

Fig. 1.6 The FT model of the Multiproc system in Figure 1.5.

**Failure mode.** We suppose that the correct functioning of at least one processing unit is required for the system to be working; so, the failure of all the processing units causes the system failure. The failure of a processing unit is due to the failure of its processor, or to the contemporary failure of all

Table 1.2    The    failure    rate    for
each type of component.

| Component | Failure rate ($\lambda$) |
|-----------|-------------------------|
| Processor | 5.0E-7 $h^{-1}$ |
| Disk | 8.0E-7 $h^{-1}$ |
| Memory | 3.0E-8 $h^{-1}$ |
| Bus | 2.0E-9 $h^{-1}$ |

its internal memories together with the denied access to $R1$ and $R2$. The use
of a shared memory is not possible if it is failed or when the corresponding
bus is failed. The system failure is caused also by the impossibility to access
any hard disk; this happens if a hard disk fails or if $DBUS$ fails. The
probability of failure of the components of the system, obeys the negative
exponential distribution; Table 1.2 indicates some possible failure rates for
each type of component.

**FT model.**    Figure 1.6 shows the FT model of Multiproc. The system
failure $(TE)$ is the output of an OR gate whose input events are $DA$ (disk
access) and $CM$ (computing module); $CM$ represents the impossibility to
perform computations due to the failure of all the processing units, while
$DA$ represents the impossibility to access the hard disks. $CM$ is the output
of an AND gate whose input events are $PU1$, $PU2$ and $PU3$ representing
the failure of the corresponding processing units. $PU1$ is the output of an
OR gate having $P1$ and $MEM1$ as input events; $P1$ is a BE modelling
the failure of the processor of $PU1$, while $MEM1$ represents the failure
of the memories that $PU1$ can access. $MEM1$ is the output of an AND
gate having two inputs: $MM1$ and $SM$; $MM1$ represents the failure of
all the internal memories of $PU1$, while $SM$ models the failure of the
shared memories. $MM1$ is the output of an AND gate whose inputs are
the BE $M11$, $M12$ and $M13$. $SM$ is the output of an AND gate with
input events $BR1$ and $BR2$; $BR1$ represents the impossibility to access the
shared memory $R1$, so $BR1$ is the output of an OR gate having $R1$ and
$B1$ as input events. Similarly, $BR2$ is the output of an OR gate having
$R2$ and $B2$ as input events. The subtrees having $MEM1$, $MEM2$ and
$MEM3$ respectively as roots, share a common subtree rooted in $SM$, since
the failure of all the processing units may depend on the state of the shared
memories. Besides the occurrence of $CM$, $TE$ is caused also by $DA$ which
is the output of an OR gate whose input events are $DBUS$ and $MS$. In
particular, $MS$ is the failure of at least one disk, so $MS$ is the output of
an OR gate whose input events are $D1$ and $D2$.

## 1.2.1.2 *Fault Tree Analysis*

The *Fault Tree Analysis* (FTA) [Xing and Amari (2008)] provides a set of techniques enabling to derive both qualitative results and quantitative measures from a FT model.

**Qualitative analysis.** It supplies information about functional and logic properties of the system failure mode. One of the possible results of the qualitative analysis of a FT, is the detection of the *Minimal Cut Sets* (MCS). The MCS of a FT correspond to the minimal scenarios of BE leading the system to a failure. A FT encodes the Boolean formula $F(x_1, \ldots, x_n)$ expressed on the set of variables $\mathfrak{X} = \{x_1, \ldots, x_n\}$ corresponding to the BE of the FT. An assignment over $\mathfrak{X}$ is any mapping from $\mathfrak{X}$ to $\mathbb{B} = \{true, false\}$. An assignment $\rho$ satisfies $F$ ($\rho \models F$) if $\rho$ makes $F$ *true*. A *literal* of $\mathfrak{X}$ is either a Boolean variable $x_i \in \mathfrak{X}$ or its negation $\neg x_i$. A *cut set* $C$ of $F$ is a set literals $C = \{l_1 \ldots l_m\} \subseteq \mathfrak{X}$ such that if $\pi = \bigwedge_{j=1}^{m} l_j = true$ then $F$ is *true*. This implies that

$$\forall \rho : \rho \models \pi, \rho \models F \tag{1.8}$$

This property can also be expressed as $\pi \models F$. A cut set $C$ of $F$ is minimal (MCS) if there is no cut set $C'$ of $F$ such that $C' \subset C$. In the case of coherent FTs, any cut set is composed by literals which are non negated variables, so there is only one assignment $\rho$ satisfying the conjunction of the literals of the cut set, by mapping each variable in the cut set to *true*. In other words, a MCS of a coherent FT indicates a minimal set of components whose contemporary state of failure determines the system failure (TE).

The number of BE (variables) in a MCS is called the *order* of the MCS. The order is a significant qualitative parameter since it highlights failure sets of events that might be more critical for the system. In fact, a MCS of order 1 means that the failure of a single basic component is sufficient to determine the TE, indicating no fault tolerance with respect to that component. In a MCS of order 2, two simultaneous failures of basic components are needed. For this reason, it is useful to list the MCS in increasing order, so that the list starts with the MCS being potentially most critical.

Another form of qualitative analysis of a FT, is the *Minimal Path Sets* (MPS) detection, which is dual to the MCS detection and provides the minimal sets of components whose contemporary working state assures the working state of the system. MCS and MPS detection allows the reliability analyst to be concentrated on minimal sets of components instead of the whole system, in order to study their degree of participation to the system failure, or the way to improve the reliability of the system.

**Example case study.**   The MCS of the FT in Figure 1.6, sorted by their order, follow:

1 : $[D1]$
2 : $[D2]$
3 : $[DBUS]$
4 : $[P1P2P3]$
5 : $[B1B2M11M12M13P2P3]$
6 : $[B1R2M11M12M13P2P3]$
7 : $[R1B2M11M12M13P2P3]$
8 : $[R1R2M11M12M13P2P3]$
9 : $[B1B2P1M21M22M23P3]$
10 : $[B1B2P1P2M31M32M33]$
11 : $[B1R2P1M21M22M23P3]$
12 : $[B1R2P1P2M31M32M33]$
13 : $[R1B2P1M21M22M23P3]$
14 : $[R1B2P1P2M31M32M33]$
15 : $[R1R2P1M21M22M23P3]$
16 : $[R1R2P1P2M31M32M33]$
17 : $[B1B2M11M12M13M21M22M23P3]$
18 : $[B1R2M11M12M13M21M22M23P3]$
19 : $[R1B2M11M12M13M21M22M23P3]$
20 : $[R1R2M11M12M13M21M22M23P3]$
21 : $[B1B2M11M12M13P2M31M32M33]$
22 : $[B1R2M11M12M13P2M31M32M33]$
23 : $[R1B2M11M12M13P2M31M32M33]$
24 : $[R1R2M11M12M13P2M31M32M33]$
25 : $[B1B2P1M21M22M23M31M32M33]$
26 : $[B1R2P1M21M22M23M31M32M33]$
27 : $[R1B2P1M21M22M23M31M32M33]$
28 : $[R1R2P1M21M22M23M31M32M33]$
29 : $[B1B2M11M12M13M21M22M23M31M32M33]$
30 : $[B1R2M11M12M13M21M22M23M31M32M33]$
31 : $[R1B2M11M12M13M21M22M23M31M32M33]$
32 : $[R1R2M11M12M13M21M22M23M31M32M33]$

Looking at the MCS list we can notice that $D1$, $D2$, and $DBUS$ are single point of failures (cut set n. 1, 2, 3), while all the available processors must fail (cut set n. 4), in order to produce a system failure. Other possible causes of system failure will need a quite large combination of component faults.

**Quantitative analysis.** Several quantitative measures can be computed on the FT, such as the TE probability at time $t$ (system unreliability), the probability of occurrence of each MCS, the system *Mean Time To Failure* (MTTF), and importance factors (component criticality). Quantitative analysis requires the occurrence probability of BE. Often the failure probability of components is not directly expressed in the FT; instead, a time to failure distribution is provided, from which a failure probability at time $t$ can be derived. Typically the negative exponential distribution is applied, so that each BE $x$ is characterized by a failure rate $\lambda_x$ (Section 1.1.3), and its probability at time $t$ can be computed as

$$Pr\{x, t\} = 1 - e^{\lambda_x t} \tag{1.9}$$

MCS can also be ranked according to their probability; given the MCS $M' = \{x_1, \ldots, x_m\}$ ($m \geq 1$), since standard FTA assumes that components are statistically independent, the probability of $M'$ to be occurred at time $t$, is given by

$$Pr\{M', t\} = Pr\{\bigwedge_{i=1}^{m} x_i = true, t\} = \prod_{i=1}^{m} Pr\{x_i, t\} = \prod_{i=1}^{m}(1 - e^{\lambda_{x_i} t}) \tag{1.10}$$

The system unreliability denoted by $U(u(t))$, is a function of the basic components unreliability, where $u(t)$ is the vector of basic component failure probabilities. In FT such indicator corresponds to the TE probability to be occurred at time $t$ ($Pr\{TE, t\}$). In fact, for a given time instant $t$ and fixed BE probabilities $u(t)$, the TE probability can be derived by exploiting the results of the detected MCS and their probabilities. We can use the *inclusion-exclusion expansion*, where $C_1, \ldots, C_n$ are the MCS:

$$Pr\{TE, t\} = Pr\{\bigcup_{i=1}^{n} C_i, t\}$$

$$= \sum_{i=1}^{n} Pr\{C_i, t\} - \sum_{\forall i \forall j} Pr\{C_i \cap C_j, t\}$$

$$+ \sum_{\forall i \forall j \forall k} Pr\{C_i \cap C_j \cap C_k, t\}$$

$$+ \cdots + (-1)^{n+1} \cdot Pr\{C_1 \cap \cdots \cap C_n, t\} \tag{1.11}$$

For complex systems the above formula may be prohibitive to derive due to the relevant number of MCS and the consequent huge amount of calculation to be performed. As a result, the TE probability can be approximated by

$$Pr\{TE, t\} = \sum_{i=1}^{n} Pr\{C_i, t\} \tag{1.12}$$

Among the risk-assessment and safety-analysis objectives, the classification of components according to their criticality is very important. So, in addition to the unreliability measure of a system, it is central to assess the role that a component takes on, with regard to the system reliability. This analysis is significant to the reliability engineer both during the design phase and successively in quantifying the risk-importance of the various system components, so to find out the more cost effective solution to improve the reliability. To this purpose, several indices, commonly called *importance measures* or *importance factors*, have been proposed. They are time dependent measures and may be divided in two groups: measures computed at one point in the time, such as those discussed later, and measures whose values are obtained averaging on a time period.

The most popular importance factor is the *Birnbaum Importance* (BI) due to Birnbaum [Birnbaum (1969)] and is defined as the partial derivative of the system unreliability with respect to the unreliability of the component $i$. This measure is also known as *Marginal Impact Factor* (MIF):

$$MIF_i(t) = \frac{\partial U(u(t))}{\partial u_i(t)} \tag{1.13}$$

It is possible to show that for FT, $MIF_i(t)$ is equal to:

$$MIF_i(t) = Pr\{TE|i, t\} - Pr\{TE|\bar{i}, t\} \tag{1.14}$$

where $Pr\{TE|i, t\}$ and $Pr\{TE|\bar{i}, t\}$ are the system unreliability at time $t$, given that basic component $i$ is failed and working, respectively.

Other measures of component importance have been proposed in the literature and they can be found in textbooks [Hoyland and Rausand (1994); Kovalenko *et al.* (1997)]. Table 1.3 reports some of them. In particular, MIF can be used as a basis for evaluating the criticality that an improvement of the component $i$ reliability may play in the system reliability. CIF extends MIF to take into account exactly such factor.

DIF is also known as *Fussell-Vesely Importance factor* (FVI) [Meng (2000)] and it measures the fraction of the system unreliability involving the situations in which component $i$ has failed. In FTA it can be defined in terms of MCS: it is the probability that at least one MCS containing

Table 1.3   Importance factors.

| Name | Acronym | Definition |
|------|---------|------------|
| Marginal Importance Factor | $MIF_i(t)$ | $Pr\{TE|i,t\} - Pr\{TE|\bar{i},t\}$ |
| Critical Importance Factor | $CIF_i(t)$ | $MIF_i(t) \cdot Pr\{i,t\}/Pr\{TE,t\}$ |
| Diagnostic Impact Factor | $DIF_i(t)$ | $Pr\{i|TE,t\} = Pr\{TE \wedge i,t\}/Pr\{TE,t\}$ |
| Risk Achievement Worth | $RAW_i(t)$ | $Pr\{TE|i,t\}/Pr\{TE,t\}$ |
| Risk Reduction Worth | $RRW_i(t)$ | $Pr\{TE,t\}/Pr\{TE|\bar{i},t\}$ |

component $i$ has failed at time $t$, given that the system is also failed at time $t$.

$RAW_i$ for a given component $i$ measures the increase in system failure probability, and computed for different values of $u_i(t)$ it is a meter of the importance of maintaining the current level of reliability for $i$. RRW represents the maximum decreasing of the risk it may be expected by increasing the reliability of the component. This quantity may be useful to rank the components that are the best candidates for efforts leading to improve the system reliability.

It is worth noting that all the importance measures introduced above concern the computation of probability of events, often conditioned on the occurrence of other events. As we will see in the next chapters, this is exactly the main task performed by means of *Probabilistic Graphical Models* (PGM) which are the main topic of the present book.

In the above discussion, only single component importance factors have been introduced, but in principle it may be relevant to compute importance factors for sets of components (e.g. for MCS) as well. We will discuss some examples in the following.

**Computational issues: Binary Decision Diagrams.**   The computation of both qualitative results and quantitative measures has improved notably by the introduction of *Binary Decision Diagrams* (BDD) [Rauzy (1993)] which encode the Boolean function characterizing the TE in a very compact way. The BDD representation has an enormous practical impact on the computational efficiency of FTA: the exact value of both qualitative and quantitative measures can be derived even for large systems, without resorting to an approximate solution. A BDD can represent the Boolean formula encoded by a FT, by means of the Shannon's decomposition: if $F$ is a Boolean function on variables $x_1, \ldots, x_n$, then

$$F = x_1 \wedge F_1 \vee \neg x_1 \wedge F_0 \qquad (1.15)$$

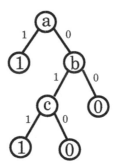

Fig. 1.7   The BDD expressing the Shannon's decomposition for the Boolean formula $F = a \vee b \wedge c$.

where $F_1$ is derived from $F$ assuming that $x_1$ is *true* $(F_1 = F|x_1 = true)$, and $F_0$ is derived from $F$ assuming that $x_1$ is *false* $(F_0 = F|x_1 = false)$.

Using recursively the Shannon's decomposition (Equation 1.15), we can express $F_1$ as $F_1 = x_2 \wedge F_{11} \vee \neg x_2 \wedge F_{10}$, and $F_0$ as $F_0 = x_2 \wedge F_{01} \vee \neg x_2 \wedge F_{00}$. Shannon's decomposition can be recursively applied until all the variables $x_1, \ldots x_n$ have been considered. The complete Shannon's decomposition can be displayed by means of a BDD which is a DAG where nodes represent variables.

Given the formula $F$, the node $x_1$ has two outgoing edges: the 1-edge points to the subgraph relative to $F_1$, while the 0-edge points to the subgraph relative to $F_0$. Typically, the 1-edge is drawn on the left side of the node, while the 0-edge is drawn on the right side. The terminal nodes are the constants 1 and 0 corresponding to *true* and *false*, respectively. Given a path from the root node to a terminal node, the value of the formula is given by the terminal node according to the values assigned to the variables, by means of the 1-edges and 0-edges, along the path.

The BDD obtained for the Boolean formula $F = a \vee b \wedge c$, is shown in Figure 1.7; we can compute the solution of the formula $F$ for any combination of values assigned to the variables $a, b, c$. For instance, the path $a \rightarrow b \rightarrow c \rightarrow 1$ indicates that if $a = 0$, $b = 1$ and $c = 1$, then $F = 1$. Another possible path is $a \rightarrow b \rightarrow 0$ and indicates that if $a = 0$ and $b = 0$, then $F = 0$.

The way to obtain the BDD equivalent to a FT is documented in [Rauzy (1993)]. Figure 1.8 shows the BDD corresponding to the FT in Figure 1.6. Once we have built the BDD, we can perform the qualitative analysis

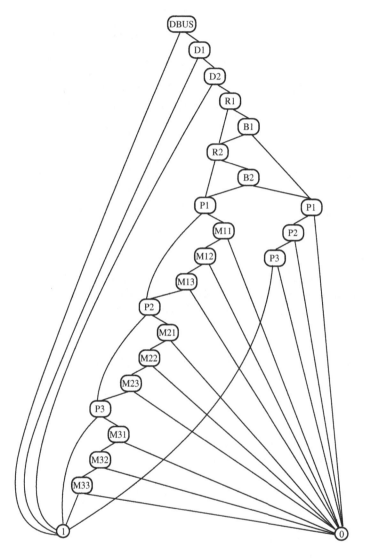

Fig. 1.8   The BDD obtained from the FT model in Figure 1.6.

(MCS detection):

$$MCS[F] = x_1 \wedge (MCS[F_1] - MCS[F_0]) \cup MC[F_0] \qquad (1.16)$$

Using recursively this formula starting from the root node and visiting the whole BDD, we can obtain all the MCS. The complexity of this algorithm is linear in the size of the BDD.

Table 1.4    Unreliability of the Multiproc system.

| time $t$ | $Pr\{TE, t\}$ | time $t$ | $Pr\{TE, t\}$ |
|---|---|---|---|
| 1000 h | 1.600717E-03 | 6000 h | 9.565979E-03 |
| 2000 h | 3.198873E-03 | 7000 h | 1.115139E-02 |
| 3000 h | 4.794473E-03 | 8000 h | 1.273428E-02 |
| 4000 h | 6.387520E-03 | 9000 h | 1.431464E-02 |
| 5000 h | 7.978020E-03 | 10000 h | 1.589248E-02 |

There are other ways to determine the MCS on the BDD. For instance, all the cut sets can be detected on the BDD by considering all the paths from the root node to the constant 1; for each of these paths, a cut set is given by the variables whose value is set to 1 (*true*) along the path. The paths from the root node to the constant 1 which do not include any other path, provide the MCS.

We can perform the quantitative analysis on the BDD. If $F(x_1, \ldots, x_n)$ is the formula encoded by the FT, the probability of the TE at a given time $t$ can be computed by means of Equation 1.17:

$$Pr\{TE, t\} = Pr\{x_1, t\} \cdot Pr\{F_1, t\}$$
$$+ (1 - Pr\{x_1, t\}) \cdot Pr\{F_0, t\} \qquad (1.17)$$

$Pr\{x_1, t\}$ is the probability at time $t$ of the BE $x_1$. Equation 1.17 has to be recursively applied to $F_1$ and $F_0$. The complexity of this algorithm is linear in the size of the BDD. Besides the system unreliability, the importance factors can be easily computed on the BDD corresponding to the FT model [Dutuit and Rauzy (2000)].

**Example case study.**    As an example, given the failure rates in Table 1.2, we can obtain the probability of TE (unreliability) for a time varying from 1000 $h$ to 10000 $h$. Such values are reported in Table 1.4.

Such results can be obtained either by manipulating MCS by means of the inclusion-exclusion expansion presented in Equation 1.11 or by means of BDD as explained above, but much more efficiently in the latter case. Of course, an efficient (but not always accurate enough) approximation of such results could also be obtained directly from MCS by exploiting Equation 1.12.

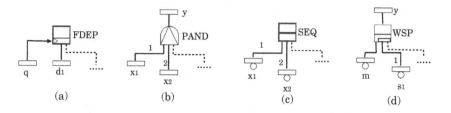

Fig. 1.9    The dynamic gates: a) FDEP; b) PAND; c) SEQ; d) WSP.

### 1.2.2    *Dynamic Fault Tree*

In FT models several assumptions hold: component failure events are assumed to be statistically independent, a component can be in two states only (working or failed), and the relations among the events are expressed by means of Boolean operators. This allows us to easily perform both the qualitative and quantitative analysis, possibly resorting to BDD. At the same time, these assumptions are a relevant limit to the modelling power of FTs, since they cannot represent dependencies involving the failure events or the state of the components. A dependency arises in the failure process when the failure behaviour of a component depends on the state of the system. One of the FT evolutions proposed in the literature is called *Dynamic Fault Tree* (DFT) [Dugan *et al.* (1992)]. In DFT, *dynamic gates* have been introduced in order to model functional dependencies, temporal dependencies and the presence of spare components.

**Functional Dependency Gate**    (FDEP) (Figure 1.9.a). An FDEP gate is connected to one trigger event $q$ and to a set of $n$ ($n \geq 1$) dependent events $d_1, \ldots, d_n$. When $q$ fails, $d_1, \ldots, d_n$ are forced to fail immediately.

**Priority And**    (PAND) (Figure 1.9.b). A PAND gate is connected to the input events $x_1, \ldots, x_n$ ($n \geq 2$) and to the output event $y$. If we indicate with $\phi(y)$ the Boolean value of $y$, $\phi(y) = true$ if both the following conditions hold:

- $\bigwedge_{i=1}^{n} x_i = true$
- $x_1, \ldots, x_n$ occurred in this order: $x_1 \prec x_2 \prec \cdots \prec x_n$, where $x \prec y$ means that $x$ precedes $y$.

The order of $x_1, \ldots, x_n$ is given by a number $(1, \ldots, n)$ assigned to each of the arcs connecting $x_1, \ldots, x_n$ to the gate.

**Warm Spare Gate**   (WSP) (Figure 1.9.d). This gate models the presence of a main component $m$ and a set of spare components $s_1, \ldots, s_m$ ($m \geq 1$) with the aim of replacing $m$ in its function if $m$ fails. $s_1, \ldots, s_m$ are called "warm" spare components because they can be in three states instead of two: dormant (or stand-by), working (or operative), failed (Figure 1.10). A spare is initially dormant and turns to the working state if it has to replace the main component; at the same time, a spare may fail both in the dormant and in the working state; the spare failure rate changes depending on its current state: if the failure rate of the spare $s_i$ is $\lambda_{s_i}$ in the working state, $\alpha_{s_i} \lambda_{s_i}$ is its failure rate in the dormant state, with $0 < \alpha_{s_i} < 1$; $\alpha_{s_i}$ is the dormancy factor of the spare $s_i$, and its aim is to express the fact that spares have a reduced failure probability during the dormancy period. If the working spare $s_i$ fails, $m$ is replaced by the spare $s_{i+1}$ instead of $s_i$. The input events of a WSP gate are the BE $m, s_1, \ldots, s_m$ modelling the failure of the main component and the failure of the spares. $s_1, \ldots, s_m$ must be ordered; the arcs connecting them to the gate have an order number varying between 1 and $m$. If $y$ is the output event of the gate, and we indicate with $\phi(y)$ the Boolean value of $y$, then

$$\phi(y) = m \wedge \bigwedge_{i=1}^{n} s_i$$

Two alternative versions of this gate exist:

- *Cold Spare* gate (CSP): $\forall s_i, \alpha_{s_i} = 0$
  The spares can not fail during the dormancy period.
- *Hot Spare* gate (HSP): $\forall s_i, \alpha_{s_i} = 1$
  The failure rate of the spares is the same in both the dormancy period and the working period.

Actually, HSP gates can be modeled as standard AND gates and they are not strictly considered as primary constructs of the DFT language.

**Sequence Enforcing Gate**   (SEQ) (Figure 1.9.c). Given a set of $n \geq 2$ events $x_1, \ldots, x_n$ connected to a SEQ gate, $x_1, \ldots, x_n$ are forced to fail in a specific order: $x_1 \prec x_2 \prec \cdots \prec x_n$. A number is associated with each of the arcs connecting $x_1, \ldots, x_n$ to the gate, in order to specify the failure order.

Also SEQ gates are not strictly a primary construct in a DFT, since they can be modeled as a special case of a CSP [Manian *et al.* (1999)]; therefore, they can be used as syntactic sugar when it is natural to emphasize the

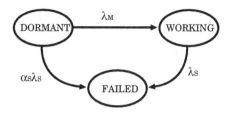

Fig. 1.10   The states of the spare $S$ depending on the main component $M$.

sequential nature of some faults. An example of DFT model is shown in Figure 1.12.

### 1.2.2.1   *A DFT Modeling Example*

We extend the example case study of *Multiproc* introduced in Section 1.2.1.1, by the addition of dependencies among several components. The system is again composed by three processing units ($PU1$, $PU2$, $PU3$), two shared memories ($R1$, $R2$), and two disks which are now a primary ($D1$) and a backup disk ($D2$). The scheme of the system is shown in Figure 1.11. Each processing unit is composed by one processor and one internal memory. In the case of $PU1$, they are $P1$ and $M1$ respectively. Both $R1$ and $R2$ are connected to the processing units by means of the bus $B$, and they can replace any internal memory if it fails. A spare memory can be in one of these three states: dormant, working, failed. $PU1$, $PU2$, $PU3$ share $D1$, while $D2$ is the backup of the data contained in $D1$. Initially, the processing units access $D1$, while $D2$ is only periodically accessed by a particular device ($BD$) for the update operations; so, we assume that in this situation, $D2$ can not fail. If $D1$ fails, the processing units access $D2$; from this moment, $D2$ may fail. Both $D1$ and $D2$ can be accessed by $PU1$, $PU2$, $PU3$, through the bus $DBUS$.

**Failure mode.** The correct functioning of at least one processing unit is required for the system to be working; so, the failure of all $PU1$, $PU2$, $PU3$ causes the whole system failure. A processing unit fails in two cases: if its processor fails, or if its internal memory fails and there are no available spare memories to replace it. A spare memory is available to replacement if it is not failed and it is not already replacing another internal memory. Moreover, both $R1$ and $R2$ functionally depend on $B$; so, if $B$ fails both $R1$ and $R2$ cannot be accessed by $PU1$, $PU2$, $PU3$, and this has the same

Table 1.5   The failure rate for each type of component.

| Component | Failure rate ($\lambda$) | Dormancy factor ($\alpha$) |
|---|---|---|
| Processor | 5.0E-7 $h^{-1}$ | |
| Disk | 8.0E-7 $h^{-1}$ | |
| Memory | 3.0E-8 $h^{-1}$ | 0.1 |
| Bus | 2.0E-9 $h^{-1}$ | |
| Backup Device | 7.0E-8 $h^{-1}$ | |

effect of the contemporary failure of $R1$ and $R2$. Another cause of failure
of the system, is the compromised access to the hard disks; this happens in
three cases: the failure of $DBUS$, the failure of both $D1$ and $D2$, and the
failure of $BD$. In particular, the failure of $BD$ is relevant only if it happens
before the failure of $D1$. In this case, when $D1$ fails and is replaced by
$D2$, this one is not updated, due to the previous failure of $BD$. If instead
$BD$ fails after the failure of $D1$, the update operation is not necessary any
more. Table 1.5 indicates the failure rate (and the dormancy factor) for
each type of component.

**DFT model.** The DFT in Figure 1.12 represents the failure mode of the
system. The $TE$ is caused by the compromised access to the hard disks
or by the failure of all the processing units, so $TE$ is the output of an $OR$
gate whose input events are $DA$ and $CM$. $DA$ is the output of an $OR$ gate
whose input events are $DBUS$, $UPD$, $MS$. $UPD$ represents the failed
update of the backup disk, and $MS$ represents the failure of both disks.
$UPD$ is the output of a PAND gate whose ordered input events are $BD$
and $D1$. So, $UPD$ occurs when both $BD$ and $D1$ have occurred, and if
$BD$ occurred before $D1$. Since $D2$ can not fail before the failure of $D1$,
$D1$ and $D2$ are connected to a SEQ gate, by means of ordered arcs. The
event $MS$ is the output of a gate of type $AND$ with $D1$ and $D2$ as input
events. The event $CM$ indicates the failure of all the processing units, so
it is the output of an $AND$ gate having $PU1$, $PU2$, $PU3$ as input events.
$PU1$ is the output of an $OR$ gate whose input events are $P1$ and $MEM1$;
in particular, $MEM1$ represents the failure of $M1$ and the contemporary
impossibility of $M1$ to be replaced by any spare memory. $MEM1$ is the
output of a WSP gate having as input events $M1$, $R1$, $R2$. $R1$ and $R2$ are
connected to the gate by means of ordered arcs. The failure of $PU2$ and
$PU3$ is modelled in a similar way. $R1$ and $R2$ are connected also to other
two WSP gates since $R1$ and $R2$ can replace also the internal memories of
the other processing units. The functional dependency of $R1$ and $R2$ on

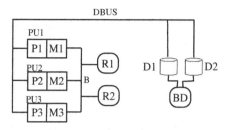

Fig. 1.11  The scheme of the Multiproc system with dependencies.

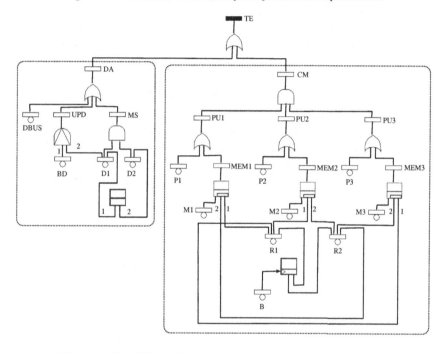

Fig. 1.12  The DFT model for the Multiproc system in Figure 1.11.

$B$ is modelled by a FDEP gate having $B$ as trigger event, $R1$ and $R2$ as dependent events.

#### 1.2.2.2  *DFT analysis*

Due to the presence of dependencies, the solution techniques used for FT are not applicable to the analysis of a DFT; this kind of model needs the *state space analysis* (see Section 1.3 below in the chapter). This requires the generation of all the possible system states and stochastic transitions between states. The way to perform the quantitative analysis of DFT models is presented in Section 1.3.2.2.

## 1.3 State Space Models

When the accuracy of combinatorial models is not enough to capture the characteristics of the system to be modelled, we can resort to state space based models; they represent the behaviour of the system in terms of reachable states and possible state transitions. The models in this category have a greater modelling power with respect to the combinatorial models, but the state space analysis may be computationally expensive. This depends on the number of states in the model: the state space size may grow exponentially with respect to the number of components in the system. When the analysis of state space based models becomes unpractical due to the high number of states, dependability measures can be obtained from these models by means of simulation. In general, state space based models are addressed to expert model designers. Examples of models in this category are *Markov Chains* (MC) and *Petri Nets* (PN) [Sahner *et al.* (1996)].

### 1.3.1 *Markov Chains*

In terms of graph, in a MC, nodes represent states, while arcs represent state transitions. A state can be considered as a specific configuration of the system holding for a time interval. The occurrence of an event may change the system configuration, so the system state. As an example, let us consider the MC depicted in Figure 1.13: a system may be initially in the normal state; this state holds until the occurrence of the malfunctioning of a component; this event may cause the transition from the normal state to the anomalous state. Then, the system may turn to the normal state, if the recovery of the component is performed, or may turn to the failed state if the component is definitively faulty.

In a MC the duration of a state is a random variable ruled by the probabilities associated with the state transitions. In *Discrete Time Markov Chains* (DTMC) [Sahner *et al.* (1996)], time is discretized according to a time step $\Delta$, so that transitions may occur at time $\Delta$, $2\Delta$, $3\Delta$, etc. So, each transition is characterized by the probability that the transition occurs when a time step is reached. In *Continuous Time Markov Chain*

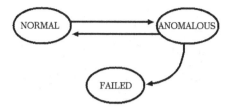

Fig. 1.13 An example of Markov Chain.

(CTMC) [Sahner *et al.* (1996)], a state transition may occur at any instant of time. In this case state transitions are characterized by the negative exponential distribution (Section 1.1.3) providing the state transition probability as a function of the time. A transition rate $\lambda$ is associated with each transition. If rates are constant, we talk about homogeneous CTMC; if rates are time dependent, we talk about non homogeneous CTMC. Both DTMC and CTMC are characterized by the initial probability vector providing for each state the probability to be in that state at time 0.

The analysis of a DTMC or CTMC can determine the values of several measures [Sahner *et al.* (1996)]. A typical one is the probability of the system to be in a specific state. This can be computed at a certain time (transient) analysis) or at infinite time (steady-state analysis).

In reliability models, the use of DTMC or CTMC becomes necessary when the system behaviour is characterized by dependent events concerning the failure mode or the recovery of the system, or by multi-state components. An example could be the case where the failure rate of a spare component changes according to the state of the main component, as shown by the CTMC in Figure 1.10. This situation cannot be represented in combinatorial model like a FT. This situation can be modelled by a DFT using the WSP gate, but the analysis of the model requires the CTMC generation (Section 1.2.2). Another case where the use of MC becomes necessary, is the repair of a failed component, performed when the failure of the subsystem occurs. Only a certain number of components may be repairable in a contemporary way, because of shared repair facilities.

### 1.3.2 *Petri Nets*

A PN contains two kinds of nodes: *places* and *transitions*. Places contain a discrete number of *tokens*; this number is called *marking*. A place graphically appears as a circle. The current state of the system is modelled by

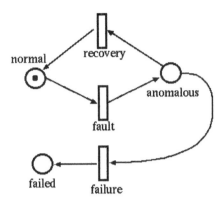

Fig. 1.14   An example of Petri Net (the multiplicity of all the arcs is 1).

the current net marking which is the number of tokens in each place of the net. Transitions are graphically represented by rectangles and are used to model the system state transitions. A transition is connected to a set of input places by means of input arcs, and to a set of output places by means of output arcs. Both kinds of arcs are characterized by a multiplicity. A transition is enabled to fire if each input place contains at least the number of tokens specified by the input arc multiplicity. When the transition fires, a certain number of tokens is consumed in input places and a certain number of tokens is produced in output places. The number of tokens consumed or produced is given by the multiplicity of the input or output arc, respectively. The firing of a transition modifies the net marking, so the system state.

**Example.**   An example of PN is shown in Figure 1.14 and corresponds to the same process represented by the MC in Figure 1.13. The initial presence of one token inside the place *normal* indicates the initial normal state of the system. In this situation, only the transition *fault* is enabled to fire; this transition models a malfunctioning. The firing of *fault* moves the token from the place *normal* to the place *anomalous*, in order to represent the anomalous state of the system. When the place *anomalous* is marked, two transitions are enabled to fire: *recovery* and *failure*. The firing of *recovery* moves the token back to the place *normal*, so that the initial situation holds again. The firing of *failure* instead, moves the token to the place *failed*, in order to model the definitive failure of the system.

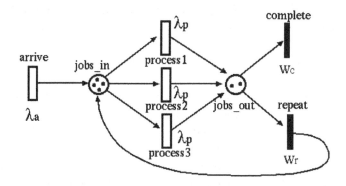

Fig. 1.15    An example of GSPN (the multiplicity of all the arcs is 1).

### 1.3.2.1   *Generalized Stochastic Petri Nets*

Several kinds of Petri Nets are present in the literature. In particular, *Generalized Stochastic Petri Nets* (GSPN) [Ajmone-Marsan *et al.* (1995)] are characterized by the presence of two types of transitions: *immediate transitions* (black rectangles) fire as soon as they are enabled; the firing of *timed transitions* (white rectangles) instead, is delayed of a period of time whose duration is a random variable ruled by a negative exponential distribution whose parameter is the *firing rate* of the timed transition. In GSPN we have a third type of arcs: *inhibitor arcs* connect a place to a transition with the aim of disabling the transition; the multiplicity of the arc indicates the minimum number of tokens inside the place, necessary to disable the transition.

In a GSPN, two or more immediate transitions may be enabled at the same time; in this case, *weights* and *priorities* can be used to rule their firing. If we use weights, higher is the weight of a transition, higher is its probability to fire. If we use priorities, the transition with highest priority fires.

**Example.** An example of GSPN is shown in Figure 1.15 and models the processing of incoming jobs by three servers. The transition *arrive* produces the tokens inside the place *jobs_in*; each of them represents one job to be processed. The transitions *process1, process2, process3* represent the processing of jobs; they are enabled if at least one token is present inside *jobs_in*. The firing of any of them moves one token from *jobs_in* to *jobs_out*; the tokens inside *jobs_out* represent the completed jobs. All the transitions above are timed, so their firing occurs with a random delay ruled by the firing rate ($\lambda_a$ or $\lambda_p$ in Figure 1.15). Actually the arrival of jobs and their processing are activities requiring time in order to be performed. If the place *jobs_out* is marked with at least one token, then two transitions are enabled to fire: *repeat* and *complete*. The firing of the transition *repeat* moves one token from *jobs_out* back to *jobs_in*, in order to model that a job has to be processed again. The firing of the transition *complete* instead, simply removes one token from *jobs_out*, in order to model that a job has been effectively completed. The transitions *repeat* and *complete* are immediate (we assume that the decision to repeat a job or not is taken in an immediate way). The presence of tokens inside *jobs_out* enables both of them, so weights can be assigned to the transitions in order to determine their probability to fire ($w_c$ and $w_r$ in Figure 1.15).

**GSPN analysis.** The analysis of a GSPN is performed on the corresponding CTMC; the GSPN analysis provides measures such as the probability of a certain marking of a place, the throughput of a transition (mean number of tokens moved by the transition per time unit), the expected number of tokens inside a specific place, etc. The analysis can be transient or steady-state; in the first case, the measures are computed at a given finite time $t$; in the second case they are computed for $t = +\infty$. In order to obtain the CTMC corresponding to a GSPN, first the *reachability graph* is generated. The reachability graph expresses all the possible markings which are reachable from the initial marking through the firing of transitions. In the reachability graph, we distinguish between *vanishing* markings and *tangible* markings. A vanishing marking enables one or more immediate transitions to fire; a tangible marking enables the firing of one or more timed transitions and enables no immediate transitions. By reducing the reachability graph to contain only tangible markings, we obtain the CTMC corresponding to the GSPN, where a state is given by a tangible marking, while a state transition is given by the firing of a timed transition.

**GSPN simulation.** The measures returned by GSPN analysis, can be obtained also by means of GSPN simulation. The use of simulation instead of analysis, is useful when the number of states (and state transitions) in the CTMC, is very high. In this situation, the analysis becomes computationally expensive, or even unfeasible.

## 1.3.2.2 *GSPN based analysis of DFT*

Due to the presence of dependencies, DFT models (Section 1.2.2) require the state space analysis. In other words, we need to obtain and solve the CTMC equivalent to the DFT in terms of stochastic process. The algorithm do derive a CTMC from a DFT is documented in [Manian *et al.* (1999)]. However, generating the CTMC directly from a DFT, may not be so straightforward, while efficient techniques to generate the CTMC from a GSPN are available. So, a possible way to perform the state space analysis of a DFT, consists of converting the DFT into the equivalent GSPN; then, the CTMC can be generated from the GSPN, and the unreliability of the system can be computed on the CTMC as the probability of a specific state. The way to convert a DFT into a GSPN is documented in [Codetta-Raiteri (2005)].

**Modules.** The state space analysis of a DFT is typically expensive in terms of computing, since the number of states tends to grows exponentially with the number of components. However, the state space analysis is strictly necessary only for the subtrees containing dynamic gates, while for the subtrees with only Boolean gates, the *combinatorial analysis* (exploiting MCS or BDD) is suitable. So, a way to reduce the computational cost of the state space analysis, consists of using this technique only with the subtrees containing dynamic gates, and using the combinatorial technique with the rest of the DFT [Gulati and Dugan (2003)]. Such approach requires the solution of subtrees in isolation; to this aim, the subtree must be independent from the rest of the DFT. So, the *modules* (independent subtrees) detection becomes necessary.

In a FT, a module is a subtree which is *structurally independent* from the rest of the FT; this holds if the events in the subtree, do not occur elsewhere in the FT [Dutuit and Rauzy (1996)]. This notion of module is still valid on a DFT, but we need also a way to classify the modules according to the analysis technique they require. If $e$ is the root of a subtree (possibly a module), $\hat{e}$ indicates the subtree.

- $\hat{e}$ is a *Combinatorial Solution Module* (CSM) if it is structurally independent and does not contain any dynamic gate. A CSM requires the combinatorial analysis.
- $\hat{e}$ is a *State space Solution Module* (SSM) if it is structurally independent and contains at least one dynamic gate. A SSM requires the state space analysis.

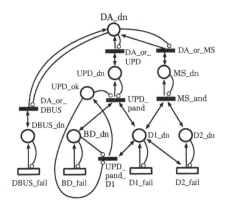

Fig. 1.16    The GSPN corresponding to the module $\widehat{DA}$ in Figure 1.12.

**Unreliability.** The main steps to compute the system unreliability at time $t$ on a DFT are: modules detection, modules classification, DFT decomposition, modules analysis and aggregation. In the decomposition step, we have to detach SSM from the DFT. The state space analysis of a SSM can be realized by converting the module into a GSPN. Then, the resulting GSPN can be analyzed returning the probability at time $t$, of the GSPN place corresponding to root event of the module being marked. In the aggregation step, we have to replace each of the detached SSM with a BE having such probability, instead of a failure rate. After the aggregation step, the DFT does not contain any dynamic gate, so it is now a CSM and can be analyzed with the combinatorial technique. In particular BDD can deal with BE characterized by a constant probability or by a failure rate.

**Example.** As an example, we compute the TE probability of the DFT in Figure 1.12, for a mission time of 10000 $h$. The SSM are $\widehat{DA}$ and $\widehat{CM}$ which are converted into GSPN as shown in Figure 1.16 and Figure 1.17 respectively. The state space analysis of $\widehat{DA}$ and $\widehat{CM}$ at time $t = 10000h$ returns these probabilities:

$Pr\{DA, t\} = Pr\{m(DA\_dn) = 1, t\} = 5.460599E\text{-}5$

$Pr\{CM, t\} = Pr\{m(CM\_dn) = 1, t\} = 1.240670E\text{-}7$

The function $m$ stands for the number of tokens (*marking*) inside a place. The state space of $\widehat{DA}$ and $\widehat{CM}$, generated from the equivalent GSPN, contains 14 states and 487 states, respectively. The state space derived from the GSPN equivalent to the whole DFT is composed by 7806 states. Thus,

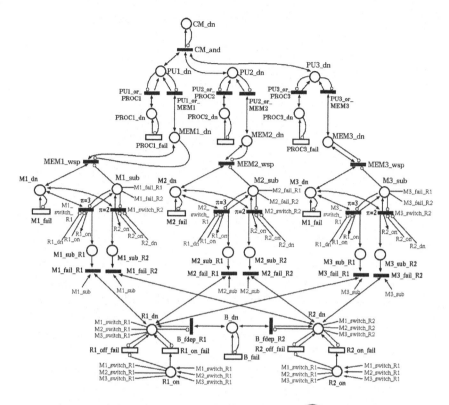

Fig. 1.17 The GSPN corresponding to the module $\widehat{CM}$ in Figure 1.12.

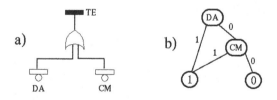

Fig. 1.18 a) The DFT model of Multiproc after the SSM analysis. b) The equivalent BDD.

it is evident the reduction of the computational cost given by the module based analysis of DFT. The replacement of the SSM with BE having the probability indicated above, produces the DFT in Figure 1.18.a; this is a CSM, so we can generate and analyze the corresponding BDD shown in

Table 1.6   Unreliability of the Multiproc system with dependencies.

| time $t$ | $Pr\{DA,t\}$ | $Pr\{CM,t\}$ | $Pr\{TE,t\}$ |
|---|---|---|---|
| 1000 h | 2.347804E-6 | 1.25E-10 | 2.347929E-06 |
| 2000 h | 5.390438E-6 | 9.99E-10 | 5.391436E-06 |
| 3000 h | 9.126738E-6 | 3.367E-9 | 9.130105E-06 |
| 4000 h | 1.355554E-5 | 7.976E-9 | 1.356352E-05 |
| 5000 h | 1.867569E-5 | 1.5567E-8 | 1.869125E-05 |
| 6000 h | 2.448601E-5 | 2.6879E-8 | 2.451289E-05 |
| 7000 h | 3.098536E-5 | 4.2651E-8 | 3.102801E-05 |
| 8000 h | 3.817258E-5 | 6.3617E-8 | 3.823620E-05 |
| 9000 h | 4.604651E-5 | 9.0513E-8 | 4.613702E-05 |
| 10000 h | 5.460599E-5 | 1.24067E-7 | 5.473005E-05 |

Figure 1.18.b; we obtain that the TE probability is 5.473005E-5. Table 1.6 reports the probabilities of the SSM and the TE, for several mission times.

**Qualitative analysis.** Some methods have been proposed to compute importance measures [Ou and Dugan (2000)], as well as to perform the qualitative analysis [Tang and Dugan (2004)] of DFT. The qualitative analysis of DFT returns the MCS and the *Minimal Cut Sequences* (MCSeq) of the system. In particular, a MCSeq is an ordered sequence of BE leading to the occurrence of the TE. MCSeq are justified by the presence in the DFT of dynamic gates requiring or forcing the event to occur in a certain temporal order.

The first reliability tool proposing modeling and analysis of DFT has been a software tool named GALILEO [Dugan *et al.* (2000); Sullivan *et al.* (1999)]; it can be used also to perform quantitative, sensitivity and qualitative analysis of DFTs.

Chapter 2

# Probabilistic Graphical Models

As we have discussed in the previous chapter, the typical approach to dependability and reliability analysis is the probabilistic one. This means that a probabilistic model of the system to be analyzed has to be constructed.

Given a set of random variables, a sound probabilistic model over such variables has to rely on the joint probability distribution over the variables. The modeler has then two main choices: either to specify the joint probability distribution directly or to devise a suitable set of independence assumptions, allowing one to derive the joint distribution indirectly. The first approach suffers from a combinatorial explosion problem: given a set of $N$ variables, the number of entries in their joint distribution is clearly exponential in $N$; asking the modeler to specify the whole set of entries in the joint probability distribution can then be prohibitive for many real-world problems. This is the problem we encountered in state space models, as discussed in the previous chapter.

On the other hand, a common assumption that allows to drastically reduce the number of required parameters is to consider every variable independent from the others: in this case, the modeler has to specify only a linear (in terms of the size of the variable set) number of entries, and the joint distribution can be easily obtained by multiplying the corresponding probabilistic parameters (as we have seen in standard FTA).

However, assuming the complete independence of the whole set of variables is clearly unrealistic in the majority of cases [1].

---

[1] A relevant exception to this situation is the task of probabilistic classification using the so called *Naive Bayes* model [Duda and Hart (1973)]. In this model, the task is to classify a given instance of an object, described in terms of different features and providing a pre-specified set of classes. The main assumption is that a given feature is independent from the others, given the class; despite the fact that this assumption is violated in several practical cases, the Naive Bayes classifier has been shown to be very

An alternative to the *complete independence assumption* is to provide more reasonable information concerning the conditional independence of specific subsets of the involved random variables. The standard tool for building this kind of models is definitely the framework of *Probabilistic Graphical Models* (PGM) [Jordan (1999); Koller and Friedman (2009); Lauritzen (2004); Whittaker (2009)]. A PGM is a type of probabilistic network having roots in different fields, and in particular in Artificial Intelligence [Pearl (1988)] and statistics [Lauritzen and Spiegelhalter (1988); Jordan (2004)]. A probabilistic graphical model is a composed by two main parts:

- a *qualitative part* represented by a graph denoting the conditional dependence structure between the random variables of interest;
- a *quantitative part* represented by a set of numerical parameters (generically called *factors*), defined over the graph structure, and through which the joint probability distribution of the random variables of the model can be defined.

The qualitative part is then a graph where nodes represent the variables of interest of the model, and edges represent dependence relations among such variables. Depending on the structure of such a graph, we can classify PGMs into three main categories:

- *undirected models*, when the underlying graph is undirected; this class of PGMs is also called *Markov Random Fields* (MRF) or *Markov Networks* [Kindermann and Snell (1980)];
- *directed models*, when the underlying graph is a DAG (Directed Acyclic Graph); in case nodes represent only random variables we have *Bayesian (Belief) Networks* (BN), while when nodes represent decision variables as well, we have *Decision Networks* (DN) (also known as *Influence Diagrams*) [Jensen and Nielsen (2007)];
- *mixed models*, when both directed and undirected edges are present in the underlying graph; in this case, the constraint is that no directed cycle is present in the graph, and we talk about *Chain Graphs* [Wermuth and Lauritzen (1990)].

Concerning the quantitative part, independently on the underlying graph, it represents a parametric specification of the joint probability distribution over the random variables of the model. The model is interpreted in such

---

robust, even when the assumption is not satisfied in practice (meaning that the class provided by the model, is often practically insensitive to the right set of dependencies) [Domingos and Pazzani (1997); Rish (2001); Zhang (2004)].

a way that the parametric specification (which depends on the class of the model) consists in a factorization of the whole joint distribution. This allows to exploit a "local" parametrization, without loosing the "global" semantics of the model (see below).

Although mixed models generalize both directed and undirected models, and although undirected models can in general represent more complicated relations among the variables, for the aim of the present book, considering the class of directed models is definitely sufficient. In particular, directed models have the advantage of exploiting the directionality of edges, in order to capture cause-effect relationships that may be really important when studying dependability issues. In the remainder of this chapter we will then briefly review the basic features of directed models.

## 2.1 Bayesian Belief Networks

Bayesian (or Belief) Networks (BN) are a widely used formalism for representing uncertain knowledge in probabilistic systems, applied to a variety of real-world problems [Cowell *et al.* (1999); Jensen and Nielsen (2007); Kjaerulff and Madsen (2008); Pearl (1988)]. BNs are directed graphical models defined by a directed acyclic graph in which random variables are assigned to each node, together with a quantitative parametrization local to each node.

**Definition 2.1.** A Bayesian Network is a pair $N = \langle G, Pr \rangle$ where:

- $G = (V, E)$ is a DAG whose nodes $V = \{X_1, X_2, \ldots X_n\}$ are a set of discrete random variables and where an edge $e = (X_i \to X_j) \in E$ from $X_i$ to $X_j$ means that $X_j$ depends on $X_i$ (often interpreted as $X_i$ causes $X_j$);
- $Pr$ is a probability distribution over $X_1, X_2, \ldots X_n$ such that

$$Pr(X_1, X_2, \ldots X_n) = \prod_{i=1}^{n} Pr(X_i | pa(X_i))$$

where $pa(X)$ is the set of parent variables of $X$ in the DAG $G$. We say that $Pr$ *factorizes* over $G$.

In the following, we will consider models where random variables are discrete. Extensions to continuous variables are possible and models where both discrete and continuous variables are present have been studied under the name of *Hybrid Bayesian Networks* (HBN) [Langseth *et al.* (2009)]. The main problem in such models is inference that can be performed exactly only when the modeled distributions are in specific forms e.g., Mixture of Truncated Exponentials (MTE) [Moral *et al.* (2001)] or Mixture of Gaussian distributions [Shenoy (2006)]; they very often requires approximate solutions, because of the computational complexity of the problem.

The advantage of the BN representation is that one can get the joint probability of the variables of the model, by specifying a set of conditional probabilities local to each variable $X_i$ and to its parents $pa(X_i)$. Since this set of conditional probability parameters can be provided in tabular form, the term *Conditional Probability Table* (CPT) is used to indicate such a parametrization.

**BN Modeling Example.** An example of BN is given in Figure 2.1; the corresponding set of CPTs is provided in Table 2.1. The model represents

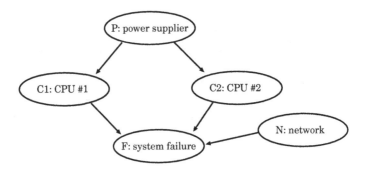

Fig. 2.1    Example of a Bayesian Network.

a fragment of a computational system composed by 2 processors $C1, C2$, connected in a network $N$ and powered through a power supplier $P$ (see Figure 2.2); the failure of the power supplier causes the failure of the processors, while if the power supplier is in the Ok state, there is a 10% probability of having a failure in each of the processors (see the CPTs of nodes $C1$ and $C2$). CPT of node $P$ models a 1% prior probability of failure for the power supplier, while the CPT of node $N$ indicates a 5% prior probability of unavailability for the network. Finally, the whole system is considered in failure mode when either the network is unavailable or both the processors are down; the system is usually working in case at least one processor is working and the network is available; however, the system may be down (due to other causes) with a small probability even in such situations (5%

Table 2.1 CPTs for
the variables P, C1,
C2, N, F (Figure 2.1)

| P=Ok | 0.99 |
|---|---|
| P=Failed | 0.01 |

| | P=Ok | P=Failed |
|---|---|---|
| C1=Ok | 0.9 | 0 |
| C1=Failed | 0.1 | 1 |

| | P=Ok | P=Failed |
|---|---|---|
| C2=Ok | 0.9 | 0 |
| C2=Failed | 0.1 | 1 |

| N=Ok | 0.95 |
|---|---|
| N=Failed | 0.05 |

| | N=Ok | | | |
|---|---|---|---|---|
| | C1=Ok | | C1=Failed | |
| | C2=Ok | C2=Failed | C2=Ok | C2=Failed |
| F=No | 0.999 | 0.95 | 0.95 | 0 |
| F=Yes | 0.001 | 0.05 | 0.05 | 1 |

| | N=Unavailable | | | |
|---|---|---|---|---|
| | C1=Ok | | C1=Failed | |
| | C2=Ok | C2=Failed | C2=Ok | C2=Failed |
| F=No | 0 | 0 | 0 | 0 |
| F=Yes | 1 | 1 | 1 | 1 |

probability of failure when one of the processors is down and 1% probability of failure when everything is ok); this uncertainty is reflected in the CPT of node $F$ (which is split in two parts in Table 2.1, for the sake of clarity), representing the system failure (and corresponding, in FTA to the TE of a FT - see Chapter 1, Section 1.2.1).

Following definition 2.1, the quantification of the BN of Figure 2.1 corresponds to the implicit specification of the whole joint probability distri-

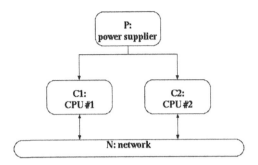

Fig. 2.2   A simple computational system.

bution of the variables of the net. Table 2.2 reports such explicit joint distribution. For example, the first row of Table 2.2 is computed as

$Pr(P = \text{Ok}, C1 = \text{Ok}, C2 = \text{Ok}, N = \text{Ok}, F = \text{No}) =$
$Pr(P = \text{Ok})Pr(C1 = \text{Ok}|P = \text{Ok})Pr(C2 = \text{Ok}|P = \text{Ok})$
$Pr(N = \text{Ok})Pr(F = \text{No}|C1 = \text{Ok}, C2 = \text{Ok}, N = \text{Ok}) =$
$0.99\ 0.9\ 0.9\ 0.95\ 0.999 = 0.7610$

The other entries of the joint probability table can be obtained similarly.

### 2.1.1   *Conditional independence and factorization*

The justification underlying the factorization of the joint distribution consists in a graph theoretical notion called *I-map*. In order to make clear this notion, let us introduce some preliminary definitions.

**Definition 2.2.** Given a DAG $G = (V, E)$ and an undirected path (also called a *trail*) $X_1, \ldots X_n$, we say that there is a *v-structure* in the trail if there exists $X_i$ in the trail such that $X_{i-1}$ and $X_{i+1}$ are parents of $X_i$ in $G$ (i.e., $X_{i-1} \to X_i \leftarrow X_{i+1}$).

**Definition 2.3.** Given a DAG $G = (V, E)$, a trail $X_1, \ldots X_n$ and a subset of nodes $Z \subseteq V$, the trail is said to be *active* given $Z$ if

- for any v-structure $X_{i-1} \to X_i \leftarrow X_{i+1}$ we have that $X_i$ or one of its descendant is in $Z$;
- no other $X_i$ not in a v-structure is in $Z$.

**Definition 2.4.** Given a DAG $G = (V, E)$, two nodes $X, Y \in V$ are said to be *d-separated* given $Z \subseteq V$ if there is no active trail between $X$ and $Y$ given $Z$. We indicate this through the notation $dsep_G(X, Y|Z)$.

Table 2.2    The joint distribution of the Bayesian Network in Figure 2.1

| P | C1 | C2 | N | F | Pr |
|---|----|----|---|---|-----|
| Ok | Ok | Ok | Ok | No | 0.7610 |
| Ok | Ok | Ok | Ok | Yes | 0.0008 |
| Ok | Ok | Ok | Unavailable | No | 0 |
| Ok | Ok | Ok | Unavailable | Yes | 0.0401 |
| Ok | Ok | Failed | Ok | No | 0.0804 |
| Ok | Ok | Failed | Ok | Yes | 0.0042 |
| Ok | Ok | Failed | Unavailable | No | 0 |
| Ok | Ok | Failed | Unavailable | Yes | 0.0045 |
| Ok | Failed | Ok | Ok | No | 0.0804 |
| Ok | Failed | Ok | Ok | Yes | 0.0042 |
| Ok | Failed | Ok | Unavailable | No | 0 |
| Ok | Failed | Ok | Unavailable | Yes | 0.0045 |
| Ok | Failed | Failed | Ok | No | 0 |
| Ok | Failed | Failed | Ok | Yes | 0.0094 |
| Ok | Failed | Failed | Unavailable | No | 0 |
| Ok | Failed | Failed | Unavailable | Yes | 0.0005 |
| Failed | Ok | Ok | Ok | No | 0 |
| Failed | Ok | Ok | Ok | Yes | 0 |
| Failed | Ok | Ok | Unavailable | No | 0 |
| Failed | Ok | Ok | Unavailable | Yes | 0 |
| Failed | Ok | Failed | Ok | No | 0 |
| Failed | Ok | Failed | Ok | Yes | 0 |
| Failed | Ok | Failed | Unavailable | No | 0 |
| Failed | Ok | Failed | Unavailable | Yes | 0 |
| Failed | Failed | Ok | Ok | No | 0 |
| Failed | Failed | Ok | Ok | Yes | 0 |
| Failed | Failed | Ok | Unavailable | No | 0 |
| Failed | Failed | Ok | Unavailable | Yes | 0 |
| Failed | Failed | Failed | Ok | No | 0 |
| Failed | Failed | Failed | Ok | Yes | 0.0095 |
| Failed | Failed | Failed | Unavailable | No | 0 |
| Failed | Failed | Failed | Unavailable | Yes | 0.0005 |

**Example.** Given the BN of Figure 2.1 it is easy to verify that the following d-separation relations hold (given that $G$ is the underlying DAG of the BN): $dsep_G(P, F|\{C1\})$; $dsep_G(C1, C2|\{P\})$; $dsep_G(C1, N|\emptyset)$. On the other hand, the following d-separation does hold: $dsep_G(C1, N|\{F\})$.

The aim of the notion of d-separation is to capture the notion of conditional independence and can be checked in an efficient way (linear in the number of edges) [Geiger *et al.* (1989)]. One of the main results of Bayesian Networks theory is indeed that, if we assume that d-separation represents conditional independence, then factorization of the joint probability exactly captures the conditional independence assumptions encoded in the DAG.

More formally: let us use the notation $(X \perp Y | Z)$ to indicate that $X$ is independent from $Y$ given the set $Z$.

**Definition 2.5.** Given a DAG $G = (V, E)$ and a probability distribution $Pr$ defined over the variables represented by $V$, consider the relation $I(G) = \{(X \perp Y | Z) : dsep_G(X, Y | Z)\}$. We say that $G$ is an *I-map* (independence map) of $Pr$, if $Pr$ satisfies $I(G)$.

Definition 2.5 states that an I-map captures conditional independence assumptions through the purely qualitative notion of d-separation. The following theorem [Pearl (1988)] completes the framework.

**Theorem 2.1.** *Given a DAG $G = (V, E)$ and a probability distribution $Pr$ defined over the variables represented by $V$, then $G$ is an I-map for $Pr$ if and only if $Pr$ factorizes over $G$*

The main consequence of this result is that the factorization of the joint distribution relies on a well-specified (and often realistic) set of conditional independence assumptions, avoiding the explicit specification of the joint probability and exploiting local conditioning.

### 2.1.2   *Causal independence*

Even if properties of BN models allows one to save a lot in the specification of the joint probability over the variables of interest, if a node $X$ has several parents, the local specification for $Pr(X | c^*)$ for each configuration $c^*$ of the parents may itself become prohibitive. For this reason, BNs introduce the possibility of exploiting the notion of *causal independence* [Heckermann and Breese (1996); Poole and Zhang (1996)] or *noisy gates*; this means that the contribution of each single parent to the child node is considered independent from the other parents, so the number of required parameters is linear with respect to the number of parents, instead of being exponential. In particular, in the case of Boolean variables, it is possible to define the noisy-OR interaction. Consider the situation shown in Figure 2.3: let $A_1, \dots A_n, B$ be binary variables (i.e. with values T=true and F=false) such that each event $A_i = $ T causes $B = $ T unless an inhibitor prevents it, and the probability for that is $q_i$, called the *inhibitor probability* for $A_i$. This means that $Pr(B = $ T$|$ only $A_i = $ T$) = 1 - q_i$. The causal independence assumption consists in considering all inhibitors as independent. This implies that

$$Pr(B = \text{T} | A_1, \dots A_n) = 1 - \prod_{j \in Y} q_j$$

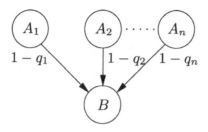

Fig. 2.3  The noisy-OR scheme.

where $Y$ is the set of indices for variables $A_j$ in state T. Standard noisy-OR models assumes that all the potential causes of $B$ are in the set $A_1, \ldots A_n$; this means that $Pr(B = \mathsf{T}|A_1 = A_2, \ldots A_n = \mathsf{F}) = 0$. In case the model does not account for all the possible causes, absent causes can be grouped in a *background* or *leak event*.

The *leak probability* is then $l = Pr(B = \mathsf{T}|A_1 = A_2 = \ldots A_n = \mathsf{F})$. CPT entries are then adjusted with the leak probability as follows:

$$Pr(B = \mathsf{T}|A_1, \ldots A_n) = 1 - (\prod_{j \in Y} q_j(1 - l))$$

Noisy-AND gates (with or without leak) can be defined in a dual way. So for example, we can indicate as $Pr(B = \mathsf{T}| \text{ only } A_i = \mathsf{F}) = p_i$, then

$$Pr(B = \mathsf{T}|A_1, \ldots A_n) = \prod_{j \in Y} p_j$$

where $Y$ is the set of indices for variables $A_j$ in state F. Similar considerations can be applied to introduce a leak.

Noisy-gates can be generalized to multi-state variables either with a generalization of the underlying Boolean function (either OR or AND) to any deterministic function [Srinivas (1993)] or to specific functions like the maximum, by considering graded variables (from the less to the more severe grade) [Henrion (1989); Diez (1993)]; the latter model is also called noisy-MAX gate.

Among the tools providing noisy gates modeling facilities we can remember GENIE [Druzdel (1999)].

### 2.1.3  *Inference*

Concerning the inference capabilities of a BN, since it represents the joint distribution over the variables of interest, then we can conclude that any kind of probabilistic computation can be performed. In particular, posterior probability queries, based on the observation of specific evidence, can be answered. In fact, if $Q$ is a set of queried variables, $e$ is a set of instantiated observed variables called the *evidence*, and $X$ is the set of all the unobserved variables, then

$$Pr(Q|e) = \frac{Pr(Q, e)}{Pr(e)} = \frac{\sum_{Z \in X - Q} Pr(X, e)}{\sum_X Pr(X, e)} \qquad (2.1)$$

Both numerator and denominator can in principle be computed from the joint distribution. Moreover, specific inference problems can be naturally casted in the framework of posterior probability computation:

- **Predictive inference.** Given any evidence $e$, the task is to compute $Pr(Q|e)$ where Q contains variables which are descendants of variables in $e$. For example, considering Figure 2.1, the computation of $Pr(F|P = 0\text{k})$.

- **Diagnostic inference.** Given any evidence $e$, the task is to compute $Pr(Q|e)$ where Q contains variables which are ancestors of variables in $e$. For example, considering Figure 2.1, the computation of $Pr(P|F = \text{Failed})$.

- **Combined inference.** Given any evidence $e$, the task is to compute $Pr(Q|e)$ where Q contains variables which are either ancestors or descendants of variables in $e$. For example, considering Figure 2.1, the computation of $Pr(C1|P = 0\text{k}, F = \text{Failed})$.

- **Explaining Away (Inter-causal reasoning).** Given evidence $e_1$ on a set of variables $E_1$, and evidence $e_2$ on some ancestors $E_2$ of $E_1$, the task is to compare $Pr(C|e_1)$ with respect to $P(C|e_1, e_2)$, where $C$ is an ancestor of variables in $E_1$ but not contained in $E_2$. For example, considering Figure 2.1, we can compute
  $Pr(N = \text{Unavailable}|F = \text{Failed}) = 0.64$
  (and thus $Pr(N = 0\text{k}|F = \text{Failed}) = 0.36$).
  However, if we observe another potential cause of a system failure, e.g. $C2 = \text{Failed}$, then we have that
  $Pr(N = \text{Unavailable}|F = \text{failed}, C2 = \text{Failed}) = 0.191 <$
  $Pr(N = \text{Unavailable}|F = \text{Failed})$;
  this "explains away" the network $N$ as a likely cause of system failure, since we have observed an alternative cause of failure (namely the second processor $C2$).

Despite the fact that Equation 2.1 can be used to perform any inference on a BN, direct exploitation of this formula requires an explicit construction of the joint distribution; this may be impractical in several real-world situations. Specific algorithms have been developed for solving the inference problem in a BN, subdivided into exact and approximate algorithms. Among exact algorithms, the most widely used is the *Belief Propagation* (BP) algorithm [Pearl (1988)] that has been developed in two main versions: the HUGIN propagation scheme [Lauritzen and Jensen (1997)] and the *Shafer-Shenoy* architecture [Shafer and Shenoy (1990)]. The idea is to compile the network into a secondary tree structure called *Junction Tree* (JT) whose nodes represent clusters of variables of the original net; inference is then performed by propagating probabilistic parameters through message-passing between the nodes of the JT, until quiescence is obtained. Marginal posterior probabilities of the variables of interest can then be computed by probabilistic marginalization using the parameters stored in a cluster containing such variables. Appendix A describes this approach to inference in more details.

A version of BP algorithm called *Loopy Belief Propagation* (LBP) has also been developed without compiling the network into a secondary structure [Murphy *et al.* (1999)], resulting however, in an approximate inference scheme.

Notice that, computing joint probabilities in case of more variables in the query, can in principle be performed by successive JT propagations, by exploiting the chain rule of probability; indeed, if $Q = \{Y_1, Y_2, \ldots Y_k\}$ and $e$ is the evidence then we have that

$$Pr(Y_1, Y_2, \ldots Y_k | e) = Pr(Y_1 | e) \times Pr(Y_2 | Y_1, e) \times \ldots \times Pr(Y_k | Y_{k-1}, \ldots Y_1, e)$$

Alternatively, a dummy node can be added to the network, with all the variables in the query set as parent nodes, and with a set of states corresponding to the joint entries to be computed. A single JT propagation can then be performed on the dummy node as the only query node. However, since both approaches may be quite costly, JT propagation (and the corresponding BP algorithm) are usually adopted when the interest is in the marginals of each single variable, or in the joint probabilities of variables that are contained in the same cluster of the JT. Other classes of algorithms can be adopted for the joint probability computation task.

Another approach to exact inference relies on a sequence of factors multiplications (where factors are CPTs or distributions resulting from CPTs multiplications), followed by a suitable elimination of variables not involved in the posterior query, by means of marginalization. Such an approach is known as *Variable Elimination* (VE) algorithm or *Factoring* [Zhang and

Poole (1994); D'Ambrosio (1995)]. In this case, the computation of the joint probability of an arbitrary set of variables is directly addressed by the algorithm.

Concerning approximate inference, the main class of algorithms is based on stochastic simulation; the idea is to repeatedly sample the values of the variables from the distribution encoded in the network, and to compute the required posterior distribution using the collected samples as estimates. Different techniques can be used from *Rejection Sampling* [Henrion (1988)], *Importance Sampling* [Fung and Chang (1990)] or *Markov Chain Monte Carlo* (MCMC) methods like *Gibbs Sampling* [Pearl (1987); Gilks *et al.* (1996)]. The accuracy of the estimation depends on the number of samples one can generate, as well as on the probability of the evidence that has been observed.

Another important problem that arises from the practical usage of probabilistic networks is the problem of finding the most likely value assignment to a set of variables, given the evidence [Jensen and Nielsen (2007); Pearl (1988)]. When the evidence is equal to the complement of the queried variables (or alternatively the query involves all the network variables but the evidence ones), the problem is known as the *Most Probable Explanation* or MPE problem. Actually, MPE is a special case of a more general problem often referred to as *Maximum A Posteriori* or MAP assignment problem. In the general MAP assignment problem, we have a set of queried variables and a set of evidence variables that not necessarily complete the whole set of network variables; a MAP is an assignment to queried variables having the maximum posterior probability, given the evidence. The practical usefulness of MAP and MPE assignments in the context of dependability analysis will be discussed in Chapter 3.

It is worth noting that, in several applications, it may be of interest to find a number of different variable assignments with a high probability, rather than only the most likely assignment (as in standard MAP/MPE definition): this problem is often referred to as "enumerating MAP assignments". The bad news is that the theoretical complexity of both enumerating as well as finding one MAP assignment is very hard (see [Kwisthout (2008)] for the details); however, some algorithms have been devised that works well in practical situations, among which the max-sum version of LBP [Winsper and Chli (2013)], best-first heuristic search [Portinale and Torasso (1997); Neapolitan (1990)] and factoring [Li and D'Ambrosio (1993)].

Finally, we want to point out that several tools for the construction and analysis of Bayesian Networks are available either as commercial tools, as for example HUGIN (www.hugin.dk), BAYESIALAB (www.bayesia.com), NETICA (www.norsys.com), and AGE-NARISK (www.agenarisk.com) or freeware software like GENIE/SMILE (genie.sis.pitt.edu), BNTOOLBOX for MatLab (bnt.googlecode.com), MS-BNX (research.microsoft.com/en-us/um/redmond/groups/adapt/msbnx) and SAMIAM (reasoning.cs.ucla.edu/samiam/). In particular, the last tool of the list (SAMIAM) is one of a few tools implementing different solutions for the MAP (and MPE) assignment problem, as well as some techniques for the sensitivity analysis on the network parameters (see [Chan and Darwiche (2004, 2006)] for a description of the implemented techniques).

## 2.2 Decision Networks

Decision Networks (DN) are decision theoretic extensions to BN and are thus still directed models [Jensen and Nielsen (2007); Kjaerulff and Madsen (2008)]. They are models that capture the need of exploiting probabilistic information in a decision making process, by exploiting the *Maximum Expected Utility* (MEU) principle [von Neumann and Morgenstern (1953); Howard and Matheson (1984)]. This means that numerical utilities are associated to the outcomes of specific variables and the expectation is taken with respect to the probabilistic distribution over such variables. More formally, we have the following definition.

**Definition 2.6.** A *decision network* is a triple $DN = \langle G, Pr, U \rangle$ where:

- $G = (V, E)$ is a DAG where:
  - $V = CN \cup DN \cup VN$ is the set of nodes (vertices) of $G$, partitioned into three disjoint subsets: $CN$ the set of *chance nodes* (graphically represented as ovals), $DN$ the set of *decision nodes* (graphically represented as rectangles), $VN$ the set of *value nodes* (graphically represented as diamonds). They represent random variables, decision variables and utility definitions respectively. Given a chance or decision node/variable $X$ we denote as $\Omega_X$ the domain of $X$ (i.e., the set of states or values of $X$), and we call $x \in \Omega_X$ an *instance* of $X^2$.
  - $E = CA \cup IA \cup FA$ is the set of arcs (edges) of $G$, partitioned into three disjoint subsets: $CA$ the set of *conditional arcs* linking

---

[2]With an abuse of notation, we use the same symbol even for a set of variables $\xi$, so that $\Omega_\xi$ denote a set of instances, one for each variable in $\xi$.

either a chance node $c$ to another chance node $c'$ (i.e., $(c \to c')$ or a decision node $d$ to a chance node of $c$ (i.e., $(d \to c)$), $IA$ the set of *informational arcs* linking either a chance node $c$ to a decision node $d$ (i.e., $(c \to d)$) or a decision node $d$ to another decision node $d'$ (i,e., $(d \to d')$), $FA$ the set of *functional arcs* linking either a chance or a decision node $n$ to a value node $v$ (i.e., $n \to v$)).

- $Pr$ is a parametrized probability distribution over $X_1, X_2, \ldots X_n$ ($X_i \in CN, 1 \leq i \leq n$) such that

$$Pr(X_1, X_2, \ldots X_n : d_1, \ldots d_m) = \prod_{i=1}^{n} Pr(X_i | pa(X_i))$$

  where $pa(X)$ is the set of parent variables (either chance or decision) of $X$ in the DAG $G$ and $d_1, \ldots d_m$ are assignments to decision variables $D_1, \ldots D_m$ where $DN = \{D_1, \ldots D_m\}$ and $d_j \in \Omega_{D_j} (1 \leq j \leq m)$. It represents the distribution over chance variables when decision variables are externally set [Cowell *et al.* (1999)].

- $U$ is the joint utility function defined as additively decomposable i.e., $U = \sum_{v \in VN} U_v$, where $U_v : \Omega_{pa(v)} \to \mathbb{R}$ is the local utility function relative to a value node $v$.

Nodes $c \in CN$ represent random (or chance) variables, whose dependence from other random or decision variables is provided by conditional arcs $CA$; nodes $d \in DN$ represent decision (action) variables, whose instantiation depends on random or decision variables connected to them through an informational arc in $IA$; nodes in $VN$ represent the definition of a suitable utility function having the input nodes (connected through functional arcs in $FA$) as parameters. It is worth noting that informational arcs entering a given decision node $D$ deliver information about what has to be known by the decision maker at the time $D$ has to be determined; this also implies that a precedence order among decisions can be forced by means of informational arcs (we will come back on this aspect in the following).

**Example.** As an example of a DN, consider Figure 2.4; it represents a DN obtained by extending the BN of Figure 2.1, to take into account the possibility of activating a spare power supplier in order to allow the CPUs to switch to it in case of failure of the primary one. The DN adds the following nodes to the BN of the original example:

- a chance node $SPS$ with the same states as node $PS$ and representing the spare power supplier;

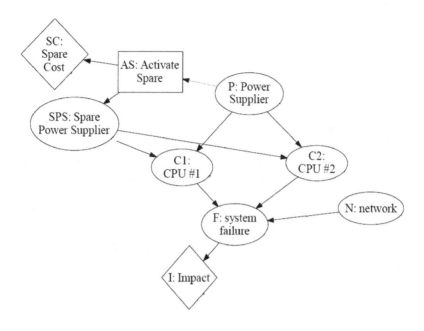

Fig. 2.4 Example of a Decision Network.

Table 2.3 CPT of CPU nodes in case of presence of spare supplier

| | P | Ok | | Failed | |
|---|---|---|---|---|---|
| | SPS | Available | Unavailable | Available | Unavailable |
| C1 | Ok | 0.9 | 0.9 | 0.9 | 0 |
| | Failed | 0.1 | 0.1 | 0.1 | 1 |

- a decision node $AS$ with states {Yes, No} modeling the choices of activating or not activating the spare supplier;
- a value node $SC$ having $AS$ as parent node and modeling the cost of activating the spare;
- a value node $I$ having $F$ as parent node and modeling the "impact" (i.e., the cost) of a system failure (or alternatively, the utility of having the system working).

Since the activation of the spare allows the CPUs to work even in presence of a fault in $PS$, the introduction of node $SPS$ changes the CPT of the CPU nodes as shown in Table 2.3 for $C1$ (of course the CPT is exactly the same for $C2$). As in the example of Figure 2.1, there is still a 10% probability of fault in the CPUs if a power supplier (either the primary $PS$

Table 2.4   CPT for the spare power supplier $SPS$

| | $AS$ | No | Yes |
|---|---|---|---|
| $SPS$ | Available | 0 | 0.99 |
| | Unavailable | 1 | 0.01 |

or the spare $SPS$) can be used, while there is definitely a fault in the CPU if no power supplier can be used.

The decision of activating the spare supplier can make the spare available, however this is not always the case, because the activation process can fail. Table 2.4 shows the CPT for the new node $SPS$, where we can notice that there is a 1% chance of failure of the activation process.

Concerning the value nodes, let us suppose that the cost of activating the spare power supplier is 100 units, and that the impact of a system failure is estimated with a loss of $10^4$ units. The utility functions on such node can then be defined as follows:

$$SC(AS = \text{Yes}) = -100 \ \ SC(AS = \text{No}) = 0$$

$$I(F = \text{No}) = 0 \ \ I(F = \text{Yes}) = -10000$$

In the DN of Figure 2.4 there is an informational arc from node $P$ to decision Node $AS$; the meaning is that the decision of activating the spare supplier has to be taken after knowing the state of the primary power supplier.

### 2.2.1   *Policies and strategies*

Definition 2.6 is a general one and, depending on additional assumptions, different models can be characterized. The most relevant ones are *Influence Diagrams* (ID) [Howard and Matheson (1984); Pearl (1988); Shachter (1988)] and *Limited Memory Influence Diagrams* (LIMID) [Lauritzen and Nilsson (2001); Maua *et al.* (2012); van Gerven and Diez (2006)]. Influence diagrams are decision networks designed for applications involving a single, non-forgetful decision maker. They obey two main assumptions: *regularity* and *no-forgetting*. The former means that there is a complete temporal order among decisions (either explicitly provided by informational arcs linking decision nodes or by considering a direct path connecting decision nodes); the latter assumption means that any disclosed information (i.e., decisions and observations made) is remembered and considered for future decisions. LIMIDs are generalizations of influence diagrams that relax the regularity and no-forgetting assumptions; they allow for decision making with limited information, as in the case of simultaneous decisions and non-communicating multiple agents. The main inference task for both IDs and LIMIDs is to find a set of decisions maximizing the expected utility. Because of the regularity assumption, in case of IDs, the decision set is a sequence, denoting the order in which decisions have to be made.

Given a sequence of decisions $\{D_1, \ldots D_m\}$, let us define as $E_i = \bigcup_{k=0}^{i-1} E_k \cup pa(D_{i+1})$ with $E_0 = pa(D_1)$; we call $E_i$ the *necessary evidence* for $D_{i+1}$.

**Definition 2.7.** Given an influence diagram and the corresponding sequence of decisions $\{D_1 \ldots D_m\}$, for any decision variable $D_i (1 \leq i \leq m)$, a policy $\delta_{D_i}$ is a function specifying an instance of $D_i$ for any configuration of its necessary evidence, that is $\delta_{D_i} : \Omega_{E_{i-1}} \to \Omega_{D_i}$. If $E_0 = \emptyset$ (i.e., the first decision $D_1$ has no parents), then $\delta_{D_1} \in \Omega_{D_1}$ (i.e., it is simply a valid state of $D_1$).

From definition 2.7 it is clear that:

- decisions are temporally ordered (regularity);
- once decisions $D_i$ has to be made, the necessary evidence for $D_i$, which is what the decision maker already knows because of the previous decisions he/she has taken, must be available to the decision maker him/herself (no-forgetting).

A different definition for the notion of policy is required for LIMIDs since, by removing the regularity and no-forgetting assumptions, only the parent set of a given decision is relevant.

**Definition 2.8.** Given a LIMID, for any decision variable $D \in DN$, a policy $\delta_D$ is a function specifying an instance of $D$ for any configuration of its parent variables, that is $\delta_D : \Omega_{pa(D)} \to \Omega_D$. If $pa(D) = \emptyset$ (i.e., $D$ has no parents), then $\delta_D \in \Omega_D$ (i.e., it is simply a valid state of $D$).

**Definition 2.9.** Given a decision network (either an ID or a LIMID), a *strategy* is a set $q = \{\delta_D : D \in DN\}$ of policies for the decisions.

Once a strategy is defined, one can compute its expected utility; given an assignment $x$ to all the the chance variables in $CN$, let $q(x)$ denote the assignment to decision variables dictated by strategy $q$, given the assignment $x$; the expected utility obtained by assigning decisions according to $q$ is the *expected utility* of strategy $q$ $(EU(q))$:

$$EU(q) = \sum_{x \in CM} Pr(x : q(x))U(x, q(x))$$

**Definition 2.10.** Given a decision network, an *optimal strategy* is a strategy $q^*$ such that $EU(q^*) \geq EU(q)$ for all strategy $q$.

As we previously mentioned, computing the optimal strategy is the main inference task in a decision network. Different algorithms can be adopted to this end; the most relevant ones are *Cooper's algorithm* for influence diagrams [Cooper (1988)] and the Single Policy Updating (SPU) algorithm for LIMID [Lauritzen and Nilsson (2001)][3].

**Example of MEU Strategy**  Consider again the DN of Figure 2.4, only a decision node is present, so there is no need to temporally order the decisions; the only policy has to be defined for decision $AS$, conditioned from the state of chance node $P$ (informational arc from $P$ to $AS$). The DN can then be interpreted as either an ID or a LIMID indifferently.

It can be shown that the MEU strategy (composed by a single policy defined on $AS$) is

$$q = \{\delta_{AS}\}$$

$$\delta_{AS}(P = \text{Ok}) = \text{No} \ (EU_1 = -688.19)$$

$$\delta_{AS}(P = \text{Failed}) = \text{Yes} \ (EU_2 = -881.31)$$

This means that, if the primary power supplier is working, then the best decision is to avoid the activation of the spare supplier, and the expected cost is 688.19 units. On the other hand, if the primary supplier fails, then the best decision is to activate the spare, and in this case, the expected cost is 881.31 (which is a larger cost, since the activation is not for free, and the probability of having a system failure is slightly larger than in the previous case).

In details, inference on the DN provides the following values:

$Pr(F = \text{Yes}|P = \text{Ok}, AS = \text{No}) = 0.068819$

$Pr(F = \text{Yes}|P = \text{Failed}, AS = \text{Yes}) = 0.078131$

This means that the computation of the EU is the following:

---

[3]Actually, SPU is in general a sub-optimal algorithm, providing in some cases a strategy which is just a local maximum; recently, an optimal algorithm for LIMIDs has been proposed in [Maua *et al.* (2012)] exploiting a variable elimination approach.

$EU_1 = Pr(F = \text{Yes}|P = \text{Ok}, AS = \text{No})\ I(F = \text{Yes}) = 0.068819\ (-10^4) = -688.19$

$EU_2 = Pr(F = \text{Yes}|P = \text{Failed}, AS = \text{Yes})\ (I(F = \text{Yes}) + SC(AS = \text{Yes})) = 0.078131\ (-10^4 + 100) = -881.31$

Any other strategy $q'$ using a policy different from $\delta_{AS}$ (as shown above), will result in a smaller expected utility.

Finally, in order to have an example of a sequence of decisions, let us extend the model of Figure 2.4 by adding the possibility of using a second spare supplier as shown in Figure 2.5. Both the activation of the first and

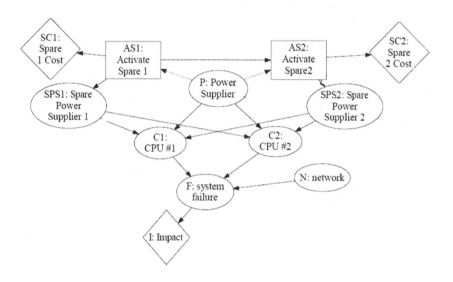

Fig. 2.5    Extending the model in Figure 2.4 with a second spare.

second spare are conditioned on knowing the state of the primary power supplier, so there are informational arcs from $P$ to $AS1$ and from $P$ to $AS2$. However, depending on the particular decision framework we want to use, we can adopt an ID (influence diagram) model or a LIMID model. Figure 2.5 shows the typical situation modeled in an ID: decision must be temporally ordered, and then an arc is present between consecutive decisions. In particular, in this example we assume that the activation of the spare $SPS1$ has to be considered before the activation of $SPS2$, thus an arc from decision node $AS1$ to decision node $AS2$ is present in the DN. By interpreting this model as an ID, we have then to build a strategy composed by two policies: a policy $\delta_{AS1} : \Omega_P \to \Omega_{AS1}$ (i.e., from a state of $P$ to a state of $AS1$), and a policy $\delta_{AS2} : \Omega_P \times \Omega_{AS1} \to \Omega_{AS2}$ (i.e., from a combination of states of $P$ and $AS1$ to a state of $AS2$). In particular, policy $\delta_{AS2}$ has to take into account the state of the previous decision $AS1$, because of the non-forgetting property of IDs, while both policies have to consider the state of $P$ because of the informational arcs entering the decision nodes.

Performing the inference on this ID results in two optimal strategies $q_1 = \{\delta_{AS1}^1, \delta_{AS2}\}$ and $q_2 = \{\delta_{AS1}^2, \delta_{AS2}\}$ where:

$$\delta_{AS1}^1(P = \text{Ok}) = \text{No} \ (EU = -688.19)$$
$$\delta_{AS1}^1(P = \text{Failed}) = \text{No} \ (EU = -881.31)$$
$$\delta_{AS1}^2(P = \text{Ok}) = \text{No} \ (EU = -688.19)$$
$$\delta_{AS1}^2(P = \text{Failed}) = \text{Yes} \ (EU = -881.31)$$

Thus, we can conclude that, concerning the first decision (to activate or not the spare $SPS1$), if the main power supplier is working, then we do not have to activate the spare, but if the main supplier is failed, then it is indifferent to activate or not the spare. This is because the ID interpretation of the DN has a global view on all the possible decisions: if the power supplier fails, then we can avoid to activate the first spare, since it is always possible to activate the second at the same cost. Indeed, the best policy for $AS2$ results to be

$$\delta_{AS2}(P = \text{Ok}, AS1 = \text{No}) = \text{No} \ (EU = -688.19)$$
$$\delta_{AS2}(P = \text{Ok}, AS1 = \text{Yes}) = \text{No} \ (EU = -788.19)$$
$$\delta_{AS2}(P = \text{Failed}, AS1 = \text{No}) = \text{Yes} \ (EU = -881.31)$$
$$\delta_{AS2}(P = \text{Failed}, AS1 = \text{Yes}) = \text{No} \ (EU = -881.31)$$

So the decision maker has to perform the following steps:

- asking for the state of $P$;
- if $P$ is working, first avoid the activation of $SPS1$, then avoid the activation of $SPS2$ (resulting in an expected cost of 688.19 units);
- if $P$ is failed, then he/she can indifferently decide to activate or not $SPS1$,
  - if $SPS1$ is not activated, then he/she has to activate $SPS2$ (resulting in an expected cost of 881.31 units);
  - if $SPS1$ is activated, then he/she has to avoid the activation of $SPS2$ (resulting in an expected cost of 881.31 units as well).

Notice that this model does not properly take into account at the decision level, the fact that the first spare can be unavailable, even if we decide to activate it. Indeed, in case $P$ fails and we decide to perform $AS1$, we then avoid the activation of $SPS2$ (the execution of $AS2$), without considering the possibility of a failure in the execution of $AS1$ (resulting in $SPS1$ in the Unavailable state). To address this problem, a further informational arc can be added to the model, in particular an informational arc from $SPS1$ to $AS2$. In this case, policy $\delta_{AS2}$ is defined taking into account states of $P$, $AS1$ and $SPS1$ as well. For example, it can be easily verified using a DN tool (e.g. GENIE/SMILE) that if $P$ is failed, and $AS1$ has been performed, but $SPS1$ is unavailable, then the best action is to perform $AS2$; this results in an expected cost of 981.31 units, which is 100 units more than the previous expected cost, since now we spend 100 unit to activate $SPS2$. On the other hand, in this case, avoiding the activation of the second spare results in an expected cost of 10100 units, which is definitely not optimal. This can be intuitively understood as follows: if $P$ fails and both the spares are unavailable, then the whole system fails, with a cost or impact of 10000 units (to which we add 100 units of cost because of the execution of $AS1$).

An alternative interpretation to the decision model is to consider it as a LIMID. In such a case, we are not forced to temporally order the decisions, so we can avoid the arc from $AS1$ to $AS2$ in Figure 2.5. This means that we do not have an explicit order in the activation of the spares (thus it is not totally correct to talk about the "first" and the "second" spare, but rather about "spare #1" and "spare #2").

If we perform SPU (LIMID inference) on the resulting network (for example using the HUGIN tool) we can obtain as optimal policies either $q_1 = \{\delta^1_{AS1}, \delta^1_{AS2}\}$ or $q_2 = \{\delta^2_{AS1}, \delta^2_{AS2}\}$, where

$$\delta^1_{AS1}(P = \texttt{Ok}) = \texttt{No}$$
$$\delta^1_{AS1}(P = \texttt{Failed}) = \texttt{Yes}$$
$$\delta^1_{AS2}(P = \texttt{Ok}) = \texttt{No}$$
$$\delta^1_{AS2}(P = \texttt{Failed}) = \texttt{No}$$

and

$$\delta^2_{AS1}(P = \texttt{Ok}) = \texttt{No}$$
$$\delta^2_{AS1}(P = \texttt{Failed}) = \texttt{No}$$
$$\delta^2_{AS2}(P = \texttt{Ok}) = \texttt{No}$$
$$\delta^2_{AS2}(P = \texttt{Failed}) = \texttt{Yes}$$

Of course, if we want to consider the potential unavailability of a spare after the activation attempt, then we have to force an order on the decisions also with the LIMID, by adding an arc from $SPS1$ to $AS2$, or from $SPS2$ to $AS1$, in case we try first $AS1$ or $AS2$ respectively. In these cases, the resulting model is equivalent to the ID with the same temporal ordering.

## 2.3  Dynamic Models

Dynamic Bayesian Networks (DBN) [Dean and Kanazawa (1990); Dagum *et al.* (1992); Murphy (2002)] extend the formalism of Bayesian Networks, by providing an explicit discrete temporal dimension. They represent a probability distribution over the possible histories of a time-invariant process; the advantage with respect to a classical probabilistic temporal model like Markov Chains is that a DBN is a stochastic transition model factored over a number of random variables, over which a set of conditional dependence assumptions is defined (see also [Portinale (1992); Console *et al.* (1992, 1994)] for alternative approaches to the modeling and analysis of this kind of problems).

While a DBN can in general represent semi-Markovian stochastic processes of order $k - 1$, providing the modeling for $k$ time slices, the term DBN is usually adopted when $k = 2$ (only 2 time slices are considered in order to model the system temporal evolution); for this reason such models are also called 2-TBN or 2-*time-slice Temporal Bayesian Network*.

Given a set of time-dependent state variables $X_1 \ldots X_n$ and given a BN $N$ defined on such variables, a DBN is essentially a replication of $N$ over two time slices $t$ and $t + \Delta$, with $\Delta$ being the so called discretization step (usually assumed to be 1 time unit), with the addition of a set of arcs representing the transition model. Letting $X_i^t$ denote the copy of variable $X_i$ at time slice $t$, the transition model is defined through a distribution (usually in the form of a CPT)

$$Pr\{X_i^{t+\Delta} | X_i^t, Y^t, Y^{t+\Delta}\}$$

where $Y^t$ is any set of variables at slice $t$ other than $X_i$ while $Y^{t+\Delta}$ is any set of variables at slice $t + \Delta$ other than $X_i$.

In standard DBN models, we assume the parameters of the CPTs are time-invariant, i.e., the model is *time-homogeneous* or *stationary*[4]. Time

---

[4]If we need to model time-dependent parameters, then they can be added to the state-space and treated as random variables [Grzegorczyk and Husmeier (2009)]

invariance ensures that the dependency model of the variables is the same at any point in time.

Arcs interconnecting nodes at different slices are called *inter-slice edges*, while arcs interconnecting nodes at the same slice are called *intra-slice edges*. The semantics of a DBN can be defined by unrolling the 2-TBN until we have T time-slices (being T a predefined time horizon). The resulting joint distribution is then given by

$$Pr\{X_{1...T}\} = \prod_{t=1}^{T} \prod_{i=1}^{n} Pr\{X_i^t | Pa(X_i^t)\}$$

where $X_{1...T} = \bigcup_{t=1}^{T} \bigcup_{i=1}^{n} X_i^t$

Following the above definition, it should be clear that a DBN represents a Discrete-Time Markov Chain or DTMC (see Chapter 1, Section 1.3.1), where the state space is defined as the Cartesian product of all the variables. The two slices of a DBN are often called the *anterior* and the *ulterior* layer (corresponding to time point $t$ and $t + \Delta$ respectively).

Finally, it is useful to define the set of *canonical variables* as $\{Y : Y^t \in \bigcup_k Pa(X_k^{t+\Delta})\}$; they are the variables having a direct edge from the anterior level to another variable in the ulterior level. A DBN is in *canonical form* if only the canonical variables are represented at slice $t$ (i.e. the anterior layer contains only variables having influence on the same variable or on another variable at the ulterior level).

**DBN Modeling Example.** Figure 2.6 shows an example of a DBN in canonical form, where node $X$ is labelled as $X$ at the anterior layer, and as $X\#$ at the ulterior layer. Given a DBN in canonical form, inter-slice edges connecting a variable in the anterior layer to the same variable in the ulterior layer are called *temporal arcs* (indicated as thick arcs in Figure 2.6); in other words, a temporal arc connects variable $X_i^t$ to variable $X_i^{t+\Delta}$ (in Figure 2.6 they connect a node $X$ with node $X\#$). Temporal arcs are just a syntactic sugar; they just evidence the nodes they are connecting as copies of the same variable at different slices. It follows that no variable in the ulterior layer may have more than one entering temporal arc. From the semantic point of view, temporal arcs are just as any other edge in the model, however they are useful to make explicit the set of variables for which a transition model (from time $t$ to time $t + \Delta$) is provided.

Several tools explicitly use the notion of temporal arcs in their representation: examples are RADYBAN (an academic tool that will be discussed in Chapter 6) [Montani *et al.* (2008); Portinale *et al.* (2007, 2010)] and

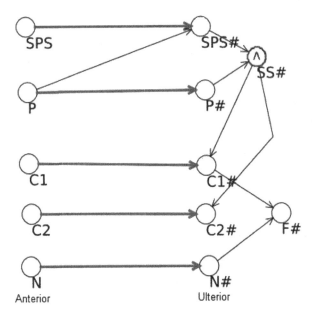

Fig. 2.6   Example of a DBN in canonical form.

BAYESIALAB [Conrady and Jouffe (2013)], a commercial tool developed by
BAYESIA CORP. (www.bayesia.com).

Considering the DBN of Figure 2.6, it represents a dynamic version of
the model in Figure 2.4 with no explicit action modeling, where the spare
power supplier $SPS$ is definitely activated in case the primary $P$ fails. In
particular:

- temporal arcs are used to model the temporal evolution of system components (i.e. modeling the conditional probability of the component
  state at the ulterior level, given the state at the anterior one);
- nodes with no connection with temporal arc represent specific subsystem conditions, like the system failure $F\#$, or the supplier system
  failure $SS\#$ (i.e. the failure of both power suppliers);
- inter-slice edge from $P$ to $SPS\#$ models the influence of the primary
  power supplier $P$ in the transition model of the spare: in particular,
  since the spare is definitely not activated until the primary fails, then
  it cannot fail when the primary is working, so there is a dependency
  from $P$ in the transition model of $SPS$;
- intra-slice edges from the supplier sub-system $SS\#$ to the CPUs model

the fact that, if both power suppliers fail, then the CPUs become unavailable and are considered in a faulty state.

We will consider in much details several of the above aspects in Chapter 4, where we relate DFT and DBN models. It is worth remarking that the DBN model allows an explicit representation of the temporal evolution of specific variables (like for instance those representing system components in the examples provided), while static models (like BN and DN) need to cast this kind of information into the prior probability of nodes having no parent; different time points of analysis will then result in different prior CPTs.

### 2.3.1 *Inference in Dynamic Bayesian Networks*

Concerning the analysis of a DBN, different kinds of inference algorithms are available. In particular, let $X^t$ be a set of variables at time $t$ and $y_{a:b}$ any stream of observation from time point $a$ to time point $b$ (i.e. a set of instantiated variables $Y_i^j$ with $a \leq j \leq b$). The following tasks can be performed on a DBN:

- **Filtering** or **Monitoring**: computing $P(X^t|y_{1:t})$, i.e. tracking the probability of the system state taking into account the stream of observations received.
- **Prediction**: computing $P(X^{t+h}|y_{1:t})$ for some horizon $h > 0$, i.e. predicting a future state taking into consideration the observations up to now (filtering is a special case of prediction with $h = 0$).
- **Smoothing**: computing $P(X^{t-l}|y_{1:t})$ for some $l < t$, i.e. estimating what happened $l$ steps in the past given all the evidence (observations) up to now.

Different algorithms, either exact (i.e. computing the exact probability value that is required by the task) or approximate can be exploited in order to implement the above tasks.

#### 2.3.1.1 *Junction Tree Inference*

In order to perform inference, a naive solution consists in unrolling the DBN to the desired time horizon; the resulting structure could then be treated as a static BN and solved through standard (either exact or approximate) inference algorithms. This is the approach used in the GENIE/SMILE tool [Druzdel (1999, 2005)].

However, unrolling the whole net could be impractical in several situations; for this reason, some algorithms that do not require to unroll the network have been proposed. The idea is to exploit both stationarity and Markovian assumptions, by working with only two time-slices. In particular, two algorithms have been proposed, using static junction tree inference on the DBN:

- the *frontier algorithm* [Zweig (1996)]; it assumes a Hidden Markov Model (HMM) [Rabiner (1989)] for the DBN, where some nodes are always observed and some others are hidden; it exploits the so called frontier set, which is the set of all hidden nodes at the current time slice $t$; since the frontier d-separates node at time $t' < t$ from nodes at time $t'' > t$, then only the joint distribution of the frontier has to be maintained for exact inference;

- the *forward interface algorithm* [Murphy (2002)]. it defines the forward interface (or simply the interface) of the DBN as the set of nodes having children in the ulterior layer; the intuition is that the interface (which is in general smaller than the frontier) has also the property of d-separating the past from the future. A junction tree can then be constructed across the anterior and the ulterior layer, by considering the canonical structure of the DBN, and by forcing the interface nodes to be contained in the same cluster. Once inference is performed at time $t$, then the cluster containing the interface is used to initialize a new copy of the junction tree, in such a way that inference can be advanced to $t + \Delta$. For this reason, this algorithm is also called *1.5JT algorithm*.

In the case of discrete state spaces, exact inference is always possible, but may be computationally prohibitive, as the complexity is exponential in the size of the forward interface. Since typically the size of the interface is about the number of persistent nodes (i.e. nodes that can be unobserved and that have children in the ulterior layer), then exact inference is intractable for large discrete DBNs. A standard approximation in the discrete case, known as the *Boyen-Koller (BK) algorithm* [Boyen and Koller (1998)], is to approximate the joint distribution over the interface as a product of marginals, splitting the interface into different clusters of more reasonable size. The BK algorithm is indeed a parametrized procedure receiving as input parameters a set of nodes (the so called *bk-clusters*), determining a partition of the interface; depending on the partition provided it may return exact (if only one bk-cluster containing the whole interface is provided, resulting in the 1.5JT algorithm) as well as approximate results, with the most aggressive approximation obtained by providing a set of singleton bk-clusters, one for each node in the interface: this version is called *fully-factorized BK*. The best approximation is obtained when no node in any one cluster is parent of a node in a different cluster within a single time slice [Boyen and Koller (1998)]. Moreover, in [Murphy (2002)] it has been shown that BK is a special case of the LBP (loopy belief propagation) algorithm.

Among the tools implementing the BK algorithm (and so the 1.5JT as well) we can remember RADYBAN [Montani *et al.* (2008)], the BNT MATLAB toolbox [Murphy (2001)] and the OPENPNL C++ library (http://sourceforge.net/projects/openpnl/). In appendix A, more details are provided about the 1.5JT and the BK algorithms for DBN.

**Example of DBN Inference.** As an example of the kind of computations that can be performed, consider again the DBN of Figure 2.6. Suppose that each component of the modeled system has an exponential failure rate, and in particular: $P$ and $SPS$ have $\lambda_P = \lambda_{PS} = 1.0E - 05$, while $N, C1$ and $C2$ have $\lambda_N = \lambda_{C1} = \lambda_{C2} = 1.0E - 06$. Moreover, let us consider a discretization step $\Delta = 1$ unit (i.e., if failure rates are given in fault per hour, then $\Delta = 1$ hour).

A first interesting task consists in trying to predict (i.e. to monitor with no evidence) the probability of a system failure over time. Figure 2.7 plots the probability of a system failure predicted every 100 hours until $t = 10000$ hours. In this case, the inference task to consider is the filtering (or monitoring), with an empty stream of observations; results shown in Figure 2.7 are obtained with an implementation of the 1.5JT algorithm with the RADYBAN tool.

Another possible computation is the filtering with a given stream of observations; suppose that we observe $F(s, t)$, the system status $s$ at some given time point $t$, and in particular we get the following observation stream: $F(\text{Ok}, 2000), F(\text{Ok}, 4000), F(\text{Fault}, 6000)$. Figure 2.8 shows the probability of the faulty state of each system component (with $C$ indicating either $C1$ or $C2$), given by filtering (again using the 1.5JT implementation of RADYBAN). We can notice that, until time $t = 5000h$, the probability is conditioned on some previous evidence about a working system status, so the probability of fault is not very high. As we get the observation of system fault at time $t = 6000h$, then the probability of a fault in the components immediately rise up.

Finally, if we consider the stream of observations as before, but we perform a smoothing task, then we obtain the results shown in Figure 2.9.

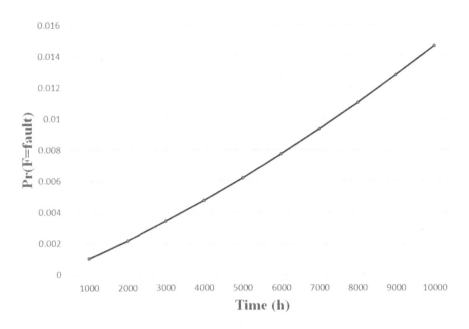

Fig. 2.7    Prediction of system failure (i.e. filtering with no evidence).

We can notice some important differences on the same queries with respect to filtering. In particular, in the example the system fails when either the network component $N$ fails or both the power suppliers $P$ and $SPS$ fail. The smoothing inference is then able to conclude that, given the system working until time $t = 4000h$, then $N$ has to be definitely working (i.e., $Pr(N = \text{Fault}) = 0$) for at least 4000 hours; moreover, since the spare supplier $SPS$ becomes active only after the failure of the primary $P$, then $SPS$ must be ok as well, until time $t = 4000h$ (if $SPS$ was down, then $P$ would have been down as well, and so the whole system). From $t = 6000h$ the results of smoothing and filtering coincide, since $t = 6000h$ is the last time point providing evidence. In a tool like RADyBaN we can also compute joint probabilities among the queried variables. In the above smoothing example, this allows one to obtain, for each time point of interest, the most probable assignment over the system components, given the whole stream of observations. Suppose we are interested in knowing the joint state of the components at the time of the last observation (i.e. when we see the system failure) and to compare it with the previous time point with a query; in the example we compute the following top two most

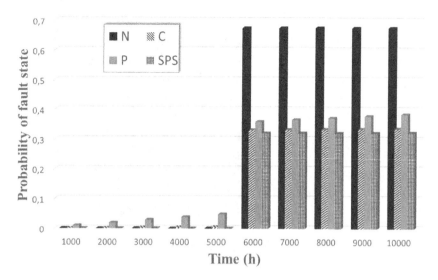

Fig. 2.8 Probability of component faults, under observation of the system status: Filtering.

probable assignments:

$t = 5000$:

$Pr(N = \texttt{Fault}, C = \texttt{Ok}, P = \texttt{Ok}, SPS = \texttt{Ok}) = 0.3191$

$Pr(N = \texttt{Ok}, C = \texttt{Ok}, P = \texttt{Fault}, SPS = \texttt{Ok}) = 0.1745$

$t = 6000$:

$Pr(N = \texttt{Fault}, C = \texttt{Ok}, P = \texttt{Ok}, SPS = \texttt{Ok}) = 0.6309$

$Pr(N = \texttt{Ok}, C = \texttt{Fault}, P = \texttt{Fault}, SPS = \texttt{Fault}) = 0.3199$

By looking at the results, we can obtain some relevant diagnostic information: for instance, we can conclude that after 5000 hours the most probable joint state of the components was the occurrence of a single failure of $N$; the same could be concluded after 6000 hours, but with a probability of failure that is almost the double. The second most probable assignment after 5000 hours is that only the primary supplier was failed, while after 6000 hours we can conclude that all the power suppliers and the CPUs are the second most probable cause of the system failure.

Considerations similar to the above ones are very important in dependability analysis; we will come back on some of these issues in the next chapters.

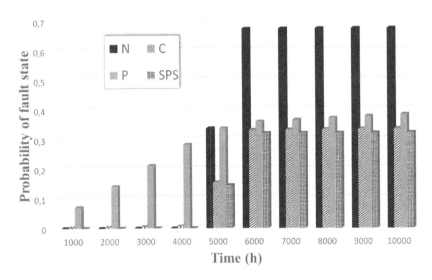

Fig. 2.9   Probability of component faults, under observation of the system status: Smoothing.

### 2.3.1.2 *Stochastic Simulation*

As for static BNs, very popular approximate algorithms are also those based on stochastic simulation; in the DBN framework we distinguish stochastic (or sampling) algorithms in two different modalities: off-line and on-line. As we have mentioned in the case of static BNs, offline methods are usually based on importance sampling (also known as likelihood weighting) or Monte Carlo Markov Chain (MCMC) [Gilks *et al.* (1996)]. On-line methods usually use particle filtering (PF), also known as sequential importance sampling (SIS) or sequential Monte Carlo [Gordon (1993)]. The main difference between off-line and on-line inference is that, in the latter we do not wait until all the evidence is collected in order to start inference; on the contrary, inference is performed as soon as new evidence is gathered at the current time. In particular, PF maintains a constant set of $N$ samples, called particles. First, an initial population of $N$ samples is created from the initial distribution at time $t = 0$; then, at each time point the following steps are repeated:

- each sample is propagated forward at time $t' = t + \Delta$, by sampling the next state of every unobserved variable, given the current state at time $t$;

- each sample is weighted by the likelihood of the current observed evidence;
- the population is resampled to generate a new population of $N$ samples, where each sample is selected with a probability which is proportional to its weight.

The resampling step is necessary in order to avoid a large increase of the approximation error, by introducing a dependence from the evidence observed.

Sampling algorithms have several advantages over deterministic approximation algorithms like BK or general LBP: they are easy to implement, they work on almost any kind of model, they can convert heuristics into provably correct algorithms by using them as proposal distributions, and they are guaranteed to give asymptotically the exact answer. The main disadvantage of sampling algorithms is speed: because of the need of several samples, they are often significantly slower than deterministic methods, often making them unsuitable for large models. A possible mitigation of this drawback is the combination of both exact and stochastic inference. This is for instance the basic idea of Rao-Blackwellisation [Casella and Robert (1996)]; in this methodology some of the variables are integrated out using exact inference, while sampling is applied to the remaining ones; when combined with particle filtering, the resulting algorithm is called Rao-Blackwellised particle filtering (RBPF) [Doucet *et al.* (2000)].

Concerning current implementations in available tools, we can point out that likelihood weighting, is implemented as approximate algorithm (for both static BNs and DBNs) in the BAYESIALAB [Conrady and Jouffe (2013)] and GENIE/SMILE tools [Druzdel (2005)].

To conclude this section on dynamic graphical models, it is worth mentioning the possibility of extending the DBN representation with actions and rewards or utilities, obtaining the so-called Dynamic Decision Networks (DDN) [Poole and Mackworth (2010)]. In a DDN, action and utility nodes are added to a DBN representation, just as in the static case (see Section 2.2). Also in this case, if we assume a first-order Markovian model, then only two time-slices need to be represented.

As DBNs are a factored representation of a Markov Chain, DDNs are a factored representation of a finite-horizon Markov Decision Process (MDP) [Puterman (1994)] or in general of a Partially Observable Markov Decision Process (POMDP) [Cassandra *et al.* (1994)]. It is worth noting that, if action nodes are instantiated, then a DDN model becomes a 2-TBN, and standard inference algorithms for DBNs can be exploited. We will return on this point in Chapter 8, when we will present a case study for the implementation of autonomous *Fault Detection, Identification and Recovery* (FDIR) strategies based on the DDN framework.

Chapter 3

# From Fault Trees to Bayesian Networks

As we have discussed in Chapter 1, Fault Tree Analysis (FTA) is a very popular and diffused technique for the dependability modeling and evaluation of large, safety-critical systems [Henley and Kumamoto (1981); Leveson (1995)].

The methodology is based on the following assumptions:

- events are binary events (working/not-working; ok/fault; false/true);
- events are statistically independent, thus dependent failures cannot be directly modeled (i.e., the behavior of one component cannot influence the behavior of another component);
- relationships between events and causes are deterministic and are represented by means of Boolean *AND* / *OR* gates.

We have also reported that, in FTA, the analysis is carried on in two steps: a qualitative step in which the logical expression of the *Top Event* (TE) (e.g. the system failure) is derived in terms of prime implicants (the minimal cut sets); a quantitative step in which, on the basis of the failure probabilities assigned to the basic components, the probability of occurrence of the TE is computed.

On the other hand, we have also noticed that Probabilistic Graphical Models (PGM) provide a robust, flexible and sound probabilistic method of reasoning under uncertainty. In particular, *Bayesian Networks* (BN) have been successfully proposed and applied to a variety of real-world problems [Heckerman *et al.* (1995); Pourret *et al.* (2008)], including diagnostic, monitoring and failure prediction tasks [Yongli *et al.* (2006); Romessis and Mathioudakis (2006); Mengshoel *et al.* (2008); Codetta-Raiteri and Portinale (2015)], risk management [Fenton and Neil (2012)], industrial maintenance [Jones *et al.* (2010)]. This has led to a growing interest in the use of

PGMs (and BNs in particular) in the dependability/reliability field. The history of BNs in reliability can (at least) be traced back to Barlow [Barlow (1988)] and Almond [Almond (1992)]. The first real attempt to merge the efforts of the two communities is probably the work of Almond, where he proposes the use of the GRAPHICAL-BELIEF tool for calculating reliability measures concerning a low-pressure coolant injection system for a nuclear reactor (a problem originally addressed by Martz and Waller [Martz and Waller (1990)]).

The proposal of using BNs as a framework for reliability analysis has given rise to a research trend comparing classical reliability formalisms and BNs. Combinatorial models have been deeply compared to BNs, in particular Reliability Block Diagrams (RBD) [Torres-Toledano and Sucar (1998); J and Sucar (2001)] and Fault Trees (FT) [Bobbio *et al.* (2001, 2003a)], by showing significant advantages of BNs over more traditional models. More recently, also state-space models have been compared with BN-related formalisms [Bouissou and Bon (2003); Boudali and Dugan (2005, 2006); Portinale *et al.* (2010); Portinale and Codetta-Raiteri (2009)], again by showing that the factorization of the state-space provided by BNs can produce significant advantages both in terms of modeling and analysis.

In the present chapter, we concentrate on the comparison of FTs to BNs, while in Chapter 4 we will consider the relationship between PGMs (and in particular DBN) and state-space models.

## 3.1  Mapping Fault Trees to Bayesian Networks

Dependability engineers are accustomed to deal with structured and easy-to-handle tools that provide a guideline for building up models starting from the system description. Relating models like FTs to BNs allows the analyst to conveniently combine a modular, structured and well-known (from the reliability point of view) methodology (such as FT) with the modeling and analytical power of BN. The computation of posterior probabilities, given some evidence, can be particularized to obtain very natural importance measures (like, for instance, the posterior probability of the basic components given the TE), or backtrace diagnostic information. On the other hand, the modeling flexibility of the BN formalism can accommodate various kinds of statistical dependencies that cannot be included in the FT formalism.

In order to define the conversion algorithm from FT to BN, we adopt the following convention; given a generic binary component $C$ we denote with $C = \text{T}$ (true) or simply with $C$ the component failure and with $C = \text{F}$ (false) or $\bar{C}$ the component working. The quantification of the FT requires the assignment of a probability value to each leaf node. Since the computation is performed at a given mission time $t$, the failure probabilities of the basic components at time $t$ should be provided. In the usual hypothesis that component failures are exponentially distributed, the probability of occurrence of the event $C$ ($C = \text{T} = \text{faulty}$) at time $t$ is $Pr(C,t) = 1 - e^{-\lambda_C t}$, where $\lambda_C$ is the (constant) failure rate of component $C$ (see Chapter 1, Section 1.1.3).

We show how any FT can be converted into an equivalent BN, then we show how assumptions recalled at the beginning of the chapter (Boolean statistically independent events and deterministic relationships) can be relaxed, if adopting the BN formalism.

Given a (coherent) FT, we can produce a BN in the following way:

- for each basic event $C$, create a binary node $N_C$ with no parent nodes and with states $\bar{N}_C$ ($N_C = \text{F} = \text{working}$), $N_C$ ($N_C = \text{T} = \text{faulty}$) corresponding to states $\bar{C}$ and $C$ respectively; however, if more leaves of the FT represent the same primary event (i.e., the same component), create just one root node in the BN; given an analysis time $t$, we set the CPT entries of $N_C$ as follows: $Pr(\bar{N}_C) = e^{-\lambda_C t}$ and $Pr(N_C) = 1 - e^{-\lambda_C t}$;

- for each event $E$, create a binary node $N_E$, (with states $\bar{N}_E, N_E$) corresponding to states of $E$;

- for each gate $G$ having event $E$ in the output and events $\{E_1, \ldots E_n\}$ in the input, create an edge from $N_{E_i}$ to $N_E$ for each ($1 \le i \le n$); depending on the type of $G$ ($G \in \{AND, OR, k : n\}$), create a corresponding (deterministic) CPT; Figure 3.1 shows the CPTs for AND, OR and $2 : 3$ gates ($k : n$ gates are generalized similarly);

- call *Fault* the node corresponding to the fault tree's TE. Due to the very special nature of the gates appearing in a FT, non-root nodes of the BN are actually deterministic nodes, and the corresponding CPT can be assigned automatically. The prior probabilities on the root nodes are coincident with the corresponding probabilities assigned to the leaf nodes in the FT.

**Example.** Let us illustrate in more detail the mapping algorithm through an example. Consider the redundant multiprocessor system shown in Fig-

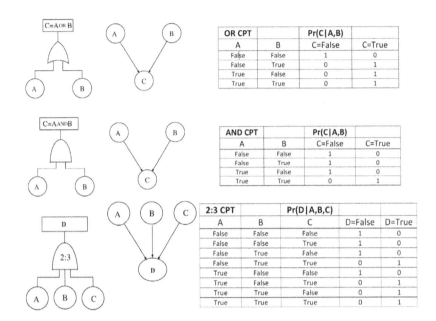

Fig. 3.1   Boolean gate representation in BN.

ure 3.2 and taken from [Malhotra and Trivedi (1995)]. The system is composed of a bus $N$ connecting two processors $P_1$ and $P_2$ having access to a local memory bank each ($M_1$ and $M_2$) and, through the bus to a shared memory bank $M_3$, so that if the local memory bank fails, the processor can use the shared one. Each processor is connected to a mirrored disk unit ($D_1$ or $D_2$). If one of the disks in the unit fails, the processor switches on the mirror. The whole system is functional if the bus $N$ is functional and one of the processing subsystems is functional. Figure 3.2 also shows the partitioning into logical subsystems, i.e., the processing subsystems $S_i$ ($i = 1, 2$); the mirrored disk units $D_i$ ($i = 1, 2$) and the memory subsystems $M_{i3}$ ($i = 1, 2$). The FT for this system is shown in Figure 3.3.

The logical expression of the $TE$ as a function of the minimal cut sets is given by the following expression:

$$TE = N + D_{11}D_{12}D_{21}D_{22} + D_{11}D_{12}M_2M_3 + D_{11}D_{12}P_2 + M_1M_3D_{21}D_{22}+$$

$$+M_1M_2M_3 + M_1M_3P_2 + P_1D_{12}D_{22} + P_1M_2M_3 + P_1P_2$$

For example, we can immediately notice, from the TE expression in terms of MCS, that the bus $N$ is a single point of failure (first MCS), that

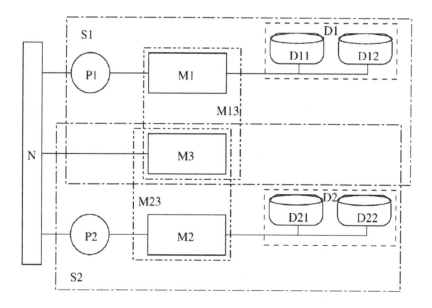

Fig. 3.2  A redundant multiprocessor system [Malhotra and Trivedi (1995)].

the failure of all the disk units is a cause of system failure (second MCS), as well as the failure of both processors (last MCS). We can interpret the other MCS similarly. The structure of the corresponding BN is represented in Figure 3.4. In order to quantify both models, the failure probabilities of each component are then assigned to the leaf nodes of the FT, and to the root nodes of the BN as prior probability. As an example, Table 3.1 reports the CPT entries for the node *Fault* (corresponding to an OR gate), for the node $S_{12}$ (corresponding to an AND gate) and the CPT of nodes $D_{ij}$ assuming an exponential failure rate $\lambda_D = 8.0E - 05$ (fault/hours) and an analysis time $t = 5000$ hours.

The mapping procedure we have described shows that each FT can be naturally converted into a BN. However, BNs are a more general formalism than FTs; for this reason, there are several modeling aspects underlying BNs that can make them very appealing for dependability analysis. In the following, we examine a number of extensions to the standard FT methodology, and we show how they can be captured in the BN framework.

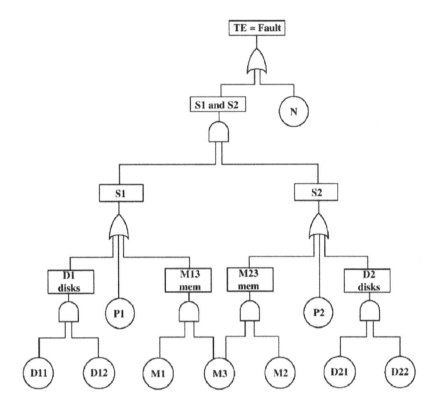

Fig. 3.3   Fault tree for the redundant multiprocessor system.

## 3.2   Common Cause Failures

Differently from FT, the dependence relations among variables in a BN are not restricted to be deterministic. This corresponds to being able to model uncertainty in the behavior of the gates, by suitably specifying the conditional probabilities in the CPT entries. Probabilistic gates may reflect an imperfect knowledge of the system behavior, or may avoid the construction of a more detailed and refined model. A typical example is the incorporation of Common Cause Failure analysis (CCF) [Mosleh (1988)]. CCF refers to dependent failures whose root causes are not explicitly modeled. In particular, CCF is a specific type of dependent failure where simultaneous (or near-simultaneous) multiple failures result from a single shared (unmodeled) cause. Common cause failures are usually modeled in FT by adding an OR gate, directly connected to the TE, in which one input is the

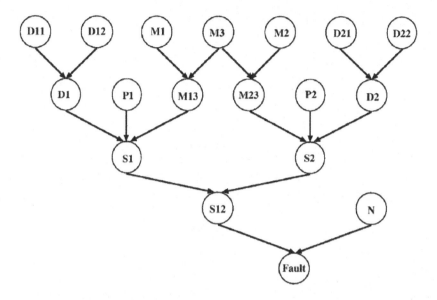

Fig. 3.4 Bayesian network for the redundant multiprocessor system (obtained from the FT of Figure 3.3).

Table 3.1 Some CPTs for the BN of Figure 3.4.

| | $S_1$ | F | | T | |
|---|---|---|---|---|---|
| | $S_2$ | F | T | F | T |
| *Fault* | F | 1 | 0 | 0 | 0 |
| | T | 0 | 1 | 1 | 1 |

| | $S_{12}$ | F | | T | |
|---|---|---|---|---|---|
| | $N$ | F | T | F | T |
| $S_{12}$ | F | 1 | 1 | 1 | 0 |
| | T | 0 | 0 | 0 | 1 |

| | F | 0.67032 |
|---|---|---|
| $D_{ij}$ | T | 0.32968 |

system failure, and the other input the CCF leaf to which the probability of failure due to common causes is assigned. In the BN formalism, such additional constructs are not necessary, since the probabilistic dependence can be included in the CPT. Figure 3.5 shows an AND gate with CCF and

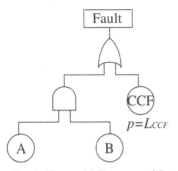

$Pr(\text{Fault}{=}T \mid A{=}F, B{=}F) = L_{CCF}$
$Pr(\text{Fault}{=}T \mid A{=}F, B{=}T) = L_{CCF}$
$Pr(\text{Fault}{=}T \mid A{=}T, B{=}F) = L_{CCF}$
$Pr(\text{Fault}{=}T \mid A{=}T, B{=}T) = 1$

Fault Tree: AND gate with     Bayesian Network: AND node with
common cause failure          common cause failure

Fig. 3.5   Modeling CCF in a FT and in a BN.

the corresponding BN. The value $L_{CCF}$ is the probability of failure of the system due to common causes, when one or both components are up.

## 3.3   Noisy Gates

Of particular interest for reliability aspects is one peculiar modeling feature often used in building BN models: *noisy gates*. As mentioned in Chapter 2, when specifying CPT entries one has to condition the value of a variable on every possible instantiation of its parent variables, making the number of required entries exponential with respect to the number of parents. By assuming that the node variable is influenced by any single parent independently of the others (causal independence), noisy gates reduce this effort by requiring a number of parameters linear in the number of parents.

Consider for example the subsystem $S_1$ in Figure 3.2: it fails if either the disk unit $D_1$ or the processor $P_1$ or the memory subsystem $M_{13}$ fails. Since node $S_1$ in the BN of Figure 3.4 has three parent nodes, this implies that the modeler has to provide eight CPT entries, in order to completely specify this local model[1]. Of course, if this local model is a strictly deterministic logical OR (as in the example), the modeler has only to specify this information, and an automatic construction of the CPT can take place (see Figure 3.1 again). Consider now the case where the logical OR interaction is *noisy* or probabilistic: even if one of the components of $S_1$ fails, there is a (possibly

---

[1]The whole local model is composed of 16 entries, but only 8 have to be provided independently because $P(Y|X) = 1 - P(\bar{Y}|X)$.

small) positive probability that the subsystem works. This corresponds to the fact that the system may maintain some functionality, or may be able to reconfigure (with some probability of reconfiguration success) in the presence of particular faults. Suppose, for example, that $S_1$ can work with probability 0.01 even if the disk unit $D_1$ has failed. Moreover, suppose that the system can also recover if other components of $S_1$ fail, but with a smaller probability (e.g., 0.005).

By adopting a noisy-OR model we can then set the following inhibitor probabilities:

$$q_{D_1} = P(\bar{S}_1|D_1, \bar{P}_1, \bar{M}_{13}) = 0.01$$

$$q_{P_1} = P(\bar{S}_1|\bar{D}_1, P_1, \bar{M}_{13}) = 0.005$$

$$q_{M_{13}} = P(\bar{S}_1|\bar{D}_1, \bar{P}_1, M_{13}) = 0.005$$

Then we can, for instance, compute the probability of the subsystem $S_1$ failed when both $D_1$ and $P_1$ have failed and $M_{13}$ is still working:

$$P(S_1|D_1, P_1, \bar{M}_{13}) = 1 - (0.01 \times 0.005) = 0.99995$$

As one can expect, such a probability is larger than the probability of $S_1$ failed given that only $D_1$ (or only $P_1$) has failed.

Suppose now that we introduce a common cause failure to $S_1$ with probability $l_{cc} = 0.02$. This accounts for the fact that we missed some unknown cause of failure, either because we do not know it precisely or because we do not deem appropriate to build up a finer representation for the system. We can model this term as a leak probability, thus the probability of failure of $S_1$, when only $M_{13}$ is working, will slightly increase as follows:

$$P(S_1|D_1, P_1, \bar{M}_{13}) = 1 - (0.01 \times 0.005 \times (1 - 0.02)) = 0.999951$$

Noisy-AND models can similarly be used to introduce uncertainty in AND gates; consider for instance, the mirrored disk subsystem $D_1$ that fails if both disks $D_{11}$ and $D_{12}$ fail. However, in a more refined view of the model, we can suppose that the mirrored connection is not perfect, and there is a small probability (e.g. 0.001) that the disk subsystem $D_1$ fails when a single disk is up (i.e., $p_{D_{11}} = P(D_1|\bar{D}_{11}, D_{12}) = p_{D_{12}} = P(D_1|\bar{D}_{11}, D_{12}) = 1 \times 10^{-3}$). By exploiting noisy-AND interaction, we can then compute the probability of $D_1$ failing when both disks are functional as $P(D_1|\bar{D}_{11}, \bar{D}_{12}) = 10^{-3} \times 10^{-3} = 1 \times 10^{-6}$.

Table 3.2   CPT for an AND gate with coverage

| $M_1$ | F | | T | |
|---|---|---|---|---|
| $M_3$ | F | T | F | T |
| $M_{13}$ F | 1 | $c$ | $c$ | 0 |
| $M_{13}$ T | 0 | $1-c$ | $1-c$ | 1 |

## 3.4   Coverage Factors

An important modelling improvement in redundant systems is to consider coverage factors [Dugan and Trivedi (1989)]. The *Coverage Factor* is defined as the probability that a single failure in a redundant system entails a complete system failure. This accounts for the fact that the recovery mechanism can be inaccurate, and that the redundancy therefore becomes inoperative, even when only one component has failed. Coverage factors may be modelled in FTs [Amari *et al.* (1999)], but they are even more naturally tackled in BNs through the use of probabilistic gates.

The coverage $c$ is defined as the probability that the reconfiguration process is able to restore the system in a working state, when a redundant element fails. We say that there is a *perfect coverage* when $c = 1$. It is worth noting that the noisy-AND gate is not the appropriate model for coverage factors. Suppose that in the memory subsystem $M_{13}$ there is a small probability (e.g. $1-c$) that the subsystem does not recover the failure of a single memory bank (i.e., $P(M_{13}|\bar{M}_1, M_3) = P(M_{13}|M_1, \bar{M}_3) = 1-c$).

If we consider the above specification as a noisy-AND model (i.e., we assume $p_{M_1} = p_{M_3} = 1-c$ as parameters for a noisy-AND), then we should compute the following

$$P(M_{13}|\bar{M}_1, \bar{M}_3) = p_{M_1} \times p_{M_3} = (1-c)^2 \geq 0$$

This probability is equal to 0 only in case of perfect coverage. In general, it implies that there is a positive probability of failure in the subsystem, even when both memory banks are functional; this is not the intended meaning of coverage. To correctly model this coverage situation the complete CPT must be specified (see Table 3.2).

## 3.5   Multi-state Variables

The use of multi-state or n-ary variables can be very useful in many applications [Garribba *et al.* (1985); Wood (1985); Kai (1990)], where it is not sufficient to restrict the component behavior to the dichotomy working/

not-working. Typical scenarios are possible that require the incorporation of multi-state components: the possible presence of various failure modes (short versus open, stuck at 0 versus stuck at 1, covered versus uncovered), the different effects of the failure modes on the system operation (e.g. fail-safe/fail-danger), or various performance levels between normal operation and failure [Wood (1985)].

By dealing with variables having more than two values, BNs allow the modeler to represent a multi-valued component by means of different states or values of the variable representing the component itself. Suppose to consider a three-state component whose states are identified as *working* (w), *fail-open* (f-o) and *fail-short* (f-s). In FT the component failure modes must be modeled as two independent binary events (w/f-o) and (w/f-s); however, to make the model correct, a XOR gate must be inserted between f-o and f-s since they are mutually exclusive events, resulting in a non-coherent FT. On the contrary, BN can include $n$-ary variables by adjusting the entries of the CPT. As already mentioned, in case of $n$-ary variables, it is also possible to generalize the noisy gate constructs, by avoiding, in some cases, the specification of the whole CPT.

## 3.6 Sequentially Dependent Failures

By using FT, another modeling issue that may be quite problematic to deal with is the problem of components failing in some dependent way. For instance, the abnormal operation of a component may induce dependent failures on other ones. Suppose for instance that we refine the description of the multiprocessor system of Figure 3.2 by adding the component power supply $(PS)$ such that, when failing, it causes a system failure, but it may also induce the processors to break down. In the FT representation, a new input $PS$ should be added to the $TE$ of Figure 3.3 to represent a new cause of system failure as shown in Figure 3.6; however, modeling the dependence between the failure of $PS$ and the failure of processor $P_i$ ($i = 1, 2$) is not possible in the FT formalism. On the other hand, in a BN this can be modeled without particular problems; in addition, the modeler may be even more precise, by resorting to a multi-state model for the power supply. Indeed, a more realistic situation could be the following: $PS$ is modeled with three possible modes: ok, defective and failed where the first mode corresponds to a nominal behavior, the second to a defective working mode where an abnormal voltage is provided, while the

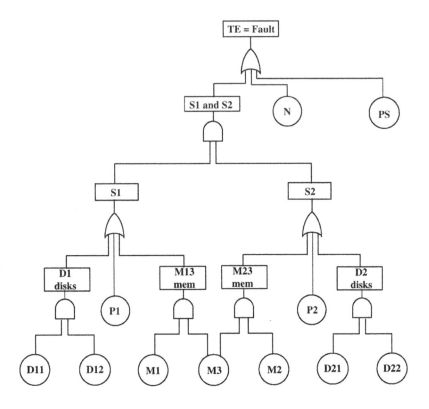

Fig. 3.6   Modified Fault tree for the redundant multiprocessor system.

last mode corresponds to a situation where $PS$ cannot work at all. Of course, the `failed` mode causes the whole system to be down, but we want to model the fact that when $PS$ is in the `defective` mode, the processors increase their conditional dependence to break down. This can be modeled in a very natural way, by considering the variable $PS$ to have three values corresponding to the above modes and by setting the entries in the CPT in a suitable way. Figure 3.7 shows the modified BN structure for the above model, while the CPT of $P_i$ ($i = 1, 2$) is reported in Table 3.3 where $\lambda_{P_i}$ is the failure rate of $P_i$ and $\alpha > 1$ is the increasing factor of the failure rate due to the defective mode of the power supply (the other modified CPT, i.e., that of node $Fault$ is simply the $OR$ of $S_{12} = $ T, $N = $ T and $PS = $ `failed`).

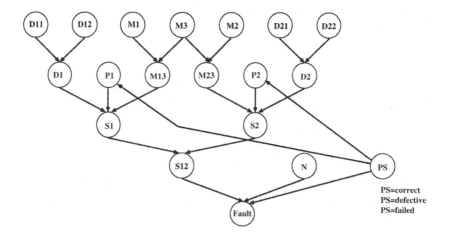

Fig. 3.7 Bayesian network obtained from the FT in Figure 3.6.

Table 3.3 CPT of processors nodes conditioned by power supply

| | *PS* | ok | defective | failed |
|---|---|---|---|---|
| $P_i$ | F | $e^{\lambda_{P_i} t}$ | $e^{\alpha \lambda_{P_i} t}$ | 0 |
| | T | $1 - e^{\lambda_{P_i} t}$ | $1 - e^{\alpha \lambda_{P_i} t}$ | 1 |

## 3.7 Dependability Analysis through BN Inference

Typical analyses performed on a FT involve both qualitative and quantitative aspects. In particular, any kind of quantitative analysis exploits the basics of the qualitative analysis, thus the minimal cut sets computation. Minimal cut sets are the prime implicants of the TE and are usually obtained by means of minimization techniques on the set of logical functions represented by the Boolean gates of the FT (see Chapter 1). Given the set of minimal cut sets, usual quantitative analysis involves:

- the computation of the overall unreliability of the system corresponding to the unreliability of the TE (i.e. $Pr(Fault)$);
- the computation of the unreliability of each identified subsystem, corresponding to the unreliability of each single gate;
- the importance of each minimal cut set, corresponding to the probability of the cut set itself, by assuming the statistical independence among components.

In particular, if each component $C_i$ has probability of failure $Pr_{C_i}$ the importance of a cut set CS is given by

$$Pr(CS) = \prod_{c_i \in CS} Pr(C_i)$$

Notice that such a quantity refers to the a-priori failure probability of each component.

As we have previously shown, any FT can be mapped into a BN where non-root nodes are deterministic. Any analysis performed on a FT can then be performed on the corresponding BN; moreover, other interesting measures can be obtained from the BN, while they cannot be directly evaluated in a FT. Let us first consider the basic analyses of a FT and how they are performed in the corresponding BN:

- *unreliability of the TE*: this corresponds to computing the prior probability of the variable *Fault*, that is $Pr(Q|E)$ with $Q = Fault$ and $E = \emptyset$;
- *unreliability of a given subsystem:* this corresponds to computing the prior probability of the corresponding variable $S_i$, that is $Pr(Q|E)$ with $Q = S_i$ and $E = \emptyset$.

Differently from the computations performed on an FT, the above computations in a BN do not require the determination of the cut sets. However, any technique used for cut set determination in the FT can be applied in the BN: indeed, the Boolean functions modeled by the gates in the FT are modeled by non-root nodes in the BN. Concerning the computation of the cut set importance, it is worth noting that BN may directly produce a more accurate measure of such an importance, being able to provide the posterior probability of each cut set given the fault. Indeed, performing inference having the node *Fault* as the evidence and root variables $R$ as queries, allows one to compute the distribution $Pr(R|Fault)$, where $R$ is a root variable. Once cut sets are known, the computation of the posterior importance is just a matter of marginalization on $Pr(R|Fault)$.

Related to the above topic, is the possibility of characterizing, in the BN setting, some standard importance measures defined in reliability theory, and in particular *Fussell-Vesely Importance* (FVI) and *Birnbaum Importance* (BI) measures [Meng (2000); Borgonovo (2007)] (see also Chapter 1). Both indices are defined with respect to a specific component of a system, and they aim at quantitatively characterizing the role and the impact of such a component in the reliability of the whole system.

In particular, the FVI index is defined as the fractional risk contribution of the component to the total risk of all scenarios involving the components. In terms of FTA, it is defined as the probability that at least one minimal cut set containing the component is failed at time $t$, given that the system is failed at time $t$; in other words the FVI of component $C$ at time $t$ is exactly the probability that component $C$ is down at time $t$ given that the system is down at time $t$, i.e. $FVI(C) = Pr(C_t|Fault_t)$. It is then clear that $FVI(C)$ can be computed on a BN as the marginal posterior probability of the failure of $C$, given the occurrence of the system failure.

On the other hand, the BI index of component $C$ ($BI(C)$) is the change in the system unavailability at time $t$ given that $C$ goes down. It can be shown that $BI(C) = Pr(Fault_t|C_t) - Pr(Fault_t|\bar{C}_t)$ [Borgonovo (2007)]; again, in the BN setting, the computation of the BI index is just a matter of posterior probability computation, in particular, the change in the probability of the system failure given that the component $C$ is down or up respectively.

The above issues introduce another aspect that is peculiar of the use of BN with respect to FT: the possibility of performing diagnostic problem-solving on the modeled system. In fact, in many cases the system analyst may be interested in determining the possible explanations of an exhibited fault in the system. Cut set determination is a step in this direction, but it may not be sufficient in certain situations. Classical diagnostic inference on a BN involves:

- computation of the posterior marginal probability distribution on each component;
- computation of the posterior joint probability distribution on subsets of components;
- computation of the posterior joint probability distribution on the set of all nodes, but the evidence ones.

The first kind of computation is perhaps the most popular one when using BN for diagnosis. One advantage is that there exist well-established algorithms, like the BP algorithm based on Junction Tree propagation discussed in Section 2.1, that can compute the marginal posterior probability of each node, by considering this task as if it was a single query (i.e. it is not necessary to perform multiple queries of the type $Pr(Q|E)$, each time considering $Q$ equal to the node for which we want the posterior distribution). Moreover, as observed above in the characterization of FVI, this kind of computation is very useful for determining the criticality of the

Table 3.4   Failure rates, prior and posterior probabilities for the multiprocessor system example.

| Component $C$ | Failure Rate $\lambda_C$ | Prior $Pr(C)$ | Posterior $Pr(C|Fault)$ |
|---|---|---|---|
| Disk $D_{ij}$ | $\lambda_D = 8.0E - 05$ | 0.32968 | 0.98438 |
| Proc $P_i$ | $\lambda_P = 5.0E - 07$ | 0.002497 | 0.02250 |
| Mem $M_j$ | $\lambda_M = 3.0E - 08$ | 0.00015 | 0.00015 |
| Bus $N$ | $\lambda_N = 2E - 09$ | 0.00001 | 0.00081 |

components of the system. The main disadvantage is that considering only the marginal posterior probability of components is not always appropriate for a precise diagnosis [Pearl (1988)]; in many cases the right way for characterizing diagnoses is to consider scenarios involving more variables (for example all the components). The other two kinds of computation address exactly this point.

Let us consider the following example, again concerning the system of Figure 3.2 and the BN of Figure 3.4. The failure distribution of all components is assumed to be exponential with the failure rates, expressed in $f/h$ (faults per hour) units given in Table 3.4. Suppose the dependability measures are required to be evaluated at a mission time $t = 5000$ $h$: the failure probability of each component, evaluated at $t = 5000$ $h$ is reported in the third column of Table 3.4. By querying the variable *Fault*, we can compute (for instance by means of a BP algorithm) the unreliability of the fault tree's TE as the (prior) probability of system failure, resulting as $Pr(Fault) = 0.01231$. If we observe a system failure at time $t$, the marginal posterior fault probabilities of each component can then be computed, and are reported on the fourth column of Table 3.4[2]. We can also notice that the most critical component is in this case each disk.

However, this information is not completely significant from the diagnostic point of view; in fact, by considering the disk units, the only way of having the fault is to assume that all the disks $D_{11}, D_{12}, D_{21}, D_{22}$ have failed at the same time (indeed, this is the only minimal cut set involving only disks). This information (the fact that all disks have to be jointly considered faulty to get the system fault) is not directly derived by marginal posteriors on components. In fact, for diagnostic purposes a more suitable analysis should consider the posterior joint probability of all the components given the system fault as evidence. This analysis corresponds to search the most probable state given the fault, over the state space represented by all the possible instantiations of the root variables (i.e. the system components).

---

[2]It is worth remembering that such probabilities are exactly the FVI index of the components.

In this case, we can determine, by means of BN inference, that the most probable diagnosis (i.e. the most probable state given the system fault) is exactly the one corresponding to the faulty value of all the disks and the normal value of all the other components; in particular, we can perform a MAP computation restricted to the component variables on the BN, and we get the following MAP assignment[3] :

$$\{\bar{N}, \bar{M}_1, \bar{M}_2, \bar{M}_3, \bar{P}_1, \bar{P}_2, D_{11}, D_{12}, D_{21}, D_{22}\}$$

with

$$Pr(\bar{N}, \bar{M}_1, \bar{M}_2, \bar{M}_3, \bar{P}_1, \bar{P}_2, D_{11}, D_{12}, D_{21}, D_{22}|Fault) = 0.95427$$

Notice that the above diagnosis does not correspond to the cut set $\{D_{11}; D_{12}; D_{21}; D_{22}\}$, since the latter does not imply that the unmentioned components are working (i.e. assigned to the normal value); anyway, the posterior probability of such cut set can be naturally computed in the BN setting by a query on all the disk variables conditioned on the observation of the fault. For example, we can compute

$$Pr(D_{11}, D12, D_{21}, D_{22}|Fault) = Pr(D_{11}|Fault)Pr(D_{12}|D_{11}, Fault)$$

$$Pr(D_{21}|D_{12}, D_{11}, Fault)Pr(D_{22}|D_{21}, D_{12}, D_{11}, Fault) =$$

$$= 0.98438 \ 0.99477 \ 0.98485 \ 0.99493 = 0.95951$$

that corresponds to the marginalization over processors, memories and bus of the MAP assignment reported above.

As we have already noticed in Section 2.1, computing MAP (or MPE) assignments is in general a computationally hard problem, both if trying to enumerate in order of probability the assignments, as well as if one tries to determine only the top one [Kwisthout (2008)]. An interesting possibility offered by BN is that there exist algorithms able to produce diagnoses (either viewed as only-root assignments or all-variable assignments) in order of their probability of occurrence, without exploring the whole state space; they are called any-time algorithms, since the user can stop the algorithm at any time, by getting an approximate answer that is improved if more time is allocated to the algorithm. An example is the algorithm based on the model described in [Portinale and Torasso (1997)] that is able to provide the most probable diagnoses (in terms of root nodes), given any observation on the model; in particular it is possible to enumerate the possible

---

[3] The result is obtained using the SamIam tool.

diagnosis assignments at any desired level of precision. In our multiprocessor system example, we can compute the most probable diagnoses, by querying the component variables with evidence on the occurrence of the *Fault* node, and by specifying a maximum admissible error $\epsilon$ in the posterior probability of the diagnoses. The algorithm is able to produce every diagnosis $d_i$ in decreasing order of their occurrence probability, with an estimate $\hat{P}r(d_i|Fault)$ such that $Pr(d_i|Fault) = \hat{P}r(d_i|Fault) \pm \epsilon$. In the example, by requiring diagnoses to be root assignments and $\epsilon = 1E - 06$, the first three diagnoses are, in order:

$$d_1 : (\bar{N}, \bar{M}_1, \bar{M}_2, \bar{M}_3, \bar{P}_1, \bar{P}_2, D_{11}, D_{12}, D_{21}, D_{22})$$

$$d_2 : (\bar{N}, \bar{M}_1, \bar{M}_2, \bar{M}_3, \bar{P}_1, P_2, D_{11}, D_{12}, \bar{D}_{21}, \bar{D}_{22})$$

$$d_3 : (\bar{N}, \bar{M}_1, \bar{M}_2, \bar{M}_3, P_1, \bar{P}_2, \bar{D}_{11}, \bar{D}_{12}, D_{21}, D_{22})$$

The first one represents the already mentioned most probable diagnosis with all disks faulty, while the second and the third one are two symmetrical diagnoses: $d_2$ represents a fault caused by disk failures in the first subsystem and a processor failure in the second; $d_3$ represents a fault caused by disk failures in the second sub-system and a processor failure in the first.

Posterior probability estimates are then computed within the given error level as

$$\hat{P}r(d_1|Fault) = 0.95422$$

$$\hat{P}r(d_i|Fault) = 9.887E - 03 \ (i = 2, 3)$$

The algorithm guarantees that any further diagnosis has a posterior probability smaller or equal than that of $d_2$ and $d_3$. It is worth noting that this result is in general obtained without exploring the whole state space, that in this case is equal to $2^{10} = 1024$ states, 10 being the number of components.

Similar results may be obtained for complete variable assignments. Notice that if the BN has only deterministic non-root nodes, a root assignment uniquely corresponds to a complete assignment with the same posterior, because given a particular assignment of modes to components, the assignment to non-root variables is deterministically obtained. This is no longer true if we introduce uncertainty at inner levels as it is usually done within the BN framework.

Chapter 4

# From Dynamic Fault Tree to Dynamic Bayesian Networks

In Chapter 3, we showed that the modeling possibilities offered by FT, can be extended by relying on BN. This allows us to relax some constraints which are typical of FT. It has been shown how FT can be directly mapped into BN, and that the basic inference techniques on the latter may be used to obtain classical parameters computed from the former. In addition, BN allow to represent local dependencies and to perform both predictive and diagnostic reasoning. In this chapter, we show how Dynamic Bayesian Networks (DBN) can provide a unified framework in which Dynamic Fault Trees (DFT) can be represented. As we have introduced in Chapter 1 (Section 1.2.2), DFT introduce four types of dynamic gates: WSP, FDEP, PAND and SEQ. WSP represents situations where spare components are available, and special cases are the CSP gate (when spares cannot fail while in stand-by mode) and the HSP gate (when spares have the same failure rate both in stand-by and in operative mode). We have also noticed that SEQ gates can be modeled as a special case of a CSP (Section 1.2.2) [Montani *et al.* (2005)], so we do not consider such gates in the following [1]. Furthermore, the FDEP gate can be generalized to the *Probabilistic Dependency* gate (PDEP) [Portinale *et al.* (2010)] where the trigger event T causes other dependent components to become unusable or inaccessible with a probability $\pi_d \leq 1$. In particular, if $\pi_d = 1$ we obtain the standard FDEP (i.e., dependent components are forced to definitely fail when the trigger occurs), while if $\pi_d < 1$ we can model different failure dependencies (we will discuss these aspects in more detail in the following).

Finally, the PAND gate reaches a failure state if and only if all of its

---

[1] The conceptual difference between the two kinds of gates is that the inputs to a SEQ do not need to be a component and its set of spares, but they can be components covering any kind of function in the DFT.

input components have failed in a preassigned order (from left to right in graphical notation).

The quantitative analysis of DFT typically requires to expand the model into its state space, and to solve the corresponding CTMC. We have previously discussed that, through a process known as modularization, it is possible to identify and solve the independent sub-trees with dynamic gates, using a different CTMC or a GSPN (much smaller than the model corresponding to the entire DFT) for each of them (Section 1.2.2). Nevertheless, there still exists the problem of state explosion. In order to alleviate this limitation, we show how is it possible to define a translation of the DFT into a DBN. With respect to CTMC, the use of a DBN allows one to take advantage of the factorization in the temporal probability model. As a matter of fact, the conditional independence assumptions enables a compact representation of the probabilistic model, allowing the system designer or analyst to avoid the complexity of specifying and using a global-state model (like a standard MC), when the dynamic module of the considered DFT is significantly large.

## 4.1 Translating Dynamic Gates

In this section, we present the conversion into DBN fragments, of the following dynamic gates: WSP, PDEP and PAND. The rules to convert Boolean gates (AND, OR, k:n) can be found in Chapter 3.

### 4.1.1 *Warm spare gate*

In a DFT, different configurations of warm spares can be designed. A simple configuration is shown in Figure 4.1, where a primary component $P$ has a set of possible spares $S_1, \ldots S_n$. Suppose the order of activation of the spares is given by their number (i.e., $S_1$ is the first, and so on): it should be clear that, in general, the failure rate of $S_k$ depends on the state of the primary component, but also on the status of every $S_h$ with $h < k$ (the change from dormant to operative status of a given spare depends on the status of spares that can be used before it). This is true in case of a strict WSP gate (i.e., a dormancy factor $0 < \alpha < 1$) and of a CSP ($\alpha = 0$). In case of HSP gate, such a dependence does not exist, since the failure rate of the spare does not change with the status of the other spares; actually HSP are equivalent to standard AND gates (they are used to emphasize the role of

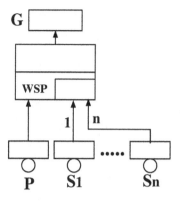

Fig. 4.1   A WSP gate with multiple spares.

each component as either primary or spare). Figure 4.2 shows the structure of the DBN modeling a WSP gate with one primary component $P$ and two spares $S_1$ and $S_2$, to be activated in the given order. Table 4.1 reports the

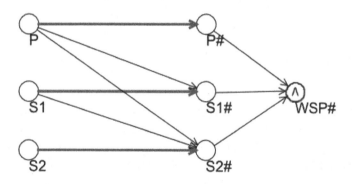

Fig. 4.2   DBN modeling a WSP gate with multiple spares.

CPTs for such a DBN (the CPT of $S2\#$ is split in two tables, for the sake of readability), where $\lambda_C$ is the (exponential) failure rate of component $C$, $\alpha$ is the gate dormancy factor and $\Delta$ is the time discretization step between the anterior and the ulterior layer of the DBN. As usual in dependability, the key is false=working and true=failed. We can notice that, even if spares have three actual states (dormant, operative and failed), in this case it is sufficient to model just two possible states as for the primary

Table 4.1  CPTs for the DBN of Figure 4.2

|  | P=false | P=true |
|---|---|---|
| P#=false | $e^{-\lambda_P \Delta}$ | 0 |
| P#=true | $1 - e^{-\lambda_P \Delta}$ | 1 |

|  | P=false | | P=true | |
|---|---|---|---|---|
|  | S1=false | S1=true | S1=false | S1=true |
| S1#=false | $e^{-\alpha \lambda_{S1} \Delta}$ | 0 | $e^{-\lambda_{S1} \Delta}$ | 0 |
| S1#=true | $1 - e^{-\alpha \lambda_{S1} \Delta}$ | 1 | $1 - e^{-\lambda_{S1} \Delta}$ | 1 |

|  | P=false | | | |
|---|---|---|---|---|
|  | S1=false | | S1=true | |
|  | S2=false | S2=true | S2=false | S2=true |
| S2#=false | $e^{-\alpha \lambda_{S2} \Delta}$ | 0 | $e^{-\alpha \lambda_{S2} \Delta}$ | 0 |
| S2#=true | $1 - e^{-\alpha \lambda_{S2} \Delta}$ | 1 | $1 - e^{-\alpha \lambda_{S2} \Delta}$ | 1 |

|  | P=true | | | |
|---|---|---|---|---|
|  | S1=false | | S1=true | |
|  | S2=false | S2=true | S2=false | S2=true |
| S2#=false | $1 - e^{-\alpha \lambda_{S2} \Delta}$ | 0 | $e^{-\lambda_{S2} \Delta}$ | 0 |
| S2#=true | $1 - e^{-\alpha \lambda_{S2} \Delta}$ | 1 | $1 - e^{-\lambda_{S2} \Delta}$ | 1 |

component, by collapsing `dormant` and `operative` into the state `working`. This is no longer possible in case of spares that are shared with other components. In fact, when the same pool of spares is shared across a set of WSP, each principal component is allowed to request the items in the pool in a precise order, if more than one is still dormant. As an example, let us consider a situation where two components $A$ and $B$ can be substituted by two spares $SA$ and $SB$ (see Figure 4.3). In particular, $SB$ is $B$'s spare, and will substitute $A$ only if $B$ is working and $SA$ is failed. If $B$ fails, it requests the activation of $SB$, and only if $SB$ is unavailable $SA$ is activated. $SA$ is $A$'s spare and analogous considerations hold. Every gate fails if and only if its principal component and all the available (i.e. working and dormant) spares in the pool fail. The structure of the DBN corresponding to this situation is shown in Figure 4.4.

It can be observed that each component node at the ulterior layer depends on its copy at the anterior layer. Moreover, each spare depends on

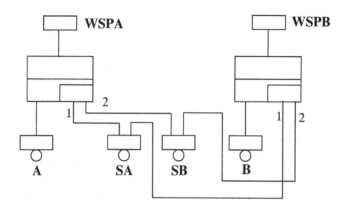

Fig. 4.3 WSP gates with sharing spares.

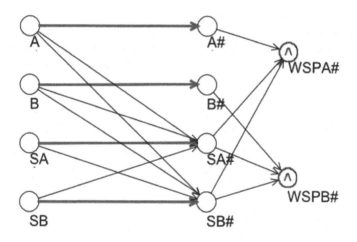

Fig. 4.4 DBN for two combined WSP gates.

the two principal components, and on the other spare. In order to model the requests of shared spares, differently from the situation of Table 4.1, in this case each spare is better modeled by keeping explicit all the possible states: dormant (d), operative on A (opA), operative on B (opB) and failed (f). On the other hand, every primary component is a classical binary variable assuming two values: working (w) and failed (f). If both principal components are working, each spare maintains a failure rate equal to $\alpha\lambda$ ($\alpha$ being the dormancy factor). On the other hand, if $A$ is

Table 4.2　CPT fragment for node $SA\#$.

| A | B | SA | SB | $SA\#=$d | $SA\#=$opA | $SA\#=$opB | $SA\#=$f |
|---|---|----|----|-----------|------------|------------|----------|
| w | w | d | f | $e^{-\alpha\lambda_{SA}\Delta}$ | 0 | 0 | $1-e^{-\alpha\lambda_{SA}\Delta}$ |
| w | f | d | f | 0 | 0 | $e^{-\lambda_{SA}\Delta}$ | $1-e^{-\lambda_{SA}\Delta}$ |
| f | w | d | f | 0 | $e^{-\lambda_{SA}\Delta}$ | 0 | $1-e^{-\lambda_{SA}\Delta}$ |
| f | f | d | f | 0 | $e^{-\lambda_{SA}\Delta}$ | 0 | $1-e^{-\lambda_{SA}\Delta}$ |

down, $SA$ switches to a failure rate equal to $\lambda_{SA}$ (since the spare is now in the active mode); the same happens if $A$ is working, but $B$ and $SB$ are both failed. $SB$ works dually on its principal component $B$. Table 4.2 reports some entries of the CPT of $SA\#$, in the hypothesis that $SA$ is dormant, $SB$ is failed at time $t$, $\lambda_{SA}$ is the (exponential) failure rate of $SA$, $\alpha$ is the dormancy factor and $\Delta$ is the time discretization step between the anterior and the ulterior layer of the DBN. Notice that the network structural complexity (i.e., the number of intra-slice edges) and the size of CPTs would significantly increase as the number of shared spares increases, because the number of dependencies induced by the pool of spares increases as well.

Each WSP gate (i.e., $WSPA$ and $WSPB$) is modeled as a deterministic AND ($\wedge$) node among its three inputs: the principal components and the two spares in the pool.

### 4.1.2　*Probabilistic dependency gate*

As we mentioned, the standard FDEP gate of a DFT can be generalized by defining a new gate, called probabilistic dependency (PDEP). In the PDEP, the probability of failure of dependent components, given that the trigger has failed, is parametrized through a specific parameter $0 \le \pi_d \le 1$. The meaning of this parametrization is that, if the trigger event occurs, then there is a given chance (determined by $\pi_d$) that the failure on a dependent component will occur as well. We assume that if $\pi_d = 0$ then the occurrence of the trigger has no influence on the failure of the dependent components[2], while if $\pi_d = 1$, then the occurrence of the trigger immediately causes the failure of dependent components, modeling the standard FDEP gate.

For any $0 < \pi_d < 1$ we can assume two possible interpretations or semantics of the gate behavior:

- the trigger, once occurred, persists as active in time, increasing the fail-

---

[2]It should be clear that, for practical reasons, there is no need of modeling a PDEP gate with $\pi_d = 0$, since this is a degenerate case where the so-called "dependent components" are actually independent from the trigger.

ure rate of the dependent components, thus accelerating their eventual failure;

- the trigger, once occurred, is de-activated, with no future chance of causing the failure of the dependent components, in case such a failure did not actually occur.

We call *persistent PDEP* the former interpretation and *one-shot PDEP* the latter [3].

In case of a persistent PDEP gate, the trigger occurrence is assumed to increase the failure rate $\lambda_A$ of a dependent component $A$; in particular, the failure rate of $A$ given that the trigger has occurred is determined as $\beta\lambda_A$, being $\beta = \frac{1}{1-\pi_d}$. Of course, if $\pi_d = 0$, then the failure rate of $A$ is unchanged, while in case $\pi_d = 1$, then $\lambda_A \to \infty$ modeling the behavior of a standard FDEP gate.

In case of a one-shot PDEP gate, the interpretation of the $\pi_d$ is indeed that of a *failure probability*. Given that the trigger has occurred, then the dependent component $A$ immediately fails with probability $\pi_d$. If $A$ does not fail, then the trigger has no longer effect and the failure rate of $A$ remains unchanged. Again if $\pi_d = 0$ the trigger has no influence on $A$, while if $\pi_d = 1$ the PDEP transforms into the FDEP gate.

Persistent PDEP corresponds to potential causes of the failure of dependent components whose physical influence persists over time; this kind of gate can model situations of component degeneration due to external causes. Consider for instance a set of components, whose function is accomplished in normal conditions under the presence of a control subsystem: the unavailability of the control subsystem increases the probability of components' failure over time.

One-shot PDEP, on the other hand, can model a situation of imperfect coverage [Amari *et al.* (1999)]; suppose that a set of components depends on the availability of a given subsystem: the unavailability of such a subsystem can be "covered" by some backup mechanisms that can be activated only with a given probability. A one-shot PDEP with the subsystem event as a trigger (and with the dependent components as other inputs) can model such a situation.

Figure 4.5 and Figure 4.6 show the structure of the DBN corresponding to the different versions of a PDEP gate, with a trigger event $T$ and a

---

[3] Another probabilistic extension to the FDEP gate is presented in [Xing and Michel (2006)]; however, the semantics is different from our PDEP gate, since the dependent events are forced to occur probabilistically in mutual exclusion.

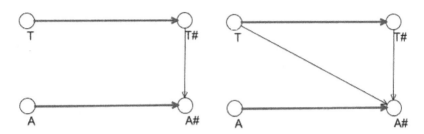

Fig. 4.5   DBN for FDEP and persistent PDEP.

Fig. 4.6   DBN for one-shot PDEP.

Table 4.3   CPT for FDEP and persistent PDEP (Figure 4.5)

|            | T#=false | | T#=true | |
|------------|----------|---------|----------|---------|
|            | A=false  | A=true  | A=false  | A=true  |
| A#=false   | $e^{-\lambda_A \Delta}$ | 0 | 0 | 0 |
| A#=true    | $1 - e^{-\lambda_A \Delta}$ | 1 | 1 | 1 |

|            | T#=false | | T#=true | |
|------------|----------|---------|----------|---------|
|            | A=false  | A=true  | A=false  | A=true  |
| A#=false   | $e^{-\lambda_A \Delta}$ | 0 | $e^{-\beta \lambda_A \Delta}$ | 0 |
| A#=true    | $1 - e^{-\lambda_A \Delta}$ | 1 | $1 - e^{-\beta \lambda_A \Delta}$ | 1 |

dependent component $A$. In particular, Figure 4.5 shows the structure of a persistent PDEP, which is the structure of a standard FDEP as well. Table 4.3 (as before split for the sake of clarity) shows the CPTs for node $A\#$ in such cases (where $\beta = \frac{1}{1-\pi_d}$). Figure 4.6 shows the structure of a one-shot PDEP, where the status of the dependent component $A$ must also depend on the trigger status at the anterior layer, since only the transition of the trigger from false state to true state may set, with probability $\pi_d$, the status of $A$ to true (failed). Table 4.4 (again split in two subtables) reports the CPT of $A\#$ in the one-shot PDEP case. Notice that the last two columns of the second subtable have the same parameters of the first two columns of the first subtable, since if the trigger becomes true, but fails to produce a failure on the dependent component, then the behavior of the latter will continue to be ruled by the standard failure rate $\lambda_A$. Third and fourth columns of the first subtable represent impossible cases, if we assume the persistence of faults (the trigger cannot switch to false state from true state), so the corresponding parameters (where the symbol / is shown) are simply ignored. Finally, the first two columns of the second

Table 4.4   CPT for one-shot PDEP (Figure 4.6)

| | T#=false | | | |
|---|---|---|---|---|
| | T=false | | T=true | |
| | A=false | A=true | A=false | A=true |
| A#=false | $e^{-\lambda_A \Delta}$ | 0 | / | / |
| A#=true | $1 - e^{-\lambda_A \Delta}$ | 1 | / | / |

| | T#=true | | | |
|---|---|---|---|---|
| | T=false | | T=true | |
| | A=false | A=true | A=false | A=true |
| A#=false | $1 - \pi_d$ | 0 | $e^{-\lambda_A \Delta}$ | 0 |
| A#=true | $\pi_d$ | 1 | $1 - e^{-\lambda_A \Delta}$ | 1 |

subtable represent the cases where the switch of the trigger from `false` to `true` causes, with probability $\pi_d$, the occurrence of $A$.

The interested reader is invited to check [Portinale *et al.* (2010)] for a discussion about the practical effect of the different versions of PDEP on a case study.

### 4.1.3   *Priority AND*

PAND gates model situations where a control component may prevent the system to crash (with ruinous consequences), because of the failure of a standard component. In such cases, a failure of the control component before the failure of the standard one prevents the recovery action of the control component, leading to a (sub)-system failure. Consider a PAND gate having two input events $A$ and $B$, in such order (i.e., the output of the gate fails if and only if both input events are failed and $A$ fails before $B$); we can model the failure sequence by introducing a new stochastic Boolean variable $PA$ representing the output of the PAND gate, that explicitly keeps track of the order in which $A$ and $B$ fail. Variable $PA$ at the anterior layer (time $t$) is initialized to `false` (i.e., at the initial stage, we assume that the PAND event has not occurred yet). Variable $PA\#$ at the ulterior layer (time $t + \Delta$) depends on all the variables at the anterior layer, and on the component variables at the ulterior layer as well (i.e., $A\#$ and $B\#$). In this way, the CPT for $PA\#$ can be set in order to model the following deterministic Boolean function:

- $PA\# = $ **true** if $A = $ **true**, $B = $ **false** and $B\# = $ **true** (i.e., $Pr\{PA\#|A, \overline{B}, B\#, \overline{PA}\} = 1$); this represents the fact that $A$ fails

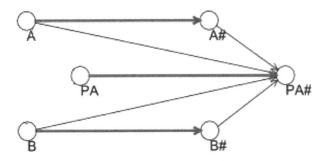

Fig. 4.7   DBN for the PAND gate.

before $B$, and that the output of the gate becomes true as soon as $B$ fails as well;

- $PA\#$ = true if $PA$ = true; this represents the persistence of the true state of the output of the gate (i.e. $Pr\{PA\#|PA, \text{any value of other parents}\} = 1$)

Figure 4.7 shows the resulting DBN.

Given the fact that a DBN is a discrete time model, an hypothesis on how to deal with contemporary faults of $A$ and $B$ has to be made; two alternatives are possible: either to set the PAND output to true (i.e., assuming that a contemporary fault of the components is equivalent to the faults in the expected order for the PAND fault) or to set the output to false (i.e., assuming that only the strict expected order is able to provide a failure). In the continuous time case (e.g., when using CTMC), this is not necessary, since a contemporary fault of the components can never occur.

## 4.2   Combining the Modules into a Single DBN

The dynamic gates we have examined in the previous section can be connected, in order to build a complex DFT. To understand which combinations can be modeled, and how we can provide an automatic translation of the DFT into the corresponding DBN, we have to recall how the gates themselves are meant to be applied.

In particular, according to [Manian *et al.* (1999)]:

(1) the dependent events of a PDEP/FDEP can only be basic events, which could be the input of another dynamic gate;

(2) WSP can have only basic events as input, and two or more spare gates can share some spare components; a set of WSP sharing a pool of spares are treated as a single module for translation (see Section 4.1.1);

(3) PAND can have basic events or spare gates as input; two or more PAND can also be combined in a cascade manner.

These simplifications let us derive a general algorithm for building the DBN corresponding to the whole DFT. The procedure follows a modular approach, since it builds the output DBN by combining the various DBN modules or fragments corresponding to the different gates. From the structural point of view, combining different fragments is relatively simple; just overlaps nodes corresponding to the same variable in different fragments. However, the quantitative combination of the conditional probabilities (i.e. the generation of the CPTs concerning the combined structure) may be rather problematic. Indeed, the structural combination will introduce new dependencies when overlapping nodes; the question is whether there exists a method of quantifying such dependencies in a modular way, by combining the CPTs of the original fragments, under a set of reasonable assumptions. We have seen in Chapter 2 that one possible answer from BN theory is the notion of *causal independence* (see Section 2.1.2).

Before looking at how this can be applied in our case, let us discuss the way to proceed, in order to obtain a complete DBN from the modules derived from each single gate. Consider a set of dynamic modules $M_1, \ldots, M_k$ of a DFT such that each $M_i$ is either a single dynamic gate or a set of WSP gates sharing spare components[4].

We can combine $M_1, \ldots, M_k$ through the nodes they share as follows:

(1) generate independently the module for each $M_i$ (call it $DBN_i$), along the lines explained in Section 4.1;

(2) connect the modules $DBN_i$ in correspondence of the nodes they share, by merging such nodes;

(3) for each merged node $X$, if after the merging there are arcs entering $X$ coming from different modules $DBN_i$, then a new CPT for $X$ is created, as follows[5]:

    **a.** add all the parents derived from DBN modules to which $X$ belongs as columns in the new CPT;

---

[4] As we have already noticed, in this case we need to generate a DBN module or fragment, by taking into account the whole set of gates sharing the spares.

[5] Notice that, if this is the case, $X$ has to be a node representing a basic component.

**b.** when the entries of the source CPTs agree on the same value, then set the corresponding entry in the new CPT to that value;

**c.** otherwise, set the entries of the CPT according to a specified combination function (see below).

Concerning the combination function, two different approaches can be adopted:

- *Causal Independence (CI)* interaction: this exploits the principles discussed in Section 2.1.2, and is a suitable choice when the influence of each module contributes to the failure of the shared component node in an "additive" way; more specifically, this means that the probability of failure of the component shared by the modules increases with the contemporary presence of the causes of failure from the different modules;

- *Most Severe Prevailing (MSP)* interaction: in this case the new CPT entries are computed as the maximum value of the entries in the CPTs of the source modules; this is a suitable choice when the most severe cause of failure prevails over the others.

In order to better clarify these issues let us consider some examples.

**Example 1.** A persistent PDEP gate has a trigger $T$ and a dependent component $S$; a WSP gate has a primary component $P$ and $S$ as spare component. The two DBN modules obtained by translating the two dynamic gates are merged by overlapping the variables corresponding to the shared component $S$, i.e., variables $S$ and $S\#$. Figure 4.8 shows the resulting DBN structure, with the different DBN modules highlighted as rectangles.

The only CPT to update is the one of variable $S\#$, having $S, T\#$ as parents in the PDEP module and $S, P$ in the WSP module: the resulting CPT must then have $S, T\#, P$ as parents. The question is how to fill the entries of the merged CPT, by combining the entries of the original ones. First of all consider the "source" CPTs concerning the PDEP and the WSP gate as shown in Table 4.5 and Table 4.6 respectively.

It is worth noting that in this case, since the spare component $S$ is involved in more than one dynamic gate, we cannot exploit the simplification adopted in the DBN of Figure 4.1, where `dormant` and `operative` states of the spare can be collapsed into one single `working` state. In Tables 4.5 and 4.6 we adopted the shorthands d for `dormant`, op for `operative` and f for `failed`. As usual, symbol / represents impossible entries (e.g., it is

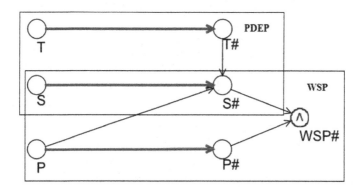

Fig. 4.8   DBN merging a module from a PDEP and a module from a WSP (shared on component $S$).

Table 4.5   CPT for a persistent PDEP gate with parameter $\pi_d$ where $p_d = 1 - e^{-\frac{\lambda_S \Delta}{1 - \pi_d}}$ and with dormancy factor $\alpha$ for $S$

| | T#=false | | | T#=true | | |
|---|---|---|---|---|---|---|
| | S=d | S=op | S=f | S=d | S=op | S=f |
| S#=d | $e^{-\alpha\lambda_S\Delta}$ | 0 | 0 | $1 - p_d$ | 0 | 0 |
| S#=op | 0 | $e^{-\lambda_S\Delta}$ | 0 | 0 | $1 - p_d$ | 0 |
| S#=f | $1 - e^{-\alpha\lambda_S\Delta}$ | $1 - e^{-\lambda_S\Delta}$ | 1 | $p_d$ | $p_d$ | 1 |

Table 4.6   CPT for a WSP gate with spare dormancy factor $\alpha$

| | P=false | | | P=true | | |
|---|---|---|---|---|---|---|
| | S=d | S=op | S=f | S=d | S=op | S=f |
| S#=d | $e^{-\alpha\lambda_S\Delta}$ | / | 0 | / | 0 | 0 |
| S#=op | 0 | / | 0 | / | $e^{-\lambda_S\Delta}$ | 0 |
| S#=f | $1 - e^{-\alpha\lambda_S\Delta}$ | / | 1 | / | $1 - e^{\lambda_S\Delta}$ | 1 |

not possible that $S = $ op and $P = $ false). Table 4.7 shows the CPT that is obtained by merging the two DBN modules of Figure 4.8.

Source entries in agreement with each other produce the CPT entries explicitly shown in Table 4.7; concerning entries $\mathcal{P}_1$ and $\mathcal{P}_2$, they represent the result of the interaction rule adopted (i.e. either CI or MSP). In case of CI interaction we get the following:

- $\mathcal{P}_1 = 1 - e^{-\gamma\lambda_S\Delta}$ where $\gamma = \frac{1}{1 - \pi_d} + \alpha = \beta + \alpha$.
  Indeed, from Table 4.5 we have that
  $Pr\{S\# = \text{f}|T\# = \text{true}, S = \text{d}\} = p_d$,
  while from Table 4.6 we have that

Table 4.7    CPT obtained from combining CPTs from Tables 4.5 and 4.6

| | T#=false | | | | | |
| --- | --- | --- | --- | --- | --- | --- |
| | P=false | | | P=true | | |
| | S=d | S=op | S=f | S=d | S=op | S=f |
| S#=d | $e^{\alpha\lambda_S\Delta}$ | / | 0 | / | 0 | 0 |
| S#=op | 0 | / | 0 | / | $e^{\lambda_S\Delta}$ | 0 |
| S#=f | $1-e^{\alpha\lambda_S\Delta}$ | / | 1 | / | $1-e^{\lambda_S\Delta}$ | 1 |

| | T#=true | | | | | |
| --- | --- | --- | --- | --- | --- | --- |
| | P=false | | | P=true | | |
| | S=d | S=op | S=f | S=d | S=op | S=f |
| S#=d | $1-\mathcal{P}_1$ | / | 0 | / | 0 | 0 |
| S#=op | 0 | / | 0 | / | $1-\mathcal{P}_2$ | 0 |
| S#=f | $\mathcal{P}_1$ | / | 1 | / | $\mathcal{P}_2$ | 1 |

$Pr\{S\# = \mathtt{f}|P = \mathtt{false}, S = \mathtt{d}\} = 1 - e^{-\alpha\lambda_S\Delta}$.

It follows that

$\mathcal{P}_1 = Pr\{S\# = \mathtt{f}|T\# = \mathtt{true}, P = \mathtt{false}, S = \mathtt{d}\} =$
$1 - (1 - p_d)(1 - (1 - e^{-\alpha\lambda_S\Delta}))$.

It is then a matter of algebraic manipulation to obtain the above expression.

- $\mathcal{P}_2 = 1 - e^{-\gamma\lambda_S\Delta}$ where $\gamma = \frac{1}{1-\pi_d} + 1 = \beta + 1$.

Indeed, from Table 4.5 we have that

$Pr\{S\# = \mathtt{f}|T\# = \mathtt{true}, S = \mathtt{op}\} = p_d$,

while from Table 4.6 we have that

$Pr\{S\# = \mathtt{f}|P = \mathtt{true}, S = \mathtt{op}\} = 1 - e^{-\lambda_S\Delta}$.

It follows that

$\mathcal{P}_1 = Pr\{S\# = \mathtt{f}|T\# = \mathtt{true}, P = \mathtt{true}, S = \mathtt{op}\} =$
$1 - (1 - p_d)(1 - (1 - e^{-\lambda_S\Delta}))$.

Again, it is just a matter of algebraic manipulation to obtain the above expression.

We can notice that, as expected, the second situation is a particular case of the first (when $\alpha = 1$ i.e., the spare is operative); moreover, the final failure rate of the spare component is incremented with respect to the contribution of each single cause of failure (which is the factor $\beta$ for the PDEP and the factor $\alpha$ for the WSP).

If the MSP interaction is adopted, we obtain the following

- $\mathcal{P}_1 = \max(p_d, 1 - e^{-\alpha\lambda_S\Delta}) = \max(1 - e^{-\beta\lambda_S\Delta}, 1 - e^{-\alpha\lambda_S\Delta})$

Table 4.8    CPTs for $P\#$ from PDEP1 and PDEP2 (Figure 4.9)

|  | T1#=false | | T1#=true | |
|---|---|---|---|---|
|  | P=false | P=true | P=false | P=true |
| P#=false | $e^{-\lambda_P\Delta}$ | 0 | $1-p_1$ | 0 |
| P#=true | $1-e^{-\lambda_P\Delta}$ | 1 | $p_1$ | 1 |

|  | T2#=false | | T2#=true | |
|---|---|---|---|---|
|  | P=false | P=true | P=false | P=true |
| P#=false | $e^{-\lambda_P\Delta}$ | 0 | $1-p_2$ | 0 |
| P#=true | $1-e^{-\lambda_P\Delta}$ | 1 | $p_2$ | 1 |

- $\mathcal{P}_2 = \max(p_d, 1-e^{-\lambda_S\Delta}) = \max(1-e^{-\beta\lambda_S\Delta}, 1-e^{-\lambda_S\Delta})$ (i.e., $\alpha=1$)

In other words, if $\beta > \alpha$ then the interaction scheme chooses $p_d$, otherwise it chooses $1-e^{-\alpha\lambda_S\Delta}$.

**Example 2.**   Two persistent PDEP gates, with trigger events $T1$ and $T2$ respectively, share the same dependent component $P$. They have different parameters $\pi_1$ and $\pi_2$ respectively resulting in $p_1 = 1 - e^{-\beta_1\lambda_P\Delta}$ and $p_2 = 1 - e^{-\beta_2\lambda_P\Delta}$, with $\beta_i = \frac{1}{1-\pi_i}$ ($i = 1, 2$). Figure 4.9 shows the resulting DBN structure. Table 4.8 reports the CPTs of variable $P\#$ from the first gate (PDEP1) and from the second gate (PDEP2) respectively; finally, the CPT for $P\#$ in the DBN of Figure 4.9 is shown in Table 4.9.

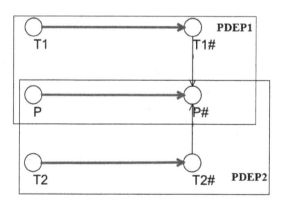

Fig. 4.9   DBN merging two persistent PDEP.

As before, source entries that are in agreement with each other produce the CPT entries explicitly shown in Table 4.9 (split in two subtables); on the

Table 4.9   CPTs for $P\#$ from DBN in Figure 4.9

| | T1#=false | | | |
|---|---|---|---|---|
| | T2#=false | | T2#=true | |
| | P=false | P=true | P=false | P=true |
| P#=false | $e^{-\lambda_P \Delta}$ | 0 | $1 - \mathcal{P}_2$ | 0 |
| P#=true | $1 - e^{-\lambda_P \Delta}$ | 1 | $\mathcal{P}_2$ | 1 |

| | T1#=true | | | |
|---|---|---|---|---|
| | T2#=false | | T2#=true | |
| | P=false | P=true | P=false | P=true |
| P#=false | $1 - \mathcal{P}_1$ | 0 | $1 - \mathcal{P}_3$ | 0 |
| P#=true | $\mathcal{P}_1$ | 1 | $\mathcal{P}_3$ | 1 |

other hand, entries resulting in the combination of different values depends on the interaction scheme.

In case of CI interaction the values obtained are the following:

- $\mathcal{P}_1 = 1 - e^{-(\beta_1 + 1)\lambda_P \Delta}$.

  $\mathcal{P}_2 = 1 - e^{-(\beta_2 + 1)\lambda_P \Delta}$.

  Indeed, concerning $\mathcal{P}_1$, from Table 4.8 we have that

  $Pr\{P\# = \text{true}|T1\# = \text{true}, P = \text{false}\} = p_1\}$

  and

  $Pr\{P\# = \text{true}|T2\# = \text{false}, P = \text{false}\} = 1 - e^{-\lambda_P \Delta}$.

  It follows that

  $\mathcal{P}_1 = Pr\{P\# = \text{true}|T1\# = \text{true}, T2\# = \text{false}, P = \text{false}\} = 1 - (1 - p_1)e^{-\lambda_P \Delta}$;

  the final expression for $\mathcal{P}_1$ is obtained by substituting the definition of $p_1 = 1 - e^{-\beta_1 \lambda_P \Delta}$. Notice that, when $\pi_1 \to 1$ (as in the case of a PDEP approaching a standard FDEP), then $\mathcal{P}_1 \approx p_1$, meaning that the influence of the standard failure rate of $P$ is negligible with respect to the influence of the active trigger.

  Similar considerations can be done for $\mathcal{P}_2$.

- $\mathcal{P}_3 = 1 - e^{-(\beta_1 + \beta_2)\lambda_P \Delta}$.

  Indeed, from Table 4.8 we have that

  $Pr\{P\# = \text{true}|T1\# = \text{true}, P = \text{false}\} = p_1\}$

  and

  $Pr\{P\# = \text{true}|T2\# = \text{true}, P = \text{false}\} = p_2$.

  It follows that

  $\mathcal{P}_1 = Pr\{P\# = \text{true}|T1\# = \text{true}, T2\# = \text{false}, P = \text{false}\} = 1 - (1 - p_1)(1 - p_2)$;

the final expression for $\mathcal{P}_3$ is obtained by substituting the definition of $p_1 = 1 - e^{-\beta_1 \lambda_P \Delta}$ and $p_2 = 1 - e^{-\beta_2 \lambda_P \Delta}$. In this case the influence of each active trigger is "added" to produce the failure on the dependent component.

In case of MSP interaction we get the following values

- $\mathcal{P}_1 = \max(p_1, 1 - e^{-\lambda_P \Delta}) = \max(1 - e^{-\beta_1 \lambda_P \Delta}, 1 - e^{-\lambda_P \Delta}) = p_1$
- $\mathcal{P}_2 = \max(p_2, 1 - e^{-\lambda_P \Delta}) = \max(1 - e^{-\beta_2 \lambda_P \Delta}, 1 - e^{-\lambda_P \Delta}) = p_2$
- $\mathcal{P}_3 = \max(p_1, p_2) = \max(1 - e^{-\beta_1 \lambda_P \Delta}, 1 - e^{-\beta_2 \lambda_P \Delta}) =$
  $\begin{cases} p_1 & \text{if } \pi_1 > \pi_2 \\ p_2 & \text{if } \pi_1 \leq \pi_2 \end{cases}$

In the first two cases, since $\beta_i > 1$ ($i = 1, 2$), then the active trigger is always prevailing over the standard failure process of $P$ (ruled by $\lambda_P$). In the third case, only the trigger having greater influence on the failure of the dependent component, that is the trigger with larger value of parameter $\pi_i$ (and thus with a larger value for $\beta_i$ as well), is considered. Differently from CI interaction, there is no additive effect here.

**Example 3.** A persistent PDEP gate with parameter $\pi_1$ (PDEP1) shares a dependent component $P$ with a one-shot PDEP gate with parameter $\pi_2$ (PDEP2), Figure 4.10 shows the corresponding DBN structure. As in

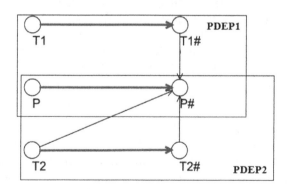

Fig. 4.10   DBN merging a persistent PDEP with a one-shot PDEP.

Example 1, the first CPT in Table 4.8 shows the conditional probabilities of variable $P\#$ from PDEP1, while the CPT of $P\#$ from PDEP2 is reported (split in two subtables) in Table 4.10.

Table 4.10    CPT for node $P\#$ from PDEP2 (parameter $\pi_2$) (Figure 4.10)

| | T2#=false | | | |
|---|---|---|---|---|
| | T2=false | | T2=true | |
| | P=false | P=true | P=false | P=true |
| P#=false | $e^{-\lambda_P \Delta}$ | 0 | / | / |
| P#=true | $1 - e^{-\lambda_P \Delta}$ | 1 | / | / |

| | T2#=true | | | |
|---|---|---|---|---|
| | T2=false | | T2=true | |
| | P=false | P=true | P=false | P=true |
| P#=false | $1 - \pi_2$ | 0 | $e^{-\lambda_P \Delta}$ | 0 |
| P#=true | $\pi_2$ | 1 | $1 - e^{-\lambda_P \Delta}$ | 1 |

The CPT resulting from the combination of the two PDEP modules can then be obtained as in the previous cases, assuming either CI or MSP interaction. As an example, if we want to compute the probability of $P\# = $ true when only $T2\# = $ true (i.e., when the second trigger becomes true before the first one, and the component $P$ is working), then we have the following:

$$P\{P\# = \text{true}|T1 = \text{false}, T2 = \text{false}, T2\# = \text{true}, P = \text{false}\} = \mathcal{P}$$

where

- $\mathcal{P} = 1 - (1 - \pi_2)e^{-\lambda_P \Delta}$ if CI interaction is assumed;
- $\mathcal{P} = \max\{\pi_2, 1 - e^{-\lambda_P \Delta}\}$ if MSP interaction is assumed

Notice that, in the usual case when $\pi_2 \approx 1$ and $0 < \lambda_P \ll 1$, both interaction schemes will produce approximately $\pi_2$ as a result (actually, MSP will exactly produce $\pi_2$).

## 4.3    Modelling Repair

Until now, we have only considered non-repairable components; this means that we have considered the persistence of faults, meaning that no component can return in a working state when failed. However, in several situations it is possible to consider repair processes. A repair process can be characterized by several aspects; for instance, the target of a repair process can be a single component or a subsystem. In the latter, the repair can be completed at the same time for all the components, or the time to repair may change according to the specific component under repair. When we repair a subsystem, we may be interested in repairing all of its components, or a minimal subset of them, allowing the subsystem to be operative again. Moreover, a repair process of a component or subsystem can be activated by the failure of the component or subsystem itself, or can be triggered by another particular event, such as the failure of a higher level subsystem. Other aspects concerning the repair can be the time to detect the failure, the number of components that can be under repair at the same time, the order of repair of the components, etc.

Defining a *repair policy* for a repair process means setting all such aspects concerning the repair. To do this, extensions to the classical DFT model have been proposed; in particular, in [Codetta-Raiteri *et al.* (2004)] a new gate called *Repair Box* (RB) is introduced, with the aim of defining different possible repair policies. An example is shown in Figure 4.11. The attributes of the RB are the repair policy, and possibly a repair rate.

The possible policies that can be defined depend on different aspects. A first kind of policy, called *Component Repair* policy (CR), concerns the repair of a single component and is activated by the failure of the component itself, as soon as this happens. The time to repair of the component is a random variable obeying the negative exponential distribution, according to the repair rate of the component.

If a RB acts according to the CR policy, then the RB has to be connected by means of an arc (a thick arc in Figure 4.11), to the basic event representing the component to be repaired. In this case, a repair rate has to be defined as a parameter of the RB; this rate rules the time to repair of the component. The effect of the repair is turning the component to the working state; this means setting to `false` the Boolean value of the basic event corresponding to the component. In this case, the RB directly determines the Boolean value of such basic event, which in turns influences the values of other events at upper levels in the DFT. The set of the events whose value is influenced in a direct or indirect way by the RB is called *coverage set* (*Cov*) [Codetta-Raiteri *et al.* (2004)] of the RB.

Concerning Figure 4.11, it depicts a portion of the larger DFT model shown in Figure 4.16; this portion represents a subsystem of the *Cardiac Assist System* (CAS) [Boudali *et al.* (2007)] described in Section 4.4. In Figure 4.11, we model the presence of the components $P$, $B$, $CS$, $SS$ composing the subsystem *CPU_unit* (their role is explained in Section 4.4). The failure relations among these components are expressed by the Boolean and dynamic gates: $P$ and $B$ are the input events of a WSP gate; this means that $P$ is the main component and in case of failure, it can be replaced by

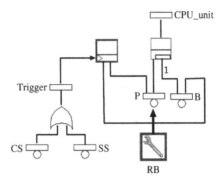

Fig. 4.11   A Repair Box (RB) modeling the repair of a component (*Component Repair* (CR) policy).

the warm spare component $B$. The FDEP gate forces the failure of both $P$ and $B$, if the event named *Trigger* occurs, i.e. if the component $CS$ or $SS$ fails. In Figure 4.11, a RB is present as well; it acts according to the CR policy and is connected to the basic event $P$. This means that as soon as $P$ fails, the corresponding repair process is activated. The repair process involves the component $P$, but it may indirectly influence the state of the subsystem containing $P$. Actually in Figure 4.11, if both $P$ and $B$ are failed, then the subsystem *CPU_unit* is failed. If we repair the main component $P$, then also *CPU_unit* turns back to the working state. Therefore the *Cov* of the RB in Figure 4.11 contains $P$ and *CPU_unit*.

A repair process may also concern a subsystem instead of a single component. In this case, several components are influenced by the repair process, and the repair of a subsystem can take place according to different policies. One possible policy is the *Subsystem Global Repair* policy (SGR), where the repair of the subsystem is activated by the failure of the subsystem itself, as soon as this occurs. Moreover, all the components in the subsystem are under repair and the repair is completed at the same time for all the components; such time is ruled by a negative exponential distribution according to the subsystem repair rate.

When we have to repair a subsystem, another possible situation is the case where the time to repair changes according to the component to be recovered. This holds in the repair policy called *Subsystem Local Repair* policy (SLR); in this case, the repair of a subsystem is triggered by the failure of the subsystem itself, as soon as it occurs. All the subsystem's components are influenced by the repair process, but the repair of each of them may take a time different from the time to repair of another component. In this situation, a specific repair rate has to be set for each component in the subsystem. In this policy, we suppose that the repair of each component is always completed, even though the repair of a subset of the components may be enough to recover the subsystem.

The SLR policy can be extended in such a way that the repair of the subsystem components is interrupted as soon as the subsystem is available again, i.e. when a minimal subset of components necessary to recover the system, is repaired. In this case, some of the subsystem components may not be repaired. Such policy is called SLR-min.

In a DFT model, the repair of a subsystem can be modeled by a RB connected by means of arcs (shows as thick-line arcs in the figures) to several events: one arc connects the event modeling the subsystem failure to the RB; such event activates the RB and is called the *trigger repair event* [Codetta-Raiteri *et al.* (2004)] of the RB. Several arcs connect the RB to the set of basic events modeling the components to be repaired; such set is called *basic coverage set* ($Cov_{BE}$) [Codetta-Raiteri *et al.* (2004)] of the RB. The effect of the RB is setting to false the Boolean value of the elements in $Cov_{BE}$, after the repair process has been completed. Actually the effect of the RB is not limited to its basic coverage set, but it influences indirectly also those events whose Boolean value depends on the basic events in $Cov_{BE}$. The union of the $Cov_{BE}$ and the set of the events indirectly influenced by the RB provides the coverage set of the RB ($Cov$) [Codetta-Raiteri *et al.* (2004)].

An example of subsystem repair is shown in the DFT model in Figure 4.12 dealing with the same subsystem modeled in Figure 4.11, but with a different repair policy: the RB in Figure 4.12 represents the repair of the subsystem *CPU_unit* instead of a single component. This RB is connected to the event *CPU_unit* triggering the activation of the RB. The $Cov_{BE}$ of the RB in Figure 4.12 is composed by the basic events $P$, $B$, $CS$, $SS$; they can be identified by the arcs connecting the RB to each of them. The coverage set of the RB contains the basic events in $Cov_{BE}$, together with the events named *Trigger* and *CPU_unit*. So, when the subsystem *CPU_unit* fails, its components ($P$, $B$, $CS$, $SS$) will be directly influenced by the repair process according to the repair policy associated with the RB. This may influence the Boolean value of the events *Trigger* and *CPU_unit*.

If the RB acts according to the SGR policy, the repair rate of the subsystem has to be set as an attribute of the RB: when *CPU_unit* fails, its repair is activated leading to the working state all its components ($P$, $B$,

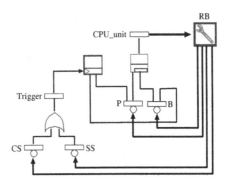

Fig. 4.12   A Repair Box (RB) modeling the repair of a subsystem, in case of *Subsystem Global Repair* (SGR) policy, *Subsystem Local Repair* (SLR) policy, or SLR-min policy.

$CS$, $SS$) and consequently to the working state of *Trigger* and *CPU_unit*; this happens after a random period of time according to the repair rate of the subsystem defined in the RB.

If instead the RB in Figure 4.12 acts according to the SLR or SLR-min policy, then a repair rate has to be set for each component as an attribute of the corresponding basic event. If the policy ruling the RB is SLR, when *CPU_unit* fails, the repair of each component of the subsystem starts and will be surely completed after a random period of time depending on the repair rate of the component. The subsystem *CPU_unit* may turn available before that the repair of all the components is completed. For instance, if $CS$, $SS$, $P$ are working, but $B$ is still under repair, *CPU_unit* is available; the repair of $B$ will be completed even though it is not strictly necessary to the availability of *CPU_unit*.

If the policy ruling the RB in Figure 4.12 is SLR-min, the repair of each component of *CPU_unit* ($P$, $B$, $CS$, $SS$) still starts as soon as the failure of *CPU_unit* occurs, but it is interrupted as soon as *CPU_unit* is available again. For instance, let us suppose that the failure of *CPU_unit* was caused by the failure of both $P$ and $B$ ($CS$ and $SS$ are still working). Then, the repair of $P$ and the repair of $B$ start. If $P$ is repaired first, then *CPU_unit* turns working again, the repair of $B$ is interrupted and $B$ keeps its failed state.

Consider now how the introduction of repair boxes in the example subsystem can be dealt with in the corresponding DBN model. First suppose that component $P$ is reparable following a CR policy, as shown in Figure 4.11, with an exponential repair rate $\mu_P$. The DBN structure cor-

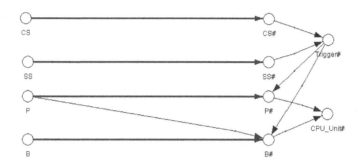

Fig. 4.13   A DBN for the CPU Unit subsystem

Table 4.11   CPT for node $P\#$ of Figure 4.13.

|  | P=false | | P=true | |
|---|---|---|---|---|
|  | Tr#=false | Tr#=true | Tr#=false | Tr#=true |
| P#=false | $e^{-\lambda_P\Delta}$ | 0 | $1-e^{-\mu_P\Delta}$ | 0 |
| P#=true | $1-e^{-\lambda_P\Delta}$ | 1 | $e^{-\mu_P\Delta}$ | 1 |

responding to such a model is the one presented in Figure 4.13. A CR policy can indeed be captured at the CPT level, by substituting the fault persistence assumption (i.e. $Pr\{P\# = \mathtt{true}|P = \mathtt{true}\} = 1$), with the corresponding repair probability. In the example, the CPT entries of node $P\#$ will becomes those shown in Table 4.11, where $\lambda_P$ and $\mu_P$ are the exponential failure and repair rates of $P$ respectively, and $Tr\#$ is a shorthand for node $Trigger\#$.

Notice that, having a repair policy only on the $P$ component does not allow to restore the $CPU\_unit$ subsystem in case of trigger occurrence, since once $P$ is repaired, the semantics of the FDEP gate assumes the immediate fault of $P$ again (i.e. $Pr\{P\# = \mathtt{true}|P = \mathtt{false}, Tr\# = \mathtt{true}\} = 1$).

Let us suppose now to have a repair policy defined at the subsystem level as shown in Figure 4.12. Depending on the particular policy adopted, different DBNs can be generated (see Figure 4.14). The main idea is to directly model the repair policy through suitable nodes representing the stochastic evolution of the different processes composing the particular policy. In case a SGR policy is employed, the resulting net structure is presented in Figure 4.14.a. Repair box nodes $RB$ and $RB\#$ are intended to represent (at the anterior and ulterior layer respectively) the "global" repair process modeled by the RepairBox $RB$ of Figure 4.12. Such nodes are Boolean

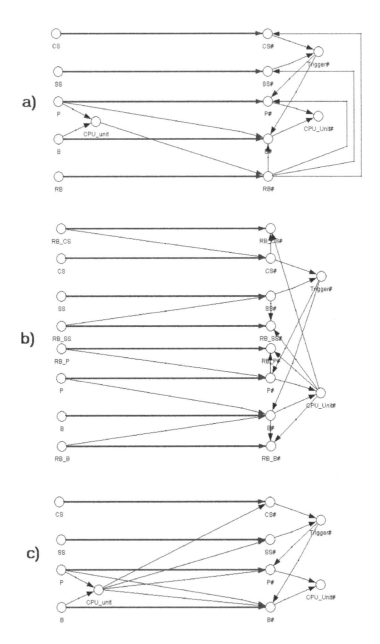

Fig. 4.14  DBN structure for SGR, SLR and SLR-min policies.

Table 4.12 CPT for node $RB\#$ =**true** under SGR policy.

| $Pr(RB\#)$ | $RB$ | $CPU\_unit$ |
|---|---|---|
| 0 | false | false |
| $e^{-\mu_{RB}\Delta}$ | false | true |
| 0 | true | false |
| any value | true | true |

Table 4.13 CPT for node $CS\#$ =**true** under SGR policy.

| $Pr(CS\#)$ | $RB$ | $CS$ |
|---|---|---|
| $1 - e^{-\lambda_{CS}\Delta}$ | false | false |
| 1 | false | true |
| 0 | true | false |
| 0 | true | true |

nodes where, in case of a SGR policy, the value **true** represents a completed repair process. This means that:

**(a)** if the repair is triggered, then the node evolves following the corresponding (global) repair rate $\mu_{RB}$;

**(b)** when the node becomes **true**, the components under repair are immediately set to be functional again (i.e. the corresponding node is reset to **false**).

Table 4.12 shows the CPT for node $RB\# = $ **true**; notice that, once $RB\#$ is set to **true**, all the subsystem components are repaired, so the $CPU\_unit$ is reset to **false**; this means that the conditioning event of the last entry is impossible (thus any value between 0 and 1 can be used there). In order to clarify the influence of the repair box node, Table 4.13 reports the CPT for node $CS\#$ =**true** (similar CPTs are derived for nodes corresponding to the other components under repair).

Another kind of repair policy introduced is the SLR policy, concerning the independent repair of a set of subsystem components, triggered by the failure event of the subsystem. If a SLR policy is adopted in the DFT of Figure 4.12, the resulting DBN is shown in Figure 4.14.b. Repair box nodes are separately introduced for each repairable component; however, in this case it is convenient to have a different interpretation of the truth value of such nodes: a repair box node $RB$ assumes value **true** if and only if the corresponding repair process is activated (and **false** otherwise); this differs from the case of SGR policy, when the **true** value means that the repair

Table 4.14    CPT for basic event node
$CS\#$=**true** under SLR policy.

| $Pr(CS\#)$ | $CS$ | $RB\_CS$ |
|---|---|---|
| $1 - e^{-\lambda_{CS}\Delta}$ | false | false |
| $1 - e^{-\lambda_{CS}\Delta}$ | false | true |
| $1$ | true | false |
| $e^{-\mu_{CS}\Delta}$ | true | true |

Table 4.15    CPT for node $RB\_CS\#$=**true** under SLR
policy.

| $Pr(RB\_CS\#)$ | $RB\_CS$ | $CS$ | $CPU\_unit\#$ |
|---|---|---|---|
| 0 | false | false | false |
| 1 | false | false | true |
| 0 | false | true | false |
| 1 | false | true | true |
| 0 | true | false | false |
| 1 | true | false | true |
| 1 | true | true | false |
| 1 | true | true | true |

is "completed". Given such an interpretation we can set a dependency between each repairable component and its repair process (the inter-slice edges between repair box nodes and basic event nodes in Figure 4.14.b). The CPT of the nodes corresponding to repairable components will then be set by considering both the failure rate (if the repair is not active) and the repair rate (if, on the contrary, the repair is active). As an example, Table 4.14 reports the CPT for node $CS\#$=**true** in Figure 4.14.b, under a SLR policy with repair rate $\mu_{CS}$ and failure rate $\lambda_{CS}$ for component $CS$. Of course, if the component is working, its failure is determined by its failure rate (first two entries of Table 4.14), if the component is faulty and the repair is not active, it will persists as faulty (third entry), while if it is faulty with an active repair process, then it will be probabilistically repaired following the corresponding repair rate (fourth entry).

Repair box nodes are, on the other hand, deterministic nodes whose value is determined by: their previous status, the component under repair and the trigger repair event. As an example, Table 4.15 reports the CPT for node $RB\_CS\#$=**true**. The repair box node is set to **true** when the trigger repair event $(CPU\_unit\#)$ is **true**; it is also kept to value **true** in case the repair is active, the component is under repair and the trigger repair event is reset to **false** by the repair of another subsystem component (seventh entry of the CPT). It is set to **false** otherwise; in particular, the fifth

Table 4.16 CPT for node $CS\#$ under
SLR-min policy.

| $Pr(CS\#)$ | $CS$ | $CPU\_unit$ |
|---|---|---|
| $1 - e^{-\lambda_{CS}\Delta}$ | false | false |
| $1 - e^{-\lambda_{CS}\Delta}$ | false | true |
| $1$ | true | false |
| $e^{-\mu_{CS}\Delta}$ | true | true |

entry of the CPT models the situation when the repair of the component is terminated.

Finally, the DBN in Figure 4.14.c models the net resulting from the compilation of the DFT of Figure 4.12 in case a SLR-min policy is adopted. In this particular case, the net structure can be simplified, without explicitly using repair box nodes, and by capturing (as in the CR policy) the repair processes at the CPT level. The only dependencies that must be taken into account are in fact, those induced by the trigger repair event on the repairable components. Table 4.16 reports the CPT for node $CS\#$=true under a SLR-min policy, with repair rate $\mu_{CS}$ and failure rate $\lambda_{CS}$ for component $CS$. Since the component is assumed to persists as faulty in case the trigger repair event is not active (i.e. third entry of the CPT in Table 4.16), then if the trigger repair event is reset to false by the repair of another component, the repair process of $CS$ is stopped. Of course, the repair process is started (and kept active) as long as both the trigger repair event and the component are faulty (fourth entry). Notice that the $CPU\_unit$ in Table 4.16 plays the same role of the repair box node $RB\_CS$ in Table 4.14.

As an example, Figure 4.15 reports the analysis of the CPU_unit subsystem, under different repair policies, using a repair rate $\mu = 0.1$ for every local and global repair process. The analysis assumes exponential failure rates: $\lambda_P = \lambda_B = 0.5E-3$ for components $P$ and $B$, $\lambda_{CS} = \lambda_{SS} = 0.2E-3$ for components $CS$ and $SS$, and a dormancy factor $\alpha_B = 0.5$ for the spare component $B$. The analysis for the CR policy involves the repair of component $P$ (Figure 4.11). As we can see, this does not increase the subsystem reliability in a significant way, with respect to the unrepairable case; on the contrary, significant improvements can be obtained by using system repair policies like those of Figure 4.12.

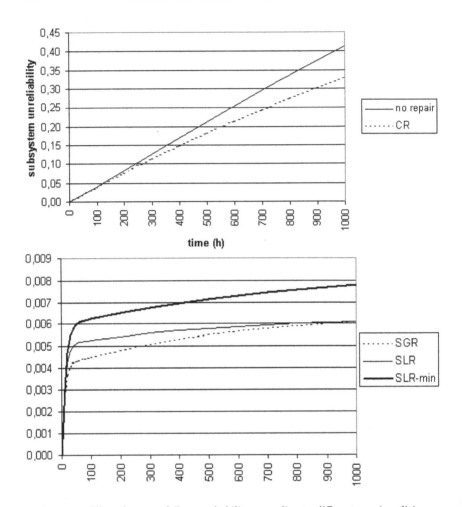

Fig. 4.15   The subsystem failure probability according to different repair policies.

## 4.4   A Case-study Example

In order to show the general capabilities of the DBN-based approach, let us consider a comprehensive case study (part of which has been already introduced in the previous section), inspired by a real-world system illustrated in [Boudali *et al.* (2007)] and representing a *Cardiac Assist System* (CAS). It is composed of three different modules named the CPU, the Motor and the Pump units. The failure of either one of the above modules causes the whole system failure. The CPU unit subsystem has already been introduced in Section 4.3. The CPU unit consists of two distinct CPUs: a primary CPU $P$ (with exponential failure rate $\lambda_P = 0.5E - 3$) and a backup warm spare CPU $B$ (with dormancy factor $\alpha_B = 0.5$ and $\lambda_B = 0.5E - 3$). Both CPUs are functionally dependent on two other components: a cross switch $CS$ (with $\lambda_{CS} = 0.2E - 3$) and a system supervisor $SS$ (with $\lambda_{SS} = 0.2E - 3$); the failure of either the above components will trigger the definite failure of the CPUs (and so the definite failure of the whole CPU unit). However, both CPUs are considered as repairable, under a CR policy, with an exponential repair rate $\mu_{CPU} = 0.1$ (corresponding to a mean time to repair $MTTR = 10$ hours).

The Motor unit consists of two motors: a primary motor $MA$ ($\lambda_{MA} = 1E - 3$) and a cold spare motor $MB$ ($\lambda_{MB} = 1E - 3$). The spare motor turns into operation when the primary fails, because of a motor switching component $MS$ ($\lambda_{MS} = 0.01E - 3$); this means that if $MS$ fails before the necessity of the switch (i.e. before the failure of $MA$), then the spare cannot become operational and the whole Motor unit fails. Finally, the Pump unit is composed by three pumps: two primary pumps $PA$ and $PB$ (with $\lambda_{PA} = \lambda_{PB} = 1E - 3$) running in parallel and a cold spare pump $PS$ ($\lambda_{PS} = 1E - 3$). The Pump unit is operational if at least one of the pump is operational.

Figure 4.16 shows the DFT for the CAS system, drawn by means of RADyBaN[Montani *et al.* (2008)]. The structure of the DBN, in canonical form, corresponding to the DFT in Figure 4.16, is shown in Figure 4.17 and is automatically generated given the DFT model, again by RADyBaN, together with the corresponding CPT quantification.

After the conversion of the DFT in the DBN, we can perform the analysis of the latter by means of the tool. First of all, let us consider the situation when the CPUs are not repairable (i.e. when the two repair boxes of the DFT in Figure 4.16 are not present or, alternatively, when the associated repair rates are 0).

Table 4.17 shows the unreliability of the system versus the mission time varying between 0 and 1000 hours (with time step 100 hours); the table compares the measures computed by RADyBaN (with discretization steps $k = 1$ hour and $k = 0.1$ hours) with those obtained by the software tool GALILEO [Sullivan *et al.* (1999)], exploiting modular decomposition of the DFT and CTMC analysis of dynamic modules.

We can notice that the results are essentially in agreement, with a small difference due to the different nature of the underlying models of the tools

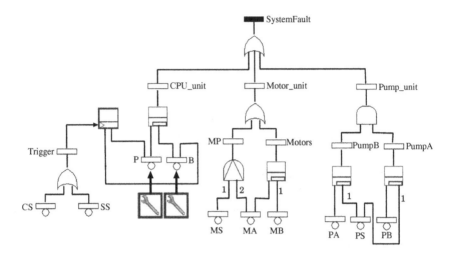

Fig. 4.16    The DFT model of CAS.

Table 4.17    The unreliability results obtained by RADYBAN and by
GALILEO if repair is not available.

| time | RADYBAN (k=1) | RADYBAN (k=0.1) | GALILEO |
|------|---------------|-----------------|---------|
| 100$h$ | 0.045978 | 0.046026 | 0.0460314 |
| 200$h$ | 0.103124 | 0.103214 | 0.103222 |
| 300$h$ | 0.169204 | 0.169327 | 0.169336 |
| 400$h$ | 0.241328 | 0.241474 | 0.241483 |
| 500$h$ | 0.316482 | 0.316645 | 0.316651 |
| 600$h$ | 0.391893 | 0.392060 | 0.392066 |
| 700$h$ | 0.465241 | 0.465408 | 0.465411 |
| 800$h$ | 0.534745 | 0.534908 | 0.534908 |
| 900$h$ | 0.599169 | 0.599322 | 0.59932 |
| 1000$h$ | 0.657763 | 0.657908 | 0.6579 |

(namely a discrete time model for RADYBAN and a continuous time model
for GALILEO). Such a difference becomes typically smaller if a smaller
discretization step is used. To perform the unreliability computation using
RADYBAN, a filtering task has been performed, by querying node System
(i.e. the Top Event) without providing any observation stream; in other
words standard prediction has been performed.

In case we want to analyze the impact of CPU repair, we can compute the system unreliability by taking into consideration the repair boxes
of Figure 4.16 with the given repair rates $\mu_{RB\_P} = \mu_{RB\_B} = 0.1$. Since

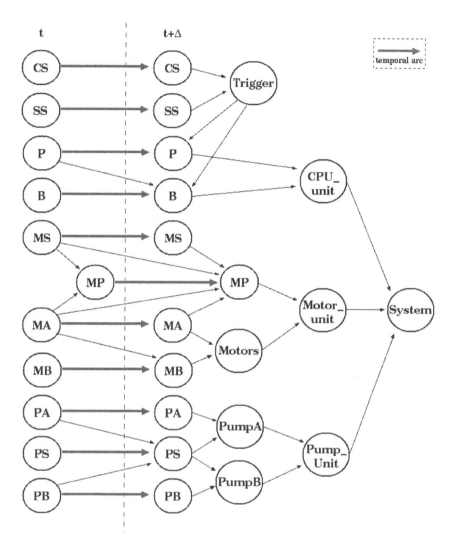

Fig. 4.17    The DBN corresponding to the DFT in Figure 4.16.

GALILEO cannot explicit model the repair of system components, we resort to a comparison with the tool DRPFTPROC having repair modeling features [Codetta-Raiteri (2005)]. The results of this comparison (when a discretization step $k = 1$ has been used for RADYBAN) are shown in Table 4.18 (second and fourth columns).

Table 4.18   The unreliability results obtained by RADYBAN and by DRPFTPROC if different repair possibilities are available.

| time | RADYBAN | | DRPFTPROC | |
|---|---|---|---|---|
| | CPU repair | CPU+Trigger repair | CPU repair | CPU+Trigger repair |
| 100$h$ | 0.044283796102 | 0.011243030429 | 0.0443301588 | 0.0112820476 |
| 200$h$ | 0.096916869283 | 0.027566317469 | 0.0951982881 | 0.0276517226 |
| 300$h$ | 0.156659856439 | 0.054836865515 | 0.155093539 | 0.0549629270 |
| 400$h$ | 0.221550568938 | 0.091957211494 | 0.220137459 | 0.0921166438 |
| 500$h$ | 0.289382189512 | 0.137252241373 | 0.288119742 | 0.137437204 |
| 600$h$ | 0.358023554087 | 0.188778832555 | 0.356905021 | 0.188981668 |
| 700$h$ | 0.425606846809 | 0.244557544589 | 0.424624354 | 0.244770740 |
| 800$h$ | 0.490624904633 | 0.302729338408 | 0.489768367 | 0.302945892 |
| 900$h$ | 0.551952958107 | 0.361649900675 | 0.551211316 | 0.361864672 |
| 1000$h$ | 0.608829379082 | 0.419938921928 | 0.608191065 | 0.420148205 |

Again we can notice the agreement between the different tools (despite the very different analysis techniques). Moreover, we can also notice that, adopting a repair policy only on the CPUs, does not increase very much the reliability of the system with respect to the unrepairable case (see Table 4.17 for a comparison with the second and fourth column of Table 4.18). This is explained by the fact that both CPUs are functionally dependent from the *Trigger* event of the DFT; this means that, once the trigger is active, then a repair on the CPUs has no effect (since the trigger is going to induce a CPU failure again, because of the FDEP gate of Figure 4.11). Of course, if we want to limit the effect of the trigger, then we can impose a repair policy on the trigger components as well. Let us suppose that also components $CS$ and $SS$ are subject to a CR policy with rate $\mu_{CS} = \mu_{SS} = 0.1$: this simply corresponds to add two repair boxes (with such rates) on the DFT of Figure 4.16, connected with $CS$ and $SS$ respectively. The results concerning the unreliability of the system, if also such repair boxes are available, are again reported in Table 4.18 (third and fifth columns). Not surprisingly, the unreliability of the system is reduced (of about 36% on average on the time slices considered), with respect to the previous case.

Notice that using four repair boxes with CR policy on the components of the *CPU_unit* subsystem is not equivalent to have a single RB with SLR policy on the *CPU_unit* event and with $Cov_{BE} = \{P, B, CS, SS\}$ (see Figure 4.12). In the latter, no repair process is started until the whole *CPU_unit* subsystem is failed, while in the example presented here the

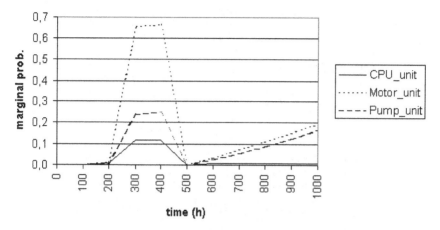

Fig. 4.18   The marginal probabilities in case of filtering. Each curve indicates the failure probability of each subsystem.

local repair processes are started as soon as the corresponding component fails[6].

Finally, we already know that DBNs offer additional analysis capabilities with respect to standard (D)FT-based tool like GALILEO and DRPFT-PROC. In particular, the possibility of exploiting explicit observations on monitorable parameters, as well as the possibility of performing smoothing inference; this allows one to rebuild the past history of the system, given a stream of observations. Consider a situation in which the CAS system (with CPU and Trigger repair available) was observed operational at time (units are hours) $t = 100$, failed at time $t = 300$ and then operational again at time $t = 500$. First of all, this stream of observations is consistent with the model, since a repair on the CPU unit can actually repair the whole system; notice that, if this stream of observation would be provided to the model without repair, an exception would be raised by the DBN inference algorithms, pointing out an inconsistency with respect to the model provided. Let $\sigma$ be the observation stream about the system behavior introduced above; a first kind of analysis we can perform consists in querying the three modules potential causes of the fault (CPU, Motor and Pump units), asking for their posterior probabilities given $\sigma$.

The results concerning the marginal probability of each subsystem over

---

[6]If an SLR policy was adopted, the upper part of the DBN in Figure 4.17 (corresponding to the subnet structure of Figure 4.13) would be substituted with the subnet shown in Figure 4.14.b.

Table 4.19    The joint probabilities in case of filtering. The
label of each column indicates the state (0 means working,
1 means failed) of the subsystems *CPU_unit*, *Motor_unit*,
*Pump_unit* respectively. Bold entries correspond to most probable configurations.

| time | 0, 0, 0 | 0, 0, 1 | 0, 1, 0 | 0, 1, 1 |
|------|---------|---------|---------|---------|
| 100 $h$ | **1.000000** | 0.000000 | 0.000000 | 0.000000 |
| 200 $h$ | **0.977576** | 0.003501 | 0.012862 | 0.000046 |
| 300 $h$ | 0.000000 | 0.228510 | **0.643095** | 0.007708 |
| 400 $h$ | 0.110162 | 0.224175 | **0.637081** | 0.022560 |
| 500 $h$ | **1.000000** | 0.000000 | 0.000000 | 0.000000 |
| 600 $h$ | **0.934621** | 0.024475 | 0.033999 | 0.000890 |
| 700 $h$ | **0.870357** | 0.051434 | 0.068166 | 0.004028 |
| 800 $h$ | **0.803337** | 0.079515 | 0.101124 | 0.010009 |
| 900 $h$ | **0.735453** | 0.107478 | 0.131794 | 0.019260 |
| 1000 $h$ | **0.668297** | 0.134277 | 0.159387 | 0.032024 |

| time | 1, 0, 0 | 1, 0, 1 | 1, 1, 0 | 1, 1, 1 |
|------|---------|---------|---------|---------|
| 100 $h$ | 0.000000 | 0.000000 | 0.000000 | 0.000000 |
| 200 $h$ | 0.005916 | 0.000021 | 0.000078 | 0.000000 |
| 300 $h$ | 0.115366 | 0.001383 | 0.003891 | 0.000047 |
| 400 $h$ | 0.000673 | 0.001357 | 0.003855 | 0.000137 |
| 500 $h$ | 0.000000 | 0.000000 | 0.000000 | 0.000000 |
| 600 $h$ | 0.005655 | 0.000148 | 0.000206 | 0.000006 |
| 700 $h$ | 0.005267 | 0.000311 | 0.000413 | 0.000024 |
| 800 $h$ | 0.004861 | 0.000481 | 0.000612 | 0.000061 |
| 900 $h$ | 0.004450 | 0.000650 | 0.000798 | 0.000117 |
| 1000 $h$ | 0.004044 | 0.000813 | 0.000964 | 0.000194 |

time, from a filtering procedure are reported in Figure 4.18; the joint probability of each possible configuration of the queried subsystems is reported
on Table 4.19. We can notice that, when the system is observed to be operational, all the three modules must be operational, while when the system
is observed to be faulty ($t = 300$), then there is a high probability that such
fault is due to the Motor unit. In particular, by looking at the joint probability entries, the most probable diagnosis is that the Motor unit is the
only module to be faulty. The CPU unit module is the less probable cause
of the fault, since it is repairable. However, as the system is observed to be
operational again at $t = 500$, then the most probable diagnosis computed at
time $t = 300$ is definitely wrong, since it should be clear that the observed
system behavior can be explained only by a failure of the CPU unit in the
interval $(100, 300]$, with a consequent repair of such a unit (which is the
only repairable unit) in the interval $(300, 500]$. This cannot be captured by
the filtering procedure (which is just a system monitoring over time); on
the other hand, the explanation can be confirmed by performing the same

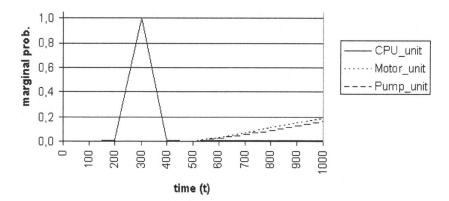

Fig. 4.19   The marginal probabilities in case of smoothing. Each curve indicates the failure probability of each subsystem.

posterior probability computation above, but under a smoothing inference procedure.

The results from a smoothing inference are reported in Figure 4.19 (marginal probabilities of the subsystems over time) and in Table 4.20 (joint probabilities of the configuration of the subsystems).

Differently from filtering inference, the above results show that before time $t = 500$ Motor and Pump units cannot be faulty, since at $t = 500$ the system must be operational; moreover, by considering that the system behavior has changed from faulty to operational in the interval $[300, 500]$, then it is certain that in such interval the CPU unit has been repaired. In particular, since repair is significantly faster than failure (because of the given repair and failure rates), smoothing can suggest that such a repair has been probably performed before $t = 400$ (since the probability of the CPU unit being operational at time $t = 400$ is close to 1). From time $t = 500$, no observation is available, so both filtering and smoothing will produce standard prediction results.

In the examples reported in this section exact algorithms (based on the calculation of the junction tree) were adopted, both for filtering and for smoothing procedures.

Table 4.20 The joint probabilities in case of smoothing. The label of each column indicates the state (0 means working, 1 means failed) of the subsystems *CPU_unit*, *Motor_unit*, *Pump_unit* respectively. Bold entries correspond to most probable configurations.

| time | 0, 0, 0 | 0, 0, 1 | 0, 1, 0 | 0, 1, 1 |
|---|---|---|---|---|
| 100 *h* | **1.000000** | 0.000000 | 0.000000 | 0.000000 |
| 200 *h* | **0.993925** | 0.000000 | 0.000000 | 0.000000 |
| 300 *h* | 0.000000 | 0.000000 | 0.000000 | 0.000000 |
| 400 *h* | **0.993925** | 0.000000 | 0.000000 | 0.000000 |
| 500 *h* | **1.000000** | 0.000000 | 0.000000 | 0.000000 |
| 600 *h* | **0.934620** | 0.024475 | 0.034000 | 0.000890 |
| 700 *h* | **0.870357** | 0.051434 | 0.068166 | 0.004028 |
| 800 *h* | **0.803337** | 0.079515 | 0.101124 | 0.010009 |
| 900 *h* | **0.735453** | 0.107478 | 0.131794 | 0.019260 |
| 1000 *h* | **0.668297** | 0.134277 | 0.159387 | 0.032024 |

| time | 1, 0, 0 | 1, 0, 1 | 1, 1, 0 | 1, 1, 1 |
|---|---|---|---|---|
| 100 *h* | 0.000000 | 0.000000 | 0.000000 | 0.000000 |
| 200 *h* | 0.006075 | 0.000000 | 0.000000 | 0.000000 |
| 300 *h* | **1.000000** | 0.000000 | 0.000000 | 0.000000 |
| 400 *h* | 0.006075 | 0.000000 | 0.000000 | 0.000000 |
| 500 *h* | 0.000000 | 0.000000 | 0.000000 | 0.000000 |
| 600 *h* | 0.005655 | 0.000148 | 0.000206 | 0.000006 |
| 700 *h* | 0.005267 | 0.000311 | 0.000413 | 0.000024 |
| 800 *h* | 0.004861 | 0.000481 | 0.000612 | 0.000061 |
| 900 *h* | 0.004450 | 0.000650 | 0.000798 | 0.000117 |
| 1000 *h* | 0.004044 | 0.000813 | 0.000964 | 0.000194 |

# Chapter 5

# Decision Theoretic Dependability

In the previous chapters, we have seen that Probabilistic Graphical Models like Bayesian Networks or Dynamic Bayesian Networks are very useful to study dependability properties of systems, such as component and system reliability, fault prediction and fault diagnosis. Concerning the maintainability aspect, while it is possible to introduce the concept of repair policy (see Chapter 4), this is limited to the possibility of modeling a stochastic repair process, with the assumption that, once a given component fails, then, with some stochastic delay, it will be eventually repaired or replaced with a working component. This is in line with the notion of maintainability as introduced in Chapter 1; however, this framework does not address the issue of preventive maintenance, and it does not deal with the problem of selecting the "best" maintenance actions or procedures.

A failure countermeasure support system is a tool aimed at efficiently determining the countermeasures (component repair, activation of spares, etc.) to be executed for remedying a failure occurring on a specific artifact, based upon information about the failure itself. Attempts to deal with these aspects have been proposed in frameworks as the Defect, Detection and Prevention (DDP) approach [Feather (2004)] or in other integrated methodologies of general Probabilistic Risk Analysis (PRA) [Bedford and Cooke (2001)]. However, there is no clear "clean" modeling strategy addressing the main issues of failure countermeasure selection.

The basic requirement to the selection of the right recovery procedure is the capability of modeling and exploiting the likelihood of a fault, the severity or impact of a fault, and the cost of the recovery itself. PGMs like Decision Networks (DN) appears then as very plausible candidates for the above tasks. As we have seen in Chapter 2, a DN augments a BN with decision (action) nodes, and it allows the definition of a utility function through which a formal (decision-theoretic) notion of "best" decision can be captured.

## 5.1   Decision Networks for Repairable Systems

In modeling a component-based repairable system with a DN we can adopt the following approach:

(1) system components and subsystem specifications are represented by multi-state random variables (each state being a behavioral mode of the component/subsystem);

(2) failure countermeasures and repair actions are modeled through decision variables;

(3) probabilistic dependencies between modeled entities, as well as the prior probability of occurrence of specific faults, are captured through local conditional probability tables in the network;

(4) costs (i.e. negative utilities) of countermeasures and repair actions are represented in value nodes depending on (i.e. having as parent nodes) the set of countermeasures under consideration; the same approach (creation of a suitable value node) can be used to quantify the impact (in terms of cost/utility) of specific system conditions, represented by the occurrence of a set of system variables (that are then set as parents of the value node which is introduced).

Concerning the analysis issues, standard inference algorithms on DNs can be exploited to perform a set of interesting tasks. It is worth remembering that in any PGM, inference algorithms provide the posterior probability of any set of variables of interest, given the observed evidence, i.e., a (possibly empty) set of instantiated variables in the network. Moreover, as explained in Chapter 2, a major measure of interest in a DN is the Expected Utility (EU) of a strategy, and a major goal is to compute the strategy providing the Maximum Expected Utility (MEU). Alternatively, we can talk about Expected Cost (EC) or Minimum Expected Cost (MEC) by simply considering costs as negative utilities. In a maintainability context dealing with failure countermeasures, it is more convenient to use the latter terminology.

Given a specific analysis time $t$ and a (possibly empty) evidence at $t$, in addition to the tasks we have already discussed with BN models, a DN can be used to solve the following interesting problems:

(1) computation of the expected cost of a strategy at time $t$;

(2) selection of the best (in terms of MEU/MEC) countermeasures/repairs to be activated at time $t$;

(3) computation of the Return on Investment (ROI) index a strategy at time $t$;

(4) selection of the best (in terms of ROI) countermeasures/repairs to be activated at time $t$;

In economic systems, the ROI index is a performance measure used to evaluate the efficiency of an investment or to compare the efficiency of a number of different investments. It represents the percentage of investment gain with respect to the investment cost. It is defined by comparing a status-quo situation and a target one, differing from the status quo in terms of a set of investments [Kim *et al.* (2012)]. In our setting, the investment is represented by a set of countermeasures or repairs and the ROI index can be defined as:

$$ROI = \frac{\Delta U - C}{C}$$

where $\Delta U$ is the difference in utility between the target and the status-quo situation, while C is the cost of the countermeasures or repairs applied. We will detail on these aspects in the following.

In the next section, we will exploit a simple case study as a guiding example to illustrate how specific failure conditions can be managed or mitigated by activating suitable countermeasures and repair actions.

## 5.2 A Repairable System

We now consider a simple repairable hydraulic/thermal system. The system (see Figure 5.1) consists of a tank containing some liquid which is renewed by means of a pump $P1$ and a valve $V1$, performing the in-flow and the out-flow tasks respectively. $P1$ can be in three different states: ok, stuck-on, stuck-off; the same holds for $V1$ that can be ok, stuck-open or stuck-closed. If ok, the component can be switched on/open or off/closed; if stuck-on/stuck-open, the component cannot be switched off/closed; if stuck-off/stuck-closed, the component cannot be switched on/open. The stuck condition of $P1$ may lead to an anomalous in-flow (low or high). The stuck condition of $V1$ may lead to an anomalous out-flow (low or high). The liquid level is ok, low or high, according to the current in-flow and out-flow. Another cause of low level may be the damage of the tank $T$, with the possible loss of liquid (tank is in state leaking). A heat source

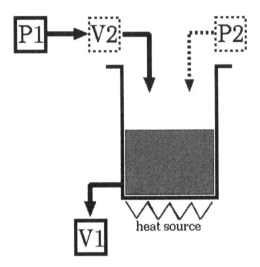

Fig. 5.1    A simple repairable system.

warms the liquid inside $T$. If the heat source is faulty, the temperature may become anomalous. A specific sensor detects the liquid temperature (ok or anomalous). Also the liquid level is monitored by a sensor; both sensors (level and temperature) are not 100% accurate and may not detect the actual level/temperature. Several actions (or decisions) can be performed in order to repair the components or recover the system:

- a secondary pump $P2$ can be activated with the goal of replacing the primary one in case of stuck-off failure; we assume $P2$ working correctly if activated, however the activation process can fail with a given probability $p_1$ (we assume $p_1 = 0.1$ in the following);
- a secondary valve $V2$ can be used to mitigate the action of $P1$ in case of stuck-on failure; also in this case, we assume $V2$ working correctly if activated, while on-demand activation of $V2$ can fail with probability $p_2$ (we also set $p_2 = 0.1$). So, the in-flow can be ok, high or low, according to the state of the primary pump and the decisions about the use/activation of $P2$, and $V2$;
- $T$ can undergo repair in case of damage (leaking);
- the heat source can be repaired if faulty;
- both the above repair actions have a small probability of failure; in the following we assume such probability to be the same for both actions (in particular $p_3 = 0.001$);

- each of these countermeasures/repairs has a cost (i.e. negative utility) if performed; we assume $CP = 100$ (cost of activating P2), $CV = 50$ (cost of activating V2), $CRH = 80$ (cost of repairing the heat source) and $CRT = 70$ (cost of repairing the leaking tank).

The overall state of the system is given by the combinations of the liquid level (ok, high, low) and temperature (normal, anomalous). We consider the system in a faulty state (the corresponding of the Top Event in a FT) if either the temperature is anomalous or if the liquid level is not ok (i.e., either low or high).

### 5.2.1 The Decision Network model

The decision network modeling the system previously introduced is shown in Figure 5.2; the state of P1 (ok, stuck-on, stuck-off) is represented

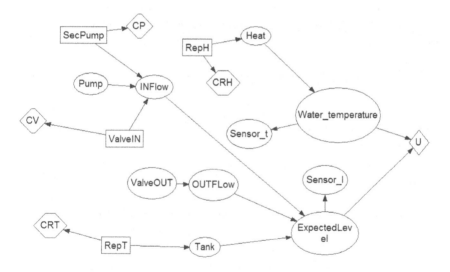

Fig. 5.2   Decision Network for the hydraulic/thermal system.

by the ternary node *Pump*. The ternary node *INFlow* models the state of the in-flow (ok, high, low). This node is influenced by *Pump* and by two decision nodes: *SecPump* represents the request for activation (states yes or no) of P2, while *ValveIN* represents the request for activation (states yes or no) of V2. The ternary node *ValveOUT* represents the state (ok, stuck-open, stuck-closed) of V1. The ternary node *OUTflow* models

Table 5.1   Utility function for the decision network of the hydraulic/thermal system.

| WaterTemperature | Ok | | | Anomalous | | |
|---|---|---|---|---|---|---|
| ExpectedLevel | Ok | High | Low | Ok | High | Low |
| Value | 0 | -2000 | -2500 | -5000 | -6000 | -6500 |

the state of the out-flow (ok, high, low), and is influenced by $ValveOUT$. The binary node $Tank$ represents the state (ok or leaking) of T. Together with $INFlow$ and $OUTFlow$, $Tank$ influences the node $ExpectedLevel$ which represents the level in T (ok, high orlow). The node $Sensor\_l$ models the detection of the level by the corresponding sensor. Therefore $Sensor\_l$ depends on $ExpectedLevel$. The node $RepT$ models the decision to repair (or not) the tank. Therefore such node influences $Tank$. The binary node $Heat$ represents the state of the heat source (ok or faulty). This node influences the binary node $Water\_temperature$ modeling the temperature of the liquid (normal or anomalous). The node $Sensor\_t$ models the detection of the temperature by the sensor. Therefore $Sensor\_t$ depends on $Temperature$. The node $RepH$ models the decision to repair (or not) the heat source. Therefore such node influences $Heat$. In the model, each of the decision nodes $(SecPump, ValveIN, RepT, RepH)$ influences a value node $(CP, CV, CRT, CRH$ respectively) representing the cost (negative utility) of the corresponding action if performed.

Finally, the value node $U$ provides the utility function for the system state. The utility is given by the combinations of liquid level and temperature. Therefore $U$ is influenced by $ControlledLevel$ and $Water\_Temperature$. Table 5.1 provides the values stored in $U$. Also in this case we assume a cost-based modeling, by considering a null cost for the nominal system behavior, and a specific cost impact value for the different faulty situations. We can notice that, because utility is modeled as a cost, utility values in Table 5.1 are all non-positive.

As any PGM, the DN can easily account for multi-state components, as well as for several sources of uncertainty in the system behavior. For example, given that each sensor has an accuracy of 85%, the CPT in Table 5.2 can be adopted for the level sensor. In particular, the CPT shows that, with probability 0.85 the sensor outputs the correct value, while the remaining probability mass is distributed on the wrong values. Table 5.3 shows the CPT fragment of node $InFlow$ modeling the uncertainty in the activation of V2 when P1 is stuck-on. The next fragment of the same CPT (Table 5.4) models the uncertainty in the success of activation (0.9 probability) of P2 when P1 is stuck-off.

Table 5.2   CPT for the level sensor.

| Sensor_l | ExpectedLevel | | |
|---|---|---|---|
|  | Ok | High | Low |
| Ok | 0.85 | 0.075 | 0.075 |
| High | 0.075 | 0.85 | 0.075 |
| Low | 0.075 | 0.075 | 0.85 |

Table 5.3   CPT for node InFlow (P1 stuck-on)

| | Pump | stuck-on | | | |
|---|---|---|---|---|---|
| | SecPump | Yes | | No | |
| | ValveIn | Yes | No | Yes | No |
| InFlow | Ok | 0.9 | 0 | 0.9 | 0 |
| | High | 0.1 | 1 | 0.1 | 1 |
| | Low | 0 | 0 | 0 | 0 |

Table 5.4   CPT for node InFlow (P1 stuck-off)

| | Pump | stuck-off | | | |
|---|---|---|---|---|---|
| | SecPump | Yes | | No | |
| | ValveIn | Yes | No | Yes | No |
| InFlow | Ok | 0.9 | 0.9 | 0 | 0 |
| | High | 0 | 0 | 0 | 0 |
| | Low | 0.1 | 0.1 | 1 | 1 |

By exploiting DN inference, we can then quantitatively analyze the system of interest from different points of view. In the following we will refer to results obtained by a clustering inference algorithm using the GENIE/SMILE tool [Druzdzel (1999); Druzdel (2005)].

### 5.2.2   *System unreliability and expected cost*

Unreliability is obtained by asking for the probability of system failure conditions, given a specific analysis time, a specific repair strategy and an empty evidence. Expected cost of a given policy is then computed by adding the cost obtained at each value node of the DN after inference. Figure 5.3 and Figure 5.4 report the system unreliability and the expected costs at different times for different repair strategies (the key for the strategies is the following: All counterm=all the countermeasures; Repair=only direct repair (tank and heat source);SecondP&V=only secondary pump and valve; No counterm=no countermeasure).

We can notice that, as expected, the system unreliability is best miti-

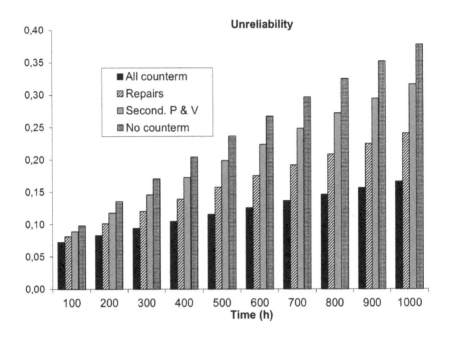

Fig. 5.3   System unreliability with respect to countermeasures or repairs.

gated by the strategy activating all the countermeasures, while the worst unreliability occurs when no countermeasure is activated; moreover, direct repair (of both tank and heat source) best mitigates unreliability than the use of spare pump and valve. However, by looking at the expected cost of the strategies, we can conclude that, until the system life does not reach 800 $h$, the best strategy (in terms of MEU/MEC) is to activate only the tank and heat source repair (except for $t = 100$ $h$ where the best choice is to do nothing). In addition, this analysis also shows that there is no clear advantage in using secondary pump and valve with respect to the do nothing strategy.

### 5.2.3   *Importance measures of components under given strategies*

As we have discussed in Section 1.2.1 and in Section 3.7, different importance indices are introduced in dependability analysis, in order to assess the role of each component in the whole system reliability. In the the current context, importance measures of components are defined with the aim

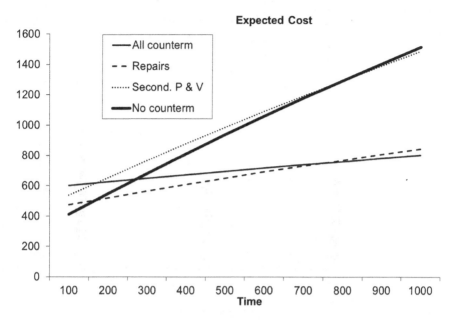

Fig. 5.4  Expected cost of strategies.

of prioritizing countermeasures or repair mechanisms to counteract fault events.

To give an idea of the role of such indices when failure countermeasures are taken into account, let us concentrate here on FVI (similar considerations apply for all other importance indices, since they can be all characterized in terms of posterior probability computation). FVI gives the likelihood of the component being down given that the system is down, thus a standard inference task in a DN. Let $C$ being a component and $m$ a faulty state of $C$; borrowing a notation from FTA, let also $TE$ (Top Event) being the system failure condition. We define $FVI(C = m) = Pr(C = m|TE)$ as the importance of fault $m$ of component $C$. When the system is subject to repair strategies, such a measure is contextually dependent on the current applied strategy. In terms of DN, this corresponds to computing the probability of node $C$ being in state $m$, given $TE$ and the current strategy as evidence. Figure 5.5 reports the FVI of the various faulty components under different strategies, computed at time $t = 100\ h$. We can notice the large importance of the heat source when either no countermeasure is applied or when only secondary pump and valve are considered; on the other

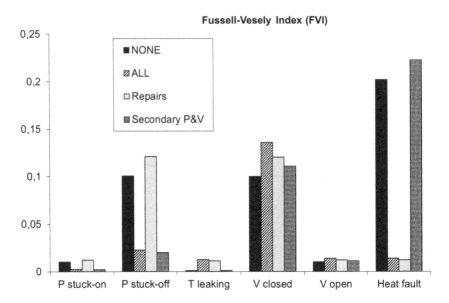

Fig. 5.5   The Fussell-Vesely index according to the applied countermeasures or repairs.

Table 5.5   Repair Strategies.

| Case ID | SecPump, ValveIN, RepT, RepH | Sensor_l | Sensor_t |
|---------|------------------------------|----------|----------|
| p1 | (No, No, No, No) | Ok | Ok |
| p2 | (No, No, No, Yes) | Ok | Anom |
| p3 | (Yes, No, No, No) | Low | Ok |
| p4 | (No, No, No, No) | High | Ok |
| p5 | (No, No, No, Yes) | High | Anom |
| p6 | (Yes, No, No, Yes) | Low | Anom |

hand, stuck-off and closed mode (of pump and valve respectively) becomes more important when direct repair is considered.

### 5.2.4   *Computation of the best repair strategy*

This is the most peculiar analysis that can be provided by the DN framework. Figure 5.6 reports the different expected costs, at different times, of the best (in terms of MEU/MEC) repair strategy conditioned on different sensor information. Table 5.5 reports the activation state of repairs in each strategy and the corresponding sensor evidence. For example, when the sensor level shows a low liquid level and the temperature appears to be anomalous, the best choice is to ask for the activation of the secondary

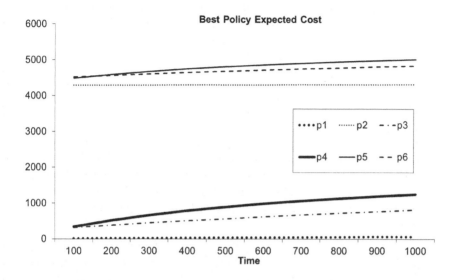

Fig. 5.6  The best strategy expected cost.

pump and to repair the heat source (*p*6 in Tab 5.5). Cases *p*1 and *p*4, as well as *p*2 and *p*5, determine the same strategy, but they have different costs, because conditioned on different evidence. From Figure 5.5 we can see that, as expected, the cost of each strategy in each case is increasing with the time at which the analysis is performed. In more details, we notice that activating the repair of the heat source in the *p*2 case (only the temperature reported as anomalous), has a cost which is not significantly increasing with time, while the same strategy increases the cost much more with time in the *p*5 case (where also a high liquid level is detected). Similar considerations hold for cases *p*1 (both sensors reporting Ok status) and *p*4 (level sensor reporting a high liquid level).

Finally, as introduced in Section 5.1, an interesting aspect related to the selection of the best repair strategy concerns the Return on Investment or ROI index. We remember here that the index is computed as

$$ROI = \frac{\Delta U - C}{C}$$

where $\Delta U$ is the difference in utility between the target and the status-quo situations to be compared (differing in the set of applied failure counter-measures), while $C$ is the cost of the repairs applied from the status-quo to the target case.

Considering a status-quo situation in which no countermeasure is ap-

Table 5.6   ROI of dif-
ferent strategies.

| Case ID | ROI |
|---------|-----|
| p2 | 1.38 |
| p3 | 0.97 |
| p5 | 1.30 |
| p6 | 0.75 |

plied, Table 5.6 reports the ROI for situations $p2, p3, p5$ and $p6$ (from Table 5.5) at time $t = 100$ $h$. For instance, we can conclude that, when only the temperature sensor reports an anomalous situation, we get a ROI of 138% if we invest in repairing the heat source ($p2$) (i.e. for each unit of investment we gain 1.38 units). Similarly we can interpret the other scenarios.

It is worth noting that optimizing the set of failure countermeasures with respect to ROI (i.e., setting the ROI as the objective function to be maximized) is in general different that optimizing them with respect to the total expected cost. Since they are different measures, modeling different facets of the potential repair strategies, then it is possible that the best strategy with respect to ROI (i.e., the one maximizing the ROI) is not the best strategy with respect to the expected cost (i.e., the one minimizing the EC).

This can be shown by computing the best set of repairs, in terms of ROI, directly on the decision network. To perform his task we can add to the DN some new value nodes (see Figure 5.7):

- a value node called *Prev* representing the value of the expected cost of the previous (status-quo) situation with respect to with ROI is computed; no parent nodes are set for *Prev* and its value is an input to the optimization problem;
- a value node called *ROI* representing the return on investment index, storing its definition in terms of change in costs of repair actions and utility of system status; parent of the *ROI* node are then the value nodes representing the costs of the actions, the node $U$ representing the utility of the system status, and the node *Prev* with respect to which we have to compute the ROI index.

Selecting the best strategy from the DN, in terms of node *ROI*, allows one to obtain the set of repair actions on which to invest, in order to have the maximum return on investment (with respect to the status-quo situation).

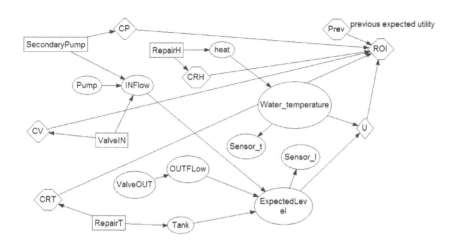

Fig. 5.7  Decision Network for the hydraulic/thermal system for ROI optimization.

To show that this does not necessarily correspond to select the MEU/MEC strategy, consider the following example. Suppose we only have observations about the tank level, and that the corresponding sensor reports a low liquid level; we do not have any information about the temperature, so the evidence in this case is just $Sensor\_l$ =low. If we perform inference at time $t = 100\ h$, then we obtain that the MEU/MEC strategy is the following:

$$s_1 : SecPump = Yes, ValveIN = No, RepairT = No, RepairH = Yes$$

corresponding to the activation of the secondary pump and of the repair procedures for the heat source (the absence of information about the actual temperature, leads to activating a potential repair of the heat source). The expected cost of this strategy results to be $EC1 = 643.06$

On the other hand, if we perform inference, on the DN of Figure 5.7, by considering the same evidence and a status-quo situation of no repair action activated (call it strategy $s_3$), then we obtain that the best strategy in terms of ROI is

$$s_2 : SecPump = Yes, ValveIN = No, RepairT = No, RepairH = No$$

Differently from the previous case, the best return on investment is obtained by the activation of the secondary pump alone, with no action performed for the heat source. The ROI index for changing from $s_3$ to $s_2$ strategy (directly computed through DN inference) results to be 92%. In details, since the EC of the no repair strategy $s_3$, under the given evidence is $EC3 = 742.81$, the

EC of the best ROI strategy $s_2$ is $EC2 = 650.79$ and the cost of activating
the secondary pump is $CP = 100$ then we obtain

$$ROI_{s_3 \to s_2} = \frac{EC3 - EC2}{CP} = \frac{742.81 - 650.79}{100} = 0.92$$

Notice that $EC2$ is already discounted from the cost $CP$; in other terms
$EC2 = U - CP$ where $U$ is the expected system utility under strategy $s_2$.
If we compare the ROI of the best strategy $s_1$ in terms of MEU/MEC, we
get the following (the cost of repairing the heat source is $CH = 80$):

$$ROI_{s_3 \to s_1} = \frac{EC3 - EC1}{CP + CH} = \frac{742.81 - 643.06}{180} = 0.55$$

We can see that, in terms of ROI, the best strategy with respect to
MEU/MEC suffered a loss of 37%.

Chapter 6

# The RADyBaN Tool: Supporting Dependability Engineers to Exploit Probabilistic Graphical Models

In this chapter, we describe a software tool which allows one to analyze a DFT relying on its conversion into a DBN. The tool is called RADy-BaN [Portinale *et al.* (2007, 2010); Montani *et al.* (2008)] which means **R**eliability **A**nalysis with **Dy**namic **Ba**yesian **N**etworks; it implements the modular algorithm described in Chapter 4 for automatically translating a DFT into the corresponding DBN; it then exploits standard algorithms for the inference on DBN, in order to compute reliability measures, and in particular the 1.5JT and BK inference algorithms (see Chapter 2).

The tool is provided with a user-friendly graphical interface, through which the user can either design the DFT and then ask for the translation, or to define the DBN directly. In fact, the first modality is the one intended to be used by people having confidence with standard reliability design tools; the aim is to provide reliability engineers with a familiar interface, by allowing them to model the system to be analyzed with a standard formalism (like a FT or a DFT); however, when the computation of specific reliability measures is requested, the compilation into the DBN is performed and inference algorithms are exploited, in order to compute the desired parameters. This is performed in a totally transparent way to the user, who could in principle be completely unaware of the underlying DBN. As we have shown in the previous chapter, the use of a PGM allows the user to be able to compute measures that are not directly computable from DFTs, but that are naturally obtainable from inference algorithms on the PGM, by means of posterior probability computations.

However, since the modeling capabilities of a DFT are rather limited, some of the extensions to DFTs described in Chapter 4, concerning probabilistic dependencies or repair policies, have been implemented in RADy-BaN; moreover, as we have already mentioned, the user can directly edit a

DBN model, either if the model has been obtained through DFT to DBN conversion or if it has been obtained from scratch. In this way, any modeling issue that cannot be directly addressed by the (extended) DFT formalism, can be explicitly dealt with a the DBN level.

## 6.1   Tool Architecture

RADYBAN has been implemented by exploiting a graphical software tool called *Draw-Net* [Codetta-Raiteri *et al.* (2006)]. *Draw-Net* provides a framework for the definition of graph-based formalisms. Each formalism is defined by means of some XML files, where the information about the types of nodes, arcs, and about the allowed connections between nodes and arcs is introduced. Graphical information (for example concerning shape and position of the nodes, color of the arcs, etc.) is also stored in the formalism definition. A Graphical User Interface (GUI) allows then the user to draw a model following the adopted formalism. The model is itself saved as an XML file and can then be provided in input to a user-defined *Solver* for any kind of analysis one wish to implement on that model.

Given the above picture, RADYBAN is then defined through the following *Draw-Net* components:

- a GUI for the editing of a DFT model (`DFTEditor`); this allows the definition of a DFT and the editing of each DFT construct;
- a GUI for the editing of a DBN model (`DBNEditor`); this allows the definition and the editing of a DBN that can be either created from scratch or loaded after being created from the DFT to DBN compilation process;
- a Solver taking as input the XML description of a DFT and producing as output an XML description of the corresponding DBN (`DFT2DBN`); this module implements the compilation process from a DFT to a DBN;
- a Solver taking as input the XML description of a DBN and implementing inference on it (`DBN analyzer`).

Figure 6.1 depicts the tool's architecture as described below. The following sections describe the functionalities of each module.

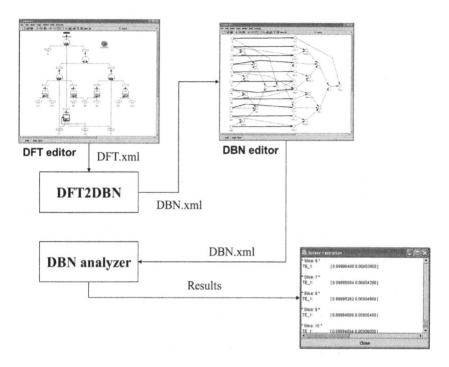

Fig. 6.1   The RADyBaN tool architecture.

## 6.2   Editing a DFT

As we have already noticed, modelling the failure modes of a system as a DBN might be complicated for a reliability engineer with experience on standard dependability formalisms, but no experience with PGMs. In such a situation, drawing the DFT model and generating automatically the corresponding DBN, is definitely more practical. In this way, the DFT becomes a high level formalism, allowing the user to express in a straightforward way the relations between the components in the failure mode of the system, whose modelling in terms of DBN primitives would be less comfortable.

The module DFTEditor allows the modeler to resort to standard DFT constructs (i.e. Boolean and dynamic gates), as well as to specify additional properties for the analysis. In fact, the user may indicate which events will be queried and which events have been observed (true or false) at a given time point, assuming discrete time. The user can also specify, on the DFT, the *analysis time step k* (i.e., defining a request for having the results of the analysis every $k$ time instants), as well as the mission time $T$ (i.e. the last point in time considered for the analysis). In other words, the output of the analysis will be the posterior probability of the queried events (both in the form of joint probability over the whole set of queried events and in the form of marginal probabilities for each single queried event) from time $t = 0$ until time $t = T$, every $k$ time instants.

Moreover, from this GUI it is also possible to select the inference algorithm (either 1.5JT or BK) and the analysis task (either filtering/prediction or smoothing). More details on this specific aspect will be provided in Section 6.5. All this information is directly inherited by the corresponding DBN when the translation occurs. In this way, the DFT is exploited as an easy and well-known formalism, to which the user is typically already familiar, through which all the needed data for DBN inference can be given as input.

Finally, particularly important from the quantitative analysis point of view is another parameter that the user can set on the DFT: the discretization step $\Delta$. Since a DBN is a discrete time formalism, a suitable discretization step must be defined in case failure specification on the system components are given in a continuous way (as usual in FT/DFT modeling). Let us suppose that a basic component $C$ is characterized by an exponential failure rate $\lambda_C$: given a discretization step $\Delta$, we characterize the failure probability of $C$ as

$$Pr\{C \text{ failed at time } t + \Delta | C \text{ working at time } t\} = 1 - e^{-\lambda_C \Delta}$$

Thus, in terms of the corresponding DBN, $\Delta$ represents the amount of time separating the anterior layer from the ulterior layer. There is a trade-off between the approximation provided by discretization and the computational effort needed for the analysis: smaller is the discretization step, more accurate are the results obtained (and closer to the continuous case computation), but greater is the time horizon required for the analysis (and thus the computation time). In fact, if failure rates are given as $f/h$ (fault per hours), and we set a mission time of $T$ hours, a discretization step $\Delta = 1\ h$ will require analysis up to step $t = T$, while a discretization step $\Delta = 10\ h$ will only require analysis up to step $t = T/10$ (since each step will count as 10 time units); this fact, in DBN inference, will result in a speed up of the computation, because a smaller number of time slices have to be considered (i.e. a time slice in the latter case approximate 10 slices in the former).

## 6.3    Editing a DBN

As we have discussed in previous chapters, PGMs (and in particular, BNs and DBNs) can be directly used as a reliability modeling and analysis tool In this case, the reliability engineer can design the model by resorting to the basic formalism features. In particular, for DBNs:

(1) for each system component, a variable is introduced at the anterior layer and replicated at the ulterior layer via a temporal arc connection;

(2) intra-slice dependencies are introduced and quantified;

(3) inter-slice dependencies are finally modeled by connecting variables at the anterior layer with those variables at the ulterior layer depending on them (i.e. that are influenced by them), and by properly quantifying such a dependence (for instance by exploiting specific failure and/or repair rates).

For example, if the modeling follows a combinatorial style, like in (D)FTs, the second point may possibly result in the introduction of new variables representing particular functionalities of the modeled system (like standard gates in a FT) [Bobbio *et al.* (2001); Langseth and Portinale (2007); Weber and Jouffe (2003)]. Both points (2) and (3) may then be involved if one has to model dynamic aspects of system functionalities like those represented by the dynamic gates of a DFT (see Chapter 4).

By means of the DBNEdit GUI, the user is allowed to directly draw the desired DBN structure, by labeling nodes (variables) with the corresponding layer (0 for the anterior and 1 for the ulterior) and by using the notion of temporal arcs (that we have depicted as thick edges in the figures) to identify temporal related copies of the same variable.

The Conditional Probability Tables (CPT) can be then elicited relying on a user friendly functionality, in which every row is automatically completed by calculating the last entry as the difference between 1 and the sum of the other values. Finally, it is possible to identify query nodes and to provide a stream of observations (i.e. evidences), each one labeled with its observation time. When the network has been fully characterized, the user can set the parameters for the analysis, and in particular the desired time horizon (i.e. the time point $T$ up to which to compute results) and the desired analysis time step $k$.

## 6.4   Compilation of a DFT into a DBN

If the analyst chooses to create his/her model through the module DFTEdit, then the solver DFT2DBN is activated to generate the DBN corresponding to the input DFT, as described in Chapter 4. The resulting DBN is formalized as XML code stored in a file which is the output of DFT2DBN. In a preliminary version of the RADYBAN tool, this XML file did not contain graphical properties (like the coordinates of the position of the DBN nodes), so it was not possible to load the resulting DBN into the module DBNEditor; this was overcome in the last version of the tool, where the output DBN of DFTEditor can actually be input for DBNEditor, allowing the analyst to possibly augment, in an incremental way, the features of the DBN, once created from an input DFT.

## 6.5   Analyzing a DBN

The analysis features provided by RADYBAN, implemented through the solver DBN analyzer, concern the computation of the posterior joint probability of the set of query variables given the evidence, starting from time $t = 0$ up to time $t = T$ (time horizon set in either DFTEditor or DBNEditor), every $k$ time instants (analysis time step again set in either DFTEditor or DBNEditor). Dependability measures can be expressed in the form of posterior probability computation as shown in Chapter 3 and Chapter 4. For this reason RADYBAN has the possibility of performing both filtering/prediction and smoothing [Murphy (2002)] on the DBN subject to the analysis. In both kind of tasks the analyst can choose between an exact inference with Murphy's 1.5JT algorithm and an approximate inference using BK algorithm; in the latter case is it possible to specify the suitable set of BK clusters or to require the most aggressive approximation called *fully factorized* BK, where each cluster is assumed to contain one single variable of the forward interface (see Chapter 2, Section 2.3.1). These algorithms have been implemented by resorting to Intel *Probabilistic Networks Library* (PNL), a set of open-source C++ libraries (see http://sourceforge.net/projects/openpnl), to which some minor adjustments have been provided. The PNL-based solver can compute both joint and marginal posterior probabilities on the queried variables, given the evidence stream. The tool has also the possibility of exploiting a C version of both 1.5JT and BK inference (specifically developed for the ARPHA

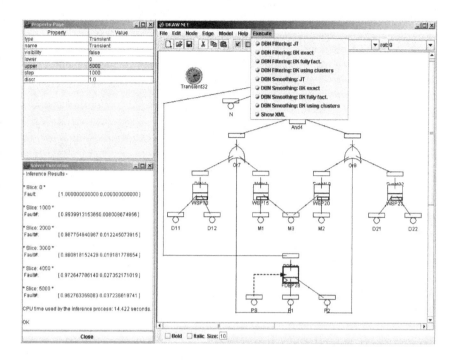

Fig. 6.2    A screenshot of the RADYBAN tool's graphical interface.

case study described in Chapter 8 of the present book), where however, only marginal probabilities can be computed. Figure 6.2 shows a screenshot of RADYBAN highlighting the DFTEditor, its Property Panel, the menu for the Solver execution and the windows containing the analysis results.

RADYBAN has been exploited in several applications and case studies, some of which are described in the present book. It has been a useful tool to demonstrate how the use of PGMs (and DBNs in particular) in dependability applications can provide significant advantages, when sophisticated modeling and quantitative analyses have to be addressed. Moreover, the possibility of defining the high-level system model relying on a widely adopted language like DFTs, has been proved quite effective in having DBNs seeped into dependability community.

More information about the tool can be obtained at the following link: http://www.di.unipmn.it/program.

# Chapter 7

# Case Study 1: Cascading Failures

## 7.1 Problem Introduction

The case study presented in this chapter concerns the problem of modeling and analyzing a set of potential situations related to cascading failures, because of dependent components. Dependencies increase the risk of failure and the vulnerability in complex critical infrastructure. As an example, most major power grid blackouts that have occurred in the past were initiated by a single event (or multiple related events) that gradually led to cascading failures and possible collapse of the entire system [Pourbeik *et al.* (2006)]. In [Rinaldi *et al.* (2001)], the authors classify dependency-related disruptions or outages as *cascading, escalating,* or *common cause.* A cascading phenomenon occurs when the failure in one component of a system induces an overload in adjacent components increasing their failure probability. If the overload can be compensated by the strength of the adjacent components, the cascade may be arrested, otherwise the cascade may become an avalanche causing a progressive and rapid disruption of all the system. Recent electrical blackouts that occurred both in USA and Europe are typical cascading phenomena, and since their effect has been catastrophic for millions of citizens, they have stimulated further research as also witnessed by the launch of public research programs in both the EU (CRUTIAL: http://crutial.rse-web.it, IRRIIS: http://www.irriis.org) and USA (The Complex Interactive Networks/Systems Initiative (CIN/SI), funded equally by EPRI and U.S. Department of Defense (DOD)).

Developing modeling frameworks for understanding interdependencies among critical infrastructures and analyzing their impact is a necessary step for building interconnected infrastructures on which a justified level of confidence can be placed with respect to their robustness to potential vulnerabilities and disruptions. Modeling can provide useful insights of how component failures might propagate and lead to disturbances on the service delivered to the users.

The definition and implementation of a modeling framework for the propagation of cascading failures is an open problem in the study of the dependability analysis of critical infrastructures. Two approaches can be accounted in the literature: a pure statistical approach and a phenomenological approach.

The aim of the *statistical approach* is to model how the appearance of a failure and the consequent overload can be redistributed, and to study the propagation of the cascade. A series of papers [Dobson *et al.* (2002, 2004, 2005)] propose a statistical model called *CASCADE* which is based on an abstract view of the cascading phenomenon. The system is assumed to be composed of many identical components randomly loaded. An initial disturbance causes some components to fail by exceeding the loading limit. The failure of a component causes a fixed load increase for other components. Models of the dynamic redistribution of the load have been explored also in [Motter and Lai (2002); Crucitti *et al.* (2004); Kinney *et al.* (2005)], where the load redistribution is based on the definition of node efficiency which is a centrality measure based on shortest paths computation. The idea of computing centrality measures using only the shortest paths has been criticized in [Newman (2005)] with the motivation that the intrinsic redundancy of the network is neglected.

In the *phenomenological approach*, an attempt is made to build a physical scenario that leads to the comprehension of the propagation of the cascading phenomenon. Typical examples of this approach in the literature can be found in [DeMarco (2001); Chowdhury and Baravc (2006); Lininger *et al.* (2007); Faza *et al.* (2007)]. In particular, [Chowdhury and Baravc (2006)] discuss the possible evolution of various failure scenarios related to the IEEE 118 bus test system. An effort to propose a formal approach to a failure scenario is discussed in [Faza *et al.* (2007)] resorting to a chain of conditional probabilities. The proposal is, however, incomplete: it does not take into account the dynamic of the cascade and it is not suitable for quantitative evaluations.

The problem of propagating or cascading failures has also been tackled in the context of standard dependability formalisms like DFT or CTMC; however, restrictions are usually assumed to limit the complexity of the problem, either at the modeling level (e.g. non-repairable binary systems as in [Wang *et al.* (2012)], or at the formalism level (e.g., combinatorial models as in [Xing and Levitin (2011)]). This chapter aims at showing that DBNs (Dynamic Bayesian Networks) can provide a very valuable framework for modeling and quantitatively analyzing dynamically dependent failure phenomena, as those arising in the propagation of cascading failures; moreover, DBN represent, at the same time, the evolution of the cascading phenomenon in a more physical way, with respect to the abstract statistical models. We show how DBN can capture the propagation of failure phenomena (Section 7.2). For the sake of illustration, we then apply the DBN model to one of the scenarios on the IEEE 118 bus test system, taken from [Chowdhury and Baravc (2006)], and we show how the model can be solved to provide quantitative results (Section 7.3).

## 7.2 Modeling Cascading Failures by Means of DBN

In the following, we consider a portion of the IEEE 118 Bus Test Case described in [Chowdhury and Baravc (2006)] and depicted in Figure 7.1. It represents a power grid with a set of nodes and a set of lines (connections among nodes); each line is represented by the pair $X - Y$, being $X$ and $Y$ the connected nodes. The test case in [Chowdhury and Baravc (2006)] discusses various cascading failure scenarios. We will concentrate on one of them, namely the one that describes the sequence of events originated from the failure of line 5-4, until they propagate up to node 12, and we show how it can be tackled by using a DBN.

For the sake of simplicity, we will concentrate on a subpart of the whole network, and in particular on the fragment delimited by the dashed oval in Figure 7.1, functionally represented in the series/parallel diagram of Figure 7.2. As illustrated in the diagram, the subnet is composed by a parallel module in series with line 11-12. The parallel module is made by two branches, the first of which, in turn, is composed by a series of two lines (5-4 and 4-11), while the second one coincides with line 5-11.

According to [Chowdhury and Baravc (2006)], we assume that each line can be in one of the following states: *working, outaged* (failed) or *overloaded*. Initially a line is working, and it may turn to the overloaded state as a consequence of the overload or the outage of another line. During the working state or the overloaded state, a line may fail. We suppose that the outage probability of all the lines is ruled by the negative exponential distribution, and that the failure rate has the same value $\lambda$ for all the working lines. Moreover, we assume that the value of the failure rate of a

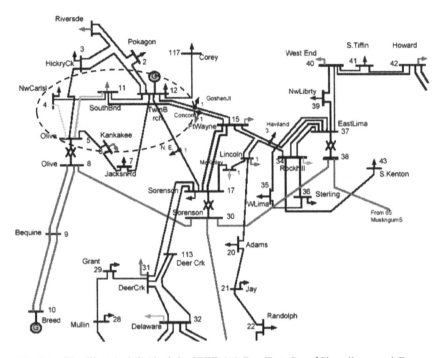

Fig. 7.1   The Electrical Grid of the IEEE 118 Bus Test Case [Chowdhury and Baravc (2006)].

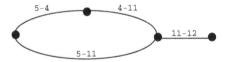

Fig. 7.2   Series/parallel diagram for the cascading failure example.

certain line is increased during the overloaded state. In particular, if the overload of the line $l_1$ is caused by the overload of the line $l_0$ on which $l_1$ depends, the failure rate of $l_1$ becomes $\alpha\lambda$. If instead the overload of $l_1$ is caused by the outage of $l_0$, the failure rate of $l_1$ becomes $\beta\lambda$. In other words, the failure probability of an overloaded line is greater than the failure probability of a working line. Such increase depends on the cause of the overload: in particular, we assume $\beta > \alpha > 1$.

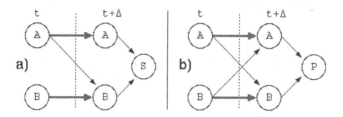

Fig. 7.3  a) DBN for the series module. b) DBN for the parallel module.

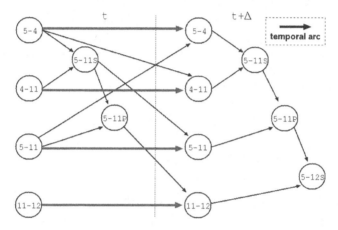

Fig. 7.4   DBN for the cascading failure example in Figure 7.2. An *S* identifies a *series* node, and a *P* identifies a *parallel* one (e.g. *5-11S* summarizes the module obtained by taking the series of 5-4 and 4-11, while *5-11P* summarizes the parallel between such a series and line 5-11 - see Figure 7.2).

## 7.2.1   *Building the DBN model*

Similarly to the approach described in Chapters 3 and 4 where FT and DFT are compiled into BN and DBN respectively, to tackle this case study, a methodology is proposed for automatically converting a series-parallel diagram, like the one in Figure 7.2, into a DBN (see also [Codetta-Raiteri *et al.* (2012)] for the details). The methodology proceeds in a modular fashion, by properly composing the translation of the simplest modules that can be found in the diagram, i.e. the *series* module and the *parallel* module, according to the rules explained in the following.

Figure 7.3.a shows the DBN translating a *series* module composed by two lines A and B (where the number of lines can be trivially extended to three or more). In the DBN, the inter-slice dependency model captures the following semantics: if line A becomes overloaded, it overloads line B at the following time slice. On the other hand, the node $S$, which summarizes the behavior of the whole module, is set as follows: if A or B fails, $S$ immediately fails. If A is overloaded, $S$ gets immediately overloaded; it can never happen that A works properly and B is overloaded. Finally, if A and B work properly, $S$ works properly.

Figure 7.3.b shows the DBN translating a *parallel* module composed by two lines A and B (where the number of lines can be trivially extended to three or more). The inter-slice dependency model captures the following semantics: if line A fails or becomes overloaded, it overloads line B at the next time slice, and vice-versa. On the other hand, the node $P$, which summarizes the behavior of the whole module, is set as follows: if both A and B fail, $P$ immediately fails. If only A fails, $P$ works properly; the same holds if only B fails. If A gets overloaded, $P$ gets immediately overloaded; the same holds if B gets overloaded. Finally, if both A and B work properly, $P$ works properly too. Therefore, all variables in Figure 7.3.a and 7.3.b are three-state variables.

All non-trivial compositions of a parallel and a series modules are managed by three rules:

(1) to connect a parallel module in series with a series module: the $P$ node summarizing the behavior of the first module affects the first line in the series module, in the inter-slice dependency model;

(2) to connect any module (series or parallel) in series with a parallel module: the $S$ or $P$ node summarizing the behavior of the first module affects the $P$ node summarizing the behavior of the second module, in the inter-slice dependency model;

(3) to connect a series module in parallel with any (series or parallel) module: the $S$ node summarizing the behavior of the first module affects the first line in the second module (if it is a series one), or all the first lines in the parallel branches (if the second module is in turn a parallel one), in the inter-slice dependency model.

Following such composition rules, we are able to translate the diagram in Figure 7.2 into the DBN in Figure 7.4. By iterating the rules application, more complex models can be automatically translated as well.

It is worth noting that in [Torres-Toledano and Sucar (1998)], an algorithm is introduced for automatically converting a Reliability Block Diagram (RBD) (which is also based on series and parallel connection types), into a static BN. In particular, according to [Torres-Toledano and Sucar (1998)], lines in parallel have to be connected through an AND node (since the overall parallel circuit fails if and only if all the lines are outaged), while lines in series have to be connected through an OR node (since the overall series circuit fails if at least one of the lines is outaged). With respect to the methodology described here, such an algorithm is limited to binary variables. On the other hand, we generalize the OR and AND nodes into the $S$ and $P$ nodes, which are multi-state (namely three-state) variables, able to account also for the overload condition. Moreover, if a line gets outaged/overloaded, the lines affected by it get overloaded, and do not directly fail: they might fail subsequently. A static BN, which could manage multi-state variables, cannot deal with this kind of temporal dependency, and this justifies the choice of relying on a DBN.

Concerning the probabilistic quantification, in the DBN model of Figure 7.4 the CPT expressing the probability that node *5-4* fails at time $t+\Delta$, depending on its state at time $t$, and on the state of its parent node *5-11* at time $t$, is the one provided in Table 7.1. The CPT expressing the probability that node *5-4* is overloaded at time $t + \Delta$ is provided in Table 7.2.

In Tables 7.1 and 7.2 it can never happen that *5-4* at time $t$ is overloaded and *5-11* at time $t$ is working, therefore any value could be inserted in the corresponding table entry; as already done in previous chapters, we adopt the symbol "/" to stand for "any value". Moreover, in Table 7.1 the probability that *5-4* is failed at time $t + \Delta$, given that *5-4* at time $t$ is working and *5-11* at time $t$ is failed, is 0. In fact, *5-4* needs to become overloaded before it fails.

### 7.2.1.1 *Modeling the repair*

The possibility of repairing outaged lines is a realistic option which can improve the overall availability of the system. The modeling approach presented here can be extended in such a way that the DBN model can represent the repair of lines as well, according to a specific repair policy. For instance, if we suppose that a line undergoes repair as soon as it becomes outaged, then the repair can be modeled directly in the CPT of the corresponding node (in this case a CR policy as described in Chapter 4, Section 4.3 is assumed). Assuming that $\mu$ is the repair rate, the CPT expressing the probability that the node *5-4* is working (Table 7.3) shows how to model both the absence of repair ($\mu = 0$) and its presence ($\mu > 0$). In

Table 7.1   CPT for node *5-4* failed (i.e. outaged), depending on its historical copy at time $t$ and on its parent node *5-11* at time $t$. $\lambda$ is the failure rate; $\alpha$ and $\beta$ are constants increasing $\lambda$ in case of overload

| **5-4 failed at $t+\Delta$** | **5-4 failed at $t$** | **5-4 over. at $t$** | **5-4 work. at $t$** |
|---|---|---|---|
| **5-11 failed at $t$** | 1 | $1\text{-}e^{-\beta\lambda\Delta}$ | 0 |
| **5-11 over. at $t$** | 1 | $1\text{-}e^{-\alpha\lambda\Delta}$ | 0 |
| **5-11 work. at $t$** | 1 | / | $1\text{-}e^{-\lambda\Delta}$ |

Table 7.2   CPT for node *5-4* overloaded

| **5-4 over. at $t+\Delta$** | **5-4 failed at $t$** | **5-4 over. at $t$** | **5-4 work. at $t$** |
|---|---|---|---|
| **5-11 failed at $t$** | 0 | $e^{-\beta\lambda\Delta}$ | 1 |
| **5-11 over. at $t$** | 0 | $e^{-\alpha\lambda\Delta}$ | 1 |
| **5-11 work. at $t$** | 0 | / | 0 |

Table 7.3   CPT for node *5-4* working, assuming the absence of repair ($\mu = 0$) or its presence ($\mu > 0$). $\mu$ is the repair rate

| **5-4 working at $t+\Delta$** | **5-4 failed at $t$** | | **5-4 over. at $t$** | | **5-4 work. at $t$** |
|---|---|---|---|---|---|
| **5-11 failed at $t$** | 0 | | 0 | | 0 |
| **5-11 over. at $t$** | 0 | | 0 | | 0 |
| **5-11 work. at $t$** | $\mu = 0$ | $\mu > 0$ | $\mu = 0$ | $\mu > 0$ | $e^{-\lambda\Delta}$ |
| | 0 | $1 - e^{-\mu\Delta}$ | / | 1 | |

presenting quantitative results in the following, we suppose that no repair policy is adopted.

### 7.2.2   *The cascading failure scenario*

In the grid portion of Figure 7.2, several cascading failure scenarios may occur as a consequence of the outage of lines. We will concentrate on one of these scenarios, namely the one that describes the sequence of events originated from the failure of line 5-4, until they propagate up to the line 11-12; initially all the lines are working, so their failure rate is $\lambda$. If the outage of line 5-4 occurs, it influences the state of the series composed by 5-4 and 4-11, which becomes outaged in turn. This series is in parallel with the line 5-11, so the outage of the series determines the overload of the line 5-11: the failure rate of 5-11 is multiplied by the constant $\beta$. The overload state of line 5-11 determines in turn the overload of the whole parallel module whose branches are the series composed by 4-5 and 5-11, and the line 5-11. Since such module composes a series together with the line 11-12, the overload state of the parallel module causes the overload state of the line 11-12 in turn. As a consequence of the overload, the failure rate of the line 11-12 is multiplied by the constant $\alpha$.

In this situation, the series may fail if at least one among the parallel module and the line 11-12 fails. In particular, in the parallel module, the line 5-4 is already outaged, and the state of the line 4-11 has no effect on the rest of the subnet. Therefore the failure of the parallel module occurs if the line 5-11, currently in overload state, fails.

## 7.3 Quantitative Results

Let us now to consider the computation if different prediction and smoothing measures by inference on the DBN model depicted in Figure 7.4, representing the behavior of the subnet in Figure 7.2 as described in Section 7.2. We report the results obtained by designing and analyzing the DBN model by means of RADYBAN (Chapter 6), assuming that the parameters $\lambda$, $\alpha$ and $\beta$ determining the failure rate of the lines in the working or overload state, are set to $1.0E - 04$, 1.2 and 1.5 respectively. Moreover, we assume that all the lines are in the working state at the initial time. In particular, we consider the scenario deriving from the outage of the line 5-4 and described at the end of Section 7.2. We suppose to observe the outage of 5-4 at time $t_1=300$ $h$ in all the experiments. Such observation is associated with the node *5-4*.

First, we predict the probability of the states of the lines 5-11 and 11-12, together with the general state of the subnet[1], for a mission time varying from 0 to 1000 $h$. To this aim, we make inference on the DBN model and we query the nodes *5-11*, *11-12* and *5-12S*.

The inference results for the general state of the subnet are reported in Table 7.4, where we can notice that the probability of the system to be working is null for times greater than 300 $h$. This is due to the observation of the outage of the line 5-4 at time $t_1=300$ $h$: this event has several cascading effects causing the overload of the whole subnet, as described in Section 7.2. Before the outage of the line 5-4, the probability of the subnet to be overloaded is very small, but it becomes close to 1 just after the outage of the line 5-4, and decreases as time elapses because of the increase

---

[1]The state of the line 4-11 is not relevant because it composes a series with the outaged line 5-4.

Table 7.4    Prediction of the subnet state probability

| time | working | overloaded | outaged | outaged (GSPN) |
|------|---------|-----------|---------|----------------|
| 100 $h$ | 0.961076 | 0.028678 | 0.010246 | 0.010257 |
| 200 $h$ | 0.923389 | 0.055636 | 0.020974 | 0.010257 |
| 300 $h$ | 0.002972 | 0.922583 | 0.074445 | 0.077806 |
| 400 $h$ | 0 | 0.900898 | 0.099101 | 0.102372 |
| 500 $h$ | 0 | 0.876898 | 0.123102 | 0.126284 |
| 600 $h$ | 0 | 0.853537 | 0.146463 | 0.149559 |
| 700 $h$ | 0 | 0.830798 | 0.169202 | 0.172213 |
| 800 $h$ | 0 | 0.808665 | 0.191335 | 0.194265 |
| 900 $h$ | 0 | 0.787121 | 0.212878 | 0.215728 |
| 1000 $h$ | 0 | 0.766152 | 0.233848 | 0.236620 |

Table 7.5    Prediction of line 5-11 state probability

| time | working | overloaded | outaged | outaged (GSPN) |
|------|---------|-----------|---------|----------------|
| 100 $h$ | 0.970638 | 0.019365 | 0.009996 | 0.009999 |
| 200 $h$ | 0.941950 | 0.038061 | 0.019989 | 0.019994 |
| 300 $h$ | 0.003063 | 0.953441 | 0.043497 | 0.044002 |
| 400 $h$ | 0 | 0.942262 | 0.057738 | 0.058235 |
| 500 $h$ | 0 | 0.928232 | 0.071767 | 0.072256 |
| 600 $h$ | 0 | 0.914412 | 0.085588 | 0.086069 |
| 700 $h$ | 0 | 0.900796 | 0.099203 | 0.099675 |
| 800 $h$ | 0 | 0.887384 | 0.112616 | 0.113080 |
| 900 $h$ | 0 | 0.874171 | 0.125828 | 0.126284 |
| 1000 $h$ | 0 | 0.861155 | 0.138844 | 0.139292 |

Table 7.6    Prediction of line 11-12 state probability

| time | working | overloaded | outaged | outaged (GSPN) |
|------|---------|-----------|---------|----------------|
| 100 $h$ | 0.961367 | 0.028657 | 0.009976 | 0.009979 |
| 200 $h$ | 0.923672 | 0.056419 | 0.019909 | 0.009979 |
| 300 $h$ | 0.006043 | 0.961559 | 0.032397 | 0.035360 |
| 400 $h$ | 0.000096 | 0.955964 | 0.043939 | 0.046866 |
| 500 $h$ | 0.000095 | 0.944561 | 0.055344 | 0.058235 |
| 600 $h$ | 0.000094 | 0.933293 | 0.066612 | 0.069469 |
| 700 $h$ | 0.000094 | 0.922160 | 0.077746 | 0.088057 |
| 800 $h$ | 0.000093 | 0.911160 | 0.088747 | 0.091536 |
| 900 $h$ | 0.000092 | 0.900291 | 0.099617 | 0.102372 |
| 1000 $h$ | 0.000091 | 0.889551 | 0.110358 | 0.113080 |

of the probability of outage of the subnet. A similar effect concerns the state probabilities of the lines 5-11 (Table 7.5) and 11-12 (Table 7.6).

The prediction results have been cross-checked by modeling and analyzing the system as a GSPN (Section 1.3.2), where the observations have been represented by properly setting the initial marking of places. The fifth column in Tables 7.4, 7.5 and 7.6 reports the outaged state probability computed on the GSPN model.

Table 7.7  Smoothing of line 5-11 state probability

| time | working | overloaded | outaged |
|------|---------|-----------|---------|
| 100 $h$ | 0.660737 | 0.339263 | 0 |
| 200 $h$ | 0.326283 | 0.673717 | 0 |
| 300 $h$ | 0 | 1.000000 | 0 |
| 400 $h$ | 0 | 0.882104 | 0.117896 |
| 500 $h$ | 0 | 0.765963 | 0.234037 |
| 600 $h$ | 0 | 0.651552 | 0.348448 |
| 700 $h$ | 0 | 0.538844 | 0.461155 |
| 800 $h$ | 0 | 0.427815 | 0.572185 |
| 900 $h$ | 0 | 0.421445 | 0.578554 |
| 1000 $h$ | 0 | 0.415170 | 0.584830 |

Besides predictions, we can compute smoothing measures on the DBN model. This can be useful in order to diagnose the possible causes of the system outage. Given the outage of the line 5-4, the outage of the whole subnet can be caused by the outage of the line 11-12, or by the outage of the line 5-11 (see Section 7.2). In order to evaluate the probability of such causes, we can execute the inference on the DBN model in Figure 7.4, but in this case we perform smoothing instead of prediction. We take into account further observations: in particular, the subnet is overloaded at time $t_1=300$ $h$ and is outaged at time $t_2=800$ $h$.

In the DBN model (see Figure 7.4), such observations are associated with the node *5-12S*, representing the state of the whole subnet. According to this, we compute the probability of line 5-11 to be working, overloaded or outaged, (Table 7.7), and of the line 11-12 (Table 7.8).

By the comparison of the values in such tables, we can notice that the probability of both lines to be working becomes zero after 300 $h$, because they become overloaded and possibly outaged as a consequence of the outage of the line 5-4 at time $t_1=300$ $h$. Moreover, we can notice that the probability of the line 5-11 to be outaged is a bit larger than the same probability concerning the line 11-12; this depends on the fact that the failure rate of the line 5-11 ($\beta\lambda$) is greater than the failure rate of 11-12 ($\alpha\lambda$), as described in Section 7.2 ($\beta > \alpha$).

If we compare the probability values of the lines 5-11 and 11-12 in the prediction experiment (Tables 7.5 and 7.6) and in the smoothing experiment (Tables 7.7 and 7.8), we can notice that the outage probability for both lines is much larger in the smoothing experiment than in the prediction one. This is due to the observation, in the smoothing experiment, of the outage of the subnet at time $t_2=800$ $h$. Such event can only be caused by the occurrence

Table 7.8   Smoothing of line 11-12 state probability

| time | working | overloaded | outaged |
|------|---------|------------|---------|
| 100 $h$ | 0.664123 | 0.335877 | 0 |
| 200 $h$ | 0.329587 | 0.670413 | 0 |
| 300 $h$ | 0.003220 | 0.996780 | 0 |
| 400 $h$ | 0 | 0.905548 | 0.094452 |
| 500 $h$ | 0 | 0.812220 | 0.187780 |
| 600 $h$ | 0 | 0.720005 | 0.279995 |
| 700 $h$ | 0 | 0.628890 | 0.371110 |
| 800 $h$ | 0 | 0.538862 | 0.461138 |
| 900 $h$ | 0 | 0.532434 | 0.467566 |
| 1000 $h$ | 0 | 0.526083 | 0.473917 |

of outage of the line 5-11 or of the outage of 11-12. The increase of the outage probability determines the decrease of the overload probability.

To conclude, this case study has shown how cascading failures can be modeled by means of the DBN framework. DBN are a powerful instrument for modeling and analyzing dynamically dependent failure phenomena. Moreover, they enable a representation of the evolution of the cascading phenomenon in a more physical way with respect to the abstract statistical models. In this study, a modular algorithm for automatically converting a series/parallel diagram into a DBN, which allows for a quick DBN creation, has also been proposed. An extension to the content of this chapter is available in [Codetta-Raiteri *et al.* (2012)].

Chapter 8

# Case Study 2: Autonomous Fault Detection, Identification and Recovery

## 8.1 Problem Introduction

The case study reported in this chapter concerns the definition of an intelligent *Fault Detection, Identification and Recovery* (FDIR) strategy for an autonomous spacecraft vehicle (in this specific case a Mars rover). This study has been performed by the authors as part of a *European Space Agency* (ESA) funded project called VERIFIM: VERIFICATION OF IMPACT FAILURES BY MODEL CHECKING[1]. In autonomous spacecraft operations, both the system behavior and the environment can exhibit various degrees of uncertainty; control software must then provide the suitable and timely reaction of the system to changes in its operational environment, as well as in the operational status of the system. The operational status of the system is dependent on the internal system dependability factors (e.g. sub-system and component reliability models), on the external environment factors affecting the system reliability and safety (e.g. thermal, radiation, illumination conditions) and on system-environment interactions (e.g. stress factors, resource utilization profiles, degradation profiles, etc.). Combinations of these factors may cause mission execution anomalies, including mission degradations and system failures. To address possible system faults and failures, the system under examination must be provided with some form of health management procedures, usually relying on the FDIR process [SalarKaleji and Dayyani (2013)]. Currently employed state-of-the-art of the FDIR is based on the design-time analysis of the faults and failure scenarios, e.g., *Failure Mode Effect Analysis* (FMEA), *Fault Tree Analysis*

---

[1]The VERIFIM study has been a joint effort of University of Piemonte Orientale (Computer Science Department) and Thales/Alenia Space, under ESA grant TEC-SWE/09259/YY (http://people.unipmn.it/dcr/verifim).

(FTA) and run-time observation of the system operational status (health monitoring). The goal is in general to timely detect faults and to start a predefined recovery procedure (often by using pre-defined look-up tables), having the goal of putting the spacecraft into a known safe configuration and transfer control to the ground operations for troubleshooting and planning actual recovery.

Standard FDIR approaches have multiple shortcomings which may significantly reduce effectiveness of the adopted procedures:

- the system, as well as its environment, is only partially observable by monitoring procedures; this introduces uncertainty in the interpretation of observations in terms of the actual system status, which is often disregarded in choosing the possible recovery.
- Recovery is essentially triggered following a reactive approach, a post-factum operation, not capable of preventive measures and prognosis for the imminent failures.

The main source of such limits is recognized to be the fact that knowledge of the general operational capabilities of the system (that should potentially be expressed in terms of causal probabilistic relations) is not usually represented on-board, making impossible to estimate the impact of the occurred faults and failures on these capabilities. Several studies have tried to address these problems, some by restricting attention to manned systems [Schwabacher *et al.* (2008)] or to systems requiring heavy human intervention [Robinson *et al.* (2003)], some others by emphasizing the prognostic phase and relying on heuristics techniques to close the FDIR cycle [Glover *et al.* (2010)].

As we have already mentioned, the goal of the VERIFIM study (http://people.unipmn.it/dcr/verifim) was to define an innovative approach to on-board FDIR; the FDIR engine exploits an on-board PGM which must take into account the system architecture, the system environment, the system-environment interaction, and the dynamic evolution in presence of uncertainty and partial observability. Moreover, the on-board FDIR engine must provide the system with diagnosis (fault detection and identification) and prognosis (fault prediction) capabilities on the operational status, to be taken into account for autonomous reactive or preventive recovery actions. To this aim, in the VERIFIM study, an on-board software prototype called ARPHA (*Anomaly Resolution and Prognostic Health management for Autonomy*) has been developed.

Before the execution of ARPHA (on-board process), the on-board model must be prepared. Because of the several aspects to be represented by the on-board model, the modelling phase (off-board process) integrates DFT as a high level modeling formalism, DBN as low level modeling formalism, and JT (Junction Tree) as an inference oriented formalism. The on-board model (i.e., the JT) is obtained through a sequence of model conversions and model enrichment.

## 8.2   The Testing Environment

We then present the testing environment that has been defined in the VER-IFIM study; it concerns the Power Supply Subsystem (PSS) of a Mars rover, an autonomous spacecraft vehicle devoted to the exploration of the Mars surface, performing specific planned operations like taking pictures, drilling the ground, moving around to explore the environment, etc. (see Figure 8.1). The attention has been focused on the following aspects.

**Solar arrays.**   We assume the presence of three solar arrays (SA), namely SA1, SA2, SA3. In particular, SA1 is composed by two redundant strings[2], while SA2 and SA3 are composed by three strings. Each SA can generate power if both the following conditions hold:

(1) at least one string is not failed;
(2) the combination of the parameters sun aspect angle (SAA), optical depth (OD), and local time (day or night) is suitable. In particular, OD is given by the presence or absence of shadow or storm.

The total amount of generated power is proportional to the number of SAs which are actually working.

**Load.**   The amount of load depends on the action performed by the rover.

**Battery.**   We assume the battery to be composed by three redundant strings. The charge of the battery may be steady, decreasing or increasing according to the current levels of load and generation by SAs. The charge of the battery may be compromised by the damage of the battery occurring in two situations: all the strings are failed, or the temperature of the battery is low.

---

[2]A string (or a cell) is a portion of a solar array or a portion of a battery.

Fig. 8.1   A Mars Rover (credit ESA).

**Scenarios.**   We are interested in four failure or anomaly scenarios. Each scenario can be recovered by specific policies:

- **S1)** low (anomaly) or very low (failure) power generation while SAA is not optimal. Recovery policies:

  - **P1)** suspension of the plan under execution, in order to reduce the load;

- **P2)** change of inclination of SA2 and SA3, in order to try to improve SAA and consequently the power generation (the tilting system cannot act on SA1).

- **S2)** low (anomaly) or very low (failure) power generation while OD is not optimal. Recovery policies:

  - **P3)** movement of the rover into another position, in order to try to avoid a shadowed area and improve OD and the power generation as a consequence;
  - **P4)** modification of the inclination of SA2 and SA3, retraction of the drill, and suspension of the plan.

- **S3)** low (anomaly) or very low (failure) battery level while drilling. Recovery policies:

  - **P4)** as above;
  - **P5)** retraction of the drill, suspension of the plan.

- **S4)** low (anomaly) or very low (failure) battery level while the battery is damaged. Recovery policies:

  - **P4)** as above.

## 8.3 Off-board Process

The off-board process starts with a fault analysis phase concerning some basic knowledge about the system faults and failures, together with some knowledge about environmental/contextual conditions and their effects and impacts on the system behavior (possibly either nominal or faulty). This phase is aimed at constructing (by standard and well-known dependability analysis procedures) a first dependability model that in the case study has been assumed to be a DFT. The produced DFT is then automatically compiled into a DBN, following the compilation process detailed in Chapter 4. The DBN model is enriched with knowledge about more specific system capabilities and failures, with particular attention to the identification of multi-state components and stochastic dependencies not captured at the DFT language level. The aim is to generate a DBN representing all the needed knowledge about failure impacts. During this phase, both knowledge about plan actions or recovery actions can be incorporated into the DBN. In ARPHA, we decided to implement the DBN analysis by resorting to JT inference algorithms. So, another role of the off-board process is the

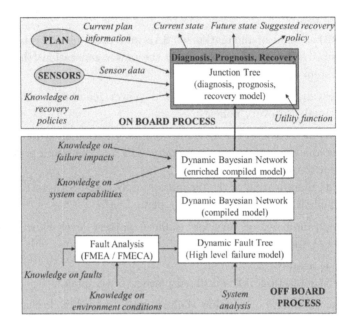

Fig. 8.2   ARPHA's off-board process and on-board process.

generation of the JT from the DBN. This is performed according to the procedures presented in appendix A

The DFT definition, its compilation into DBN, and the enrichment of the DBN are supported by the RADYBAN tool described in Chapter 6. An ad-hoc JT generator and inference engine has been implemented inside VERIFIM, in order to fulfill the requirements for on-board aircraft software as requested by ESA.

### 8.3.1   *DFT model of the case study*

The DFT model of the case study (Figure 8.3) represents the combinations of events or states leading to TE corresponding to the anomaly or failure of the whole system. TE is the output of an OR gate and occurs if the event *S1*, *S2*, *S3*, or *S4* happens. The event *S1* represents the scenario S1 and is the output of an AND gate. *S1* occurs if both the events *PowGen* and *AngleSA2* occur. They represent an anomaly/failure about the power generation (for instance, a low level of generated power) and a not optimal SAA for SA2 (we assume that SAA of SA2 is similar to SAA of SA1 and SA3). *PowGen* occurs if all the events *PowGenSA1*, *PowGenSA2* and *PowGenSA3* occur. Each of them represents the fact that a SA is not producing energy. For example, *PowGenSA1* concerns SA1 and occurs if *StringsSA1* occurs (all the strings of SA1 are failed) or *SA1perf* occurs (the combination of local time - day or night -, OD and SAA of SA1 does not allow the generation of energy). OD is not optimal in case of storm or shadow.

The event *S2* occurs if both *PowGen* and *OpticalDepth* occur. *S3* occurs if both *BattCharge* and *Drill* occur; they represent an anomaly/failure about the level of charge of the battery, and the drill action in execution respectively. *BattCharge* in turns occurs if both the events *Balance* and *BattFail* occur. *Balance* represents the fact that the use of the battery is necessary: *Balance* occurs if both *PowGen* and *Load* occur. The second event represents the presence of a load (consume of energy). The event *BattFail* models the damage of the battery, because of the failure of all its strings (event *BattStrings*) or a low temperature (event *Temp*). Finally, *S4* occurs if both the events *BattCharge* and *BattFail* occur.

The model contains two functional dependency (FDEP) gates (Section 1.2.2). The first one represents the influence of *ActionId* on other events, such as *Load*, *Drill* (in case of drilling actions), *DrillRetract* (drill in or out), *AngleSA1*, *AngleSA2*, *AngleSA3* (in case of tilting actions), *Shadow* (in case of travelling actions), and *MechShock* (possibility of mechanical shock damaging the battery strings, in case of drilling or travelling actions). *MechShock* influences in turns the events *BattString1*, *BattString2*, *BattString3* by means of the second FDEP gate.

### 8.3.2   *DBN model of the case study*

The DBN of the case study reported in Figure 8.4.a has been derived from the DFT model by following two steps:

(1) the DFT has been converted into the equivalent DBN: the structure of the DBN reflects the structure of the originating DFT: each event in the DFT corresponds to the variable in the DBN with the same name, while the DFT gates determine the influence arcs in the DBN.

(2) Then, the DBN has been enriched by increasing the size (number of possible values) of several variables and expressing more complicated relations among the variables, by editing the CPT of the variables.

The DFT contains Boolean (binary) events (variables) representing the state of components or subsystems. This lacks of modeling power in several

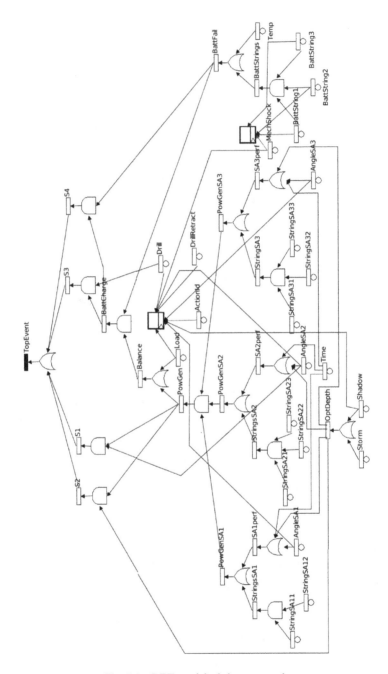

Fig. 8.3  DFT model of the case study.

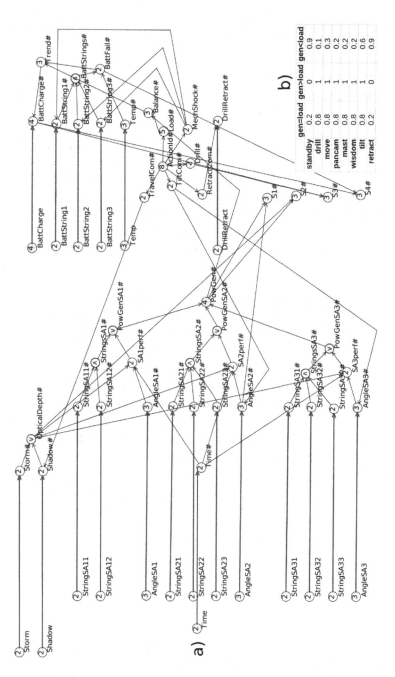

Fig. 8.4  a) DBN model of the case study. b) utility function.

cases. For instance, the level of power generation, battery charge, or load needs to be represented with a variable with more than two values, if the model has to be accurate enough to capture the aspects of the system behaviour causing its state. Moreover, the relations or dependencies holding between variables may be more complex than a Boolean or dynamic gate. For these reasons, the DBN resulting from the DFT conversion has been enriched in this sense: the variables representing SAA of each SA, and the variable *Temp* are set to be ternary (good, discrete, bad). The size of *PowGen* and *BattCharge* is set to 4 (in order to represent 4 intermediate levels of power generation and battery charge). The size of *Load* is 5 (5 levels of energy consumption). The variable *Balance* is ternary and indicates if *PowGen* is equal, higher or lower than *Load*. The size of *ActionId* is 8, in order to represent 8 actions of interest in the model. The variables *S1*, *S2*, *S3*, *S4* are ternary in order to represent the states normal, anomalous and failed in each scenario (the normal state indicates that the scenario is not occurring).

In the DBN we added some support variables, in order to reduce the number of entries in the CPT of the non binary variables, by applying the so-called "divorcing" technique [Portinale *et al.* (2010, 2007)]. The support variables are: *TravelCom*, *DrillCom* and *RetractCom* depending on *ActionId*, and *Trend* depending on *Balance* and *BattFail*. In the DBN, each variable has two instances, one for each time slice $(t, t+\Delta)$. If a variable has a temporal evolution, its two instances are connected by a "temporal" arc appearing as a thick line in Figure 8.4.a. Still in Figure 8.4.a, the observable variables are evidenced (black nodes); the values coming from the sensors will become observations for such variables during the analysis of the model. The plan actions and the recovery actions will become observations for the variable *ActionId*.

Finally, a JT is derived from the DBN model in Figure 8.4.a. and is exploited for on-board inference, concerning the diagnostic and prognostic steps; the utility function in Figure 8.4.b is exploited for Recovery (see Figure 8.5 whose details are provided in Section 8.4).

## 8.4 On-board Process

The on-board process is performed by the ARPHA prototype and operates on a JT as actual operational model, receiving observations from both sensors and plan actions (Figure 8.2). It is intended to perform Diagnosis

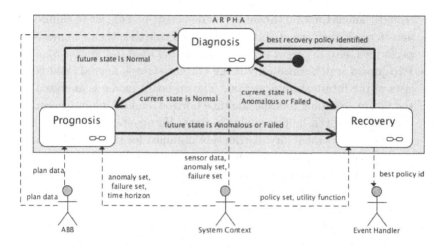

Fig. 8.5    The UML-like diagram of the functionalities of ARPHA.

(current state detection), Prognosis (future state detection) and Recovery (determination and evaluation of the best recovery policy). Figure 8.5 shows the external components (actors) that interact with ARPHA: *System Context* (memory area that contains data received from sensors, and the configuration of the system), *Autonomy Building Block* or ABB (dedicated to plan execution and plan generation), *Event Handler* (the manager of events, receiving from ARPHA the identifier of the policy to be performed, in order to recover the system).

ARPHA cyclically performs the following functionalities (Figure 8.5). Since time is discrete in DBN, each cycle is repeated at the begin of a new time step.

- **Diagnosis** begins with the retrieval of data necessary for on-board reasoning. In particular, sensor and plan data are retrieved from System Context and ABB respectively. Both kinds of data are converted in form of observations concerning specific variables of the on-board model. Observations are loaded into the on-board model; then, the model inference (analysis) is performed at the current time, by returning the probability distribution of the variables in the model. The inspection of the probabilities of specific variables, representing the system state, can provide the diagnosis at the current mission time: the possible system states are **normal** (no anomalies or failures are detected), `anomalous` (an anomaly[3] is detected) or `failed` (a failure is detected). If the current state is detected as `normal`, then Prognosis is performed, else Recovery is performed (as depicted in Figure 8.5).

- **Prognosis** is performed only if the current state is `normal`, and consists of the future state detection. The on-board model is analyzed in the future according to a specific time horizon, and taking into account observations given by future plan actions. Future state is detected according to the probability distribution obtained for the variable representing the system state. The future state can be `normal`, `anomalous`, or `failed`. In case of `normal` state, the ARPHA on-board process restarts at the next time step, with the Diagnosis phase, otherwise Recovery is performed (Figure 8.5).

- **Recovery** can be distinguished in *Reactive Recovery* (performed if the current system state is `failed`) or *Preventive Recovery* (performed in case of `anomalous` current state, `anomalous` future state, or `failed` future state). In both cases, Recovery is performed in this way: given the detected anomaly or failure, the recovery policies facing that anomaly or failure are retrieved from System Context. In particular, each recovery policy is composed by a set of recovery actions, possibly to be executed at different times. Each policy is evaluated in this way: **1)** the policy is converted into a set of observations for the on-board model variables representing actions; **2)** such observations are loaded in the on-board model which is analyzed in the future; **3)** the utility function in Figure 8.4.b provides utility values for the combinations of the possible actions and the balance between power generation and load. According to the utility function and the probability distribution of the variables involved in such function, the *expected utility* (EU) of the policy is computed. In other words, EU quantifies the future effects of the recovery policy on the system. The policy providing the best EU is selected and notified to the Event Handler for the execution. Then, the ARPHA on-board process restarts at the next time step, with Diagnosis (Figure 8.5).

ARPHA is composed by several modules: *System Context Manager, Autonomy BB Manager, Observation Generator, JT Handler, State Detector, Policy Evaluator, Event Manager, Logger*. In particular, *JT_Handler* implements the BK inference algorithm (see Chapter 2 and Appendix A) with the goal of providing the posterior probabilities over the variables of

---

[3] An anomaly is a malfunctioning possibly leading to a failure in the near future.

interest to the other components that need them (e.g. *State Detector* and *Policy Evaluator*). The details about the internal architecture of ARPHA are provided in [Portinale and Codetta-Raiteri (2011a)].

In order to perform an empirical evaluation of the approach, ARPHA has been deployed in an evaluation platform composed by a workstation linked to a PC via Ethernet cable. A rover simulator (called ROSEX) has been installed on the workstation. On the PC the TSIM environment (`www.gaisler.com`) has been installed, emulating the on-board computing hardware/OS environment (LEON3/RTEMS) (`www.rtems.org`), and the ARPHA executable. ARPHA will run in parallel to other processes of the on-board software.

## 8.5 Testing ARPHA

We provide now an example of ARPHA execution during a simulated mission; for the sake of brevity, we describe only the initial steps of the mission. Sensors data and plan data that the simulator provides are the following: OD, power generated by each SA, SAA of SA1, SA2, SA3, charge of the battery, temperature of battery, mission elapsed time, action under execution, plan under execution. Figure 8.6.a shows a graphical representation of the plan. In Figure 8.6.b we show the OD profile generated by rover simulator. Figure 8.6.c shows the power generation profile related to the OD profile in Figure 8.6.b.

At the begin of each cycle of the on-board process (Figure 8.5), the current sensor data and plan data are retrieved and converted into current or future observations for specific variables in the on-board model. Such observations are expressed as the probability distribution of the possible variable values. For example, the "wait" action in the plan at time step 3, is converted in the probability distribution $1, 0, 0, 0, 0, 0, 0, 0$ concerning the variable *ActionId* in the same step. The first value of the distribution indicates that the first possible value of the variable (0) has been observed with probability 1. This is due to the fact that *ActionId* represents in the model the current plan action (or recovery action). In particular, the value 0 corresponds to the "wait" action. An example about sensor data is the sensor *pwrsa1* providing the value 17.22273 at time step 3. This value becomes the probability distribution $1, 0$ for the values of the variable *PowGenSA1*. In other words, *PowGenSA1* is observed equal to 0 with probability 1 at the same mission step, in order to represent that SA1 is generating power in that step (the value 1 represents instead the absence of power generation).

**Diagnosis.** At time steps 0, 1, 2, ARPHA detects `normal` state as the result of both diagnosis and prognosis. Figure 8.6.d shows the output of ARPHA at time step 3 (218 Section): lines 01-04 contain the values of the sensors (generated by the rover simulator) and the plan action under execution ($SVF\_action$); lines 06-16 concern the diagnosis. In particular, at lines 07-08, the plan action ($SVF\_action=1=$"wait") performed in the current time step, is converted into the observation $ActionId = 0$; at lines 09-12, the sensor values are mapped into observations of the corresponding variable values: $pwrsa1 = 17.22273$ becomes $PowGenSA1 = 0$ (power generation by SA1 is high), $pwrsa2 = 26.67850$ becomes $PowGenSA2 = 0$ (power generation by SA2 is high), $pwrsa1 = 26.67641$ becomes $PowGenSA3 = 0$ (power generation by SA3 is high), $saa1 = 0.51575$ becomes $AngleSA1 = 0$ (SAA1 is optimal), $saa2 = 0.515750$ becomes $AngleSA2 = 0$ (SAA2 is optimal), $saa3 = 0.515750$ becomes $AngleSA3 = 0$ (SAA3 is optimal), $opticaldepth = 4.50000$ becomes $OpticalDepth = 1$ (OD is not optimal), etc. Given such observations, ARPHA performs the inference of the model at the current time step (line 13), querying the variables $S1\#$, $S2\#$, $S3\#$, $S4\#$ representing the occurrence of the scenarios (lines 14-15). The probability that $S1\# = 1$ (anomaly) or $S1\# = 2$ (failure) is lower than a predefined threshold, so S1 is not detected. The same condition holds for scenarios S2, S3, S4, so the result of diagnosis is `normal` state (line 16).

**Prognosis.** Since Diagnosis has returned `normal` state, Prognosis is activated (lines 17-26). The future actions in the plan become observations for the variable $ActionId$ (lines 18-20); then, the model inference is executed (line 21), still querying the variables $S1$, $S2$, $S3$, $S4$ (lines 22-25), but analyzing the model in the future (next four time steps). At line 22, $Pr(S2 = 2)$ is greater than a given threshold, so ARPHA detects S2 and in particular, the `failed` state (line 26).

**Recovery.** Preventive recovery is activated (lines 27-42) due to Prognosis result, with the aim of evaluating the policies P3 and P4, suitable to deal with S2. At lines 28-30, the actions inside P3 become observations in the next time steps, for the variable $ActionId$. In particular, we observe the "move" action in the future time steps 4 and 5 (line 30). Given such observations, the model is analyzed for 10 time steps in the future (line 31) and EU is computed (line 32). The same procedure is applied to P4 (lines 33-41). The actions inside P4 become evidences for *ActionId* (lines 34-39): the "tilt" action (SA inclination) is observed at time steps 4 and 5, "retract drill" is observed at time steps 6 and 7, "wait" is observed at time steps from 8 to 13. Notice that the number of actions inside a policy is not constant; therefore the duration of a policy depends on the number of actions and the duration of each action. For instance, P3 and P4 generate observations for 2 and 10 time steps in the future, respectively, because of their internal actions. According to all the previously described observations, the model is analyzed in the future, still for the next 10 time steps (line 40) and EU is computed (line 41). P4 provides a better EU, so P4 is suggested by ARPHA for execution (line 42). This is reasonably justified, since the movement in another position (P3) does not guarantee to improve power generation, while the tilting action in P4 is more effective.

In conclusion, ARPHA aims at keeping as much standard as possible the fault analysis phase, by allowing reliability engineers to build their fault models using an intuitive and familiar modelling language such as DFT. By the enrichment of the DBN obtained from the DFT, the modeler is able to address issues that are very important in the context of innovative on-board FDIR: multi-state components with different fault modes, stochastic dependencies among system components, system-environment interactions.

The presented case study has shown the steps of the modelling phase and the innovative capabilities of ARPHA: diagnosis under partial observability of the system and the environment, possibility to perform the prognosis, dealing with recovery policies composed by several actions performed at different times, evaluation of the future effects of recovery policies. Actually, ARPHA is a reasoning-based FDIR system: diagnosis, prognosis and recovery decisions derive from the analysis (inference) of the on-board model, while traditional FDIR is simply based on sensor monitoring for diagnosis, and look-up tables for recovery actions, without any prognostic capability.

The DFT formalism is rather simple, so the design of the DFT model does not require a modeller with particular skills. The DBN enrichment instead, actually requires a modeller with a specific experience in PGM modeling. In particular, the editing of CPTs needs a particular attention, in order to consider any possible situation and avoid cases not compatible with observations. In order to limit this problem, inside VERIFIM, the DFT formalism has been extended to *Extended Dynamic Fault Tree* (EDFT) [Portinale and Codetta-Raiteri (2011b)]. If an automatic translator from EDFT to DBN was developed, the effort to enrich the DBN would be less relevant, because several features may be directly modelled

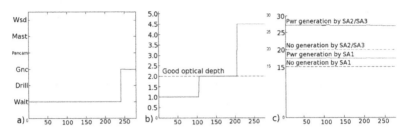

d) ARPHA's output:

```
00   *** MISSION STEP: 3 (MISSION TIME: 218 Section) ***
01   *************** ROSEX VALUES ***************
02   opticaldepht = 4.50000   pwrsa1 = 17.22273   pwrsa2 = 26.67850   pwrsa3 = 26.67641
03   saa1 = 0.51575          saa2 = 0.51575       saa3 = 0.51575       batterycharge = 90.28925
04   batttemp = 273.00000    time = 10.05112      SVF_action = 1       SVF_plan = 1
05   *********************************************
06       ## Diagnosis ##
07   Propagate PLAN STREAM
08   3:ActionId#:1 0 0 0 0 0 0
09   Propagate SENSORS STREAM
10   3:OpticalDepth#:0 1   3:PowGenSA1#:1 0    3:PowGenSA2#:1 0    3:PowGenSA3#:1 0
11   3:AngleSA1#:1 0 0     3:AngleSA2#:1 0 0    3:AngleSA3#:1 0 0   3:BattCharge#:0 0 0 1
12   3:Temp#:0 1 0         3:Time#:1 0
13   Current inference (STEP 3)
14   Pr{S1#=2}=0.000<0.590  Pr{S2#=2}=0.000<0.590  Pr{S3#=2}=0.000<0.590  Pr{S4#=2}=0.000<0.590
15   Pr{S1#=1}=0.000<0.590  Pr{S2#=1}=0.000<0.590  Pr{S3#=1}=0.000<0.590  Pr{S4#=1}=0.000<0.590
16   SYSTEM STATE: "Normal"
17       ## Prognosis ##
18   Propagate PLAN STREAM
19   4:ActionId#:1 0 0 0 0 0 0   5:ActionId#:1 0 0 0 0 0 0
20   6:ActionId#:1 0 0 0 0 0 0   7:ActionId#:0 0 1 0 0 0 0
21   Future inference (STEP 7)
22   Pr{S1#=2}=0.38471501<0.59  Pr{S2#=2}=0.60604805>=0.59          Pr{S3#=2}=0.01966910<0.59
23   Pr{S4#=2}=0.05214530<0.59  Pr{S1#=1} excluded because under recovery or minor criticality
24   Pr{S2#=2} excluded because under recovery or minor criticality   Pr{S3#=1}=0.09944675<0.59
25   Pr{S4#=1}=0.29860398<0.59
26   FUTURE SYSTEM STATE: "Failed" (S2#=2)
27       ## Preventive Recovery ##
28   Policy to convert: P3
29   Propagate POLICY STREAM
30   4:ActionId#:0 0 1 0 0 0 0   5:ActionId#:0 0 1 0 0 0 0
31   Future inference (STEP 13)
32   Utility Function = 0.0890
33   Policy to convert: P4
34   Propagate POLICY STREAM
35   4:ActionId#:0 0 0 0 0 1 0   5:ActionId#:0 0 0 0 0 1 0   6:ActionId#:0 0 0 0 0 0 1
36   7:ActionId#:0 0 0 0 0 0 1
37   8:ActionId#:1 0 0 0 0 0 0   9:ActionId#:1 0 0 0 0 0 0   10:ActionId#:1 0 0 0 0 0 0
38   11:ActionId#:1 0 0 0 0 0 0
39   12:ActionId#:1 0 0 0 0 0 0   13:ActionId#:1 0 0 0 0 0 0
40   Future inference (STEP 13)
41   Utility Function= 0.8764
42   Best policy for Preventive Recovery is P4
```

Fig. 8.6  Scenario S2: a) plan. b) Optical Depth (OD). c) Power generation by SA1, SA2, SA3. d) ARPHA's output at time step (or mission step) 3.

in EDFT form, and translated into DBN in automatic way.

Furthermore, in order to design an accurate stochastic model, knowledge about probability parameters, such as component failure rates, has to be provided. Such values may not be immediately available. Another non negligible aspect is the link between computing time and model accuracy. The complexity of the DBN model depends on the number of entries in the CPTs of variables. This number depends on the number of possible values and the number of parents of the variables. It is then usually necessary to perform a trade-off between the model accuracy and the computation time, taking into account that on-board hardware has limited computing power.

## Chapter 9

# Case Study 3: Security Assessment in Critical Infrastructures

## 9.1 Problem Introduction

We have seen in Chapter 1 that dependability is a composite concept. So far, we have mainly discussed about failure prediction and identification, that is we have essentially focused on reliability, availability, maintainability (when also repair and recovery aspects are taken into account), and indirectly on safety. In this chapter, we present a case study related to another important feature of dependability, named security or the ability of the system to protect itself against accidental or deliberate intrusions.

Security risk assessment and mitigation are important activities that must be performed "intelligently" to safely maintain any productive infrastructure, in particular critical ones like computer systems and networks. The evaluation of the possible attacks and their consequences, as well as of different countermeasure configurations can be really challenging and it may involve a lot of uncertainty; for this reason, quantitative decision making is particularly hard [Sommestad *et al.* (2009)]. The classical approach adopted by security analysts is to predefine a set of attack scenarios based on the knowledge of the systems and networks under protection. Such scenarios are very often described and modeled through different variants of so called "attack graphs" [Scheyner (2004)]. The basic idea is that, since the defended infrastructure may exhibit different penetration points and vulnerabilities, the security analyst identifies a set of intrusion goals and, by evaluating the vulnerabilities of the infrastructure, he/she tries to build attack plans (as if he/she were the attacker). Such plans can be represented as trees or graphs, modeling a goal/subgoal decomposition of the tasks to be performed by the attacker to reach his/her goals. Depending on what is actually modeled, it is possible to define different versions of the basic formalism including Attack Trees (AT) [Schneier (2000)], Attack Graphs [Scheyner (2004)], Attack/Defense Tree (ADT) [Kordy *et al.* (2012)] and Attack Countermeasure Trees (ACT) [Roy *et al.* (2011)]. In this chapter, we show how to exploit *Decision Networks* (DN) (Section 2.2) for the analysis of attack/defense scenarios in critical infrastructures [Codetta-Raiteri *et al.* (2014b,a)]. We show that they can extend modeling situations and patterns as defined by attack graph formalisms. Moreover, analysis can be performed through standard inference on DN, by allowing the analyst to adopt a rational decision making approach, concerning the assessment of specific countermeasures in terms of expected utility or costs. In order to illustrate DN suitability to security risk assessment, a case study attack scenario, concerning the Internet routing protocol BGP, will be considered. The scenario is used for showing how to derive a DN from an AT and how to perform quantitative and decision-theoretic analyses exploiting DN inference algorithms.

## 9.2    Attack Tree Based Formalisms

In order to formally specify the way in which a critical infrastructure can be attacked, specific formalisms to model threats are needed. The characterization of the attacks and the choice of the countermeasures require conceptual approaches and extended analytical tools as described in [Kroeger (2008); Shaw (2012)]. As we have previously mentioned, the security of systems can be analyzed through different formalisms which are variants of a basic version called *Attack Trees* (AT) [Schneier (2000)]. AT are very similar to FT: in an AT, attacks against a system can be represented in a tree structure, with the goal as the root node and different ways of achieving that goal as multi-level hierarchical structures based on logical (i.e. Boolean) AND/OR operators. Leaves on this hierarchy represent basic attacks; these are specific operations an attacker can put in place, in order to pursue his/her ultimate goal, the latter represented by the top node of the AT.

Even if AT constitute a very popular method for security modeling in both in industrial and academic environment, the basic AT formalism has a major limitation, namely it does not include the modeling of defense mechanisms. For this reason, extensions have been proposed to incorporate defense mechanisms or countermeasures. The most prominent extensions are *Attack Defense Tree* (ADT) [Kordy *et al.* (2012)] and *Attack Counter-measure Tree* (ACT) [Roy *et al.* (2011)]. In ACT, each countermeasure is the logical AND of two other constructs, called "detection" and "mitiga-tion" events; in other words, a countermeasure is active when the attack has been both detected and mitigated. An example of an ACT is reported in Figure 9.2. In the following, we will consider the ACT formalism, and we show how to relate it to DN.

## 9.3   Decision Networks for Attack/Defense Scenarios

An attack/defense scenario modeled through ACT techniques is essentially based on the Boolean semantics adopted for combinatorial models; even if it is possible to introduce probabilistic parameters and to compute probabilis-tic indices, a sound decision-theoretic analysis is not directly supported, as well as the modeling of uncertainty at every arbitrary level. For instance, while it is possible to introduce the probability of the occurrence of a (basic) attack or the probability of success of a countermeasure, it is not possible (due to the Boolean nature of the gates) to directly model uncertainty in the "composition" of both attack as well as defense events. This is a well known issue concerning combinatorial models in reliability (e.g., FT) which have a lot in common with ACT.

Consider for example an attack scenario on a storage system with a main disk and a mirror disk: in order to perform a successful attack, an attacker should put out of order both disks; however, there may be uncertainty on the reliability of the switching mechanism from the main disk to the mirror one, resulting in a (possibly) small probability of hav-ing the whole system out of order, even if only the main disk has been knocked-out.

Such a kind of uncertainty can be easily accounted for, by using a DN, resulting in either well-known interactions mechanisms like noisy-AND/OR or in more general probabilistic dependency (see Chapter 2). Further-more, standard inference on DN can be used to compute posterior proba-bility, given a set of observed evidence, for any variable of interest in the scenario. Several interesting indices (as importance measures of attacks) can then be computed. Finally, the determination of the suitable set of defense mechanisms can be naturally formulated as a decision problem, solved through DN inference, with a specific utility/objective function to be optimized.

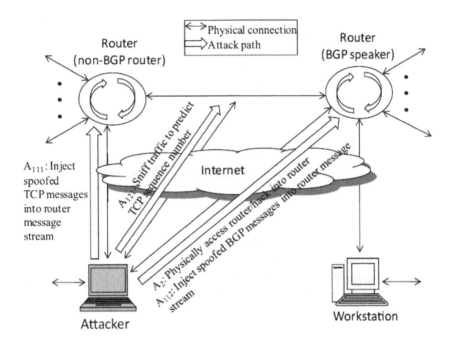

Fig. 9.1    Attack scenario for BGP session reset [Roy *et al.* (2012)].

### 9.3.1    *From Attack Countermeasure Trees to Decision Networks*

#### 9.3.1.1    *Scenario*

Consider the ACT in Figure 9.2 representing a possible attack/defense scenario concerning a BGP session as reported in [Roy *et al.* (2012)] (see Figure 9.1).    BGP (Border Gateway Protocol) is a protocol used to exchange routing information across the Internet. Undesired reset of a BGP session results in a (possibly repeated) temporary loss of Internet connectivity, that in some contexts (especially in critical activities) can produce severe economic damages. An attacker prevents two peers from exchanging routing information by repeatedly causing a BGP session in "Established" state to reset. The BGP session can be reset by injecting a spoofed TCP (Transmission Control Protocol) or BGP message into the router message stream. Such spoofed packets can often be detected by methods such as the Inter-Domain Packet Filter (IDPF) and mitigated by adding an MD5-

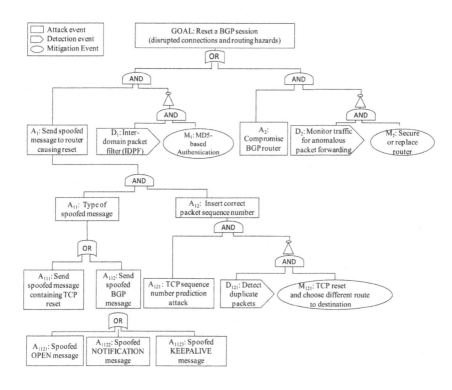

Fig. 9.2 ACT for BGP attack/defense scenario [Roy *et al.* (2012)].

based authentication (Message-Digest 5 algorithm) for packets from the source host of the spoofed packet. Building a valid TCP/BGP packet requires a valid TCP sequence number (obtained by TCP sequence number prediction). During the initial stages of a TCP sequence number attack, a spoofed packet from an attacker is usually followed by the original packet from the authentic source. Detecting such duplicate packets can be a giveaway for on-going TCP sequence number attacks. Dropping compromised connections and initiating a new connection to destination with a different route will mitigate such attacks. Spoofed TCP message with RST (reset) flag set will cause a connection to reset. Spoofed BGP messages (OPEN, NOTIFICATION or KEEPALIVE messages) received by the BGP speaker in the "Connect" or "Active" states will cause the router to reset, resulting in a denial of service. The BGP speaker can also be compromised by gaining physical or logical (hijacking a router management session) access to the router. Usually router hijacking is characterized by anomalous packet

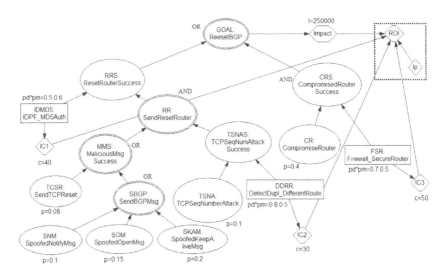

Fig. 9.3  DN for the BGP scenario. The area inside the dashed line contains the nodes necessary for ROI optimization.

forwarding, which can be detected by traffic monitoring at the router and mitigated by securing or replacing the router.

### 9.3.1.2  *Attack Countermeasure Tree*

The ACT of Figure 9.2 formalizes such a scenario and is completed by some quantitative information concerning: the *probability of occurrence of each atomic attack* (attack leaf node), the *probability of a successful detection* (detection nodes), the *probability of a successful mitigation* (mitigation nodes), the *security investment cost of countermeasures* (both detections and mitigations), the *impact or cost of each atomic attack* (from the defender point of view, representing the economic damage provided by the attack). The above quantities are then used to analyze the scenario and to compute:

(1)  the probability of occurrence of the goal;
(2)  the global impact/cost of the goal;
(3)  indices of risk given a set of attacks and/or countermeasures;
(4)  indices of importance (i.e. relevance with respect to the goal) of specific attack events.

In the following we will consider, without lack of generality, only the

Table 9.1 Modeling countermeasure success.

| TSNA | true | | false | |
|---|---|---|---|---|
| **DDRR** | inactive | active | inactive | active |
| **TSNAS=true** | 1 | 0.6 | 0 | 0 |
| **TSNAS=false** | 0 | 0.4 | 1 | 1 |

Table 9.2 Adding uncertainty to GOAL in BGP scenario.

| RRS | true | | false | |
|---|---|---|---|---|
| **CRS** | true | false | true | false |
| **GOAL=true** | 1 | 0.9802 | 1 | 0.01 |
| **GOAL=false** | 0 | 0.0198 | 0 | 0.99 |

defender point of view (dual considerations can be done when considering the attacker point of view).

### 9.3.1.3 *Decision Network generation*

A DN can be constructed either from the ACT of Figure 9.2 or directly from the specification of the BGP scenario. In the first case, we can proceed as follows:

- for each atomic attack node $A_i$ with probability of occurrence $p_{A_i}$, create a binary chance node $X_{A_i}$ with values true (occurrence of attack) and false; set the CPT of $X_{A_i}$ such that $P[X_{A_i} = true] = p_{A_i}$;
- for each countermeasure (i.e. a pair $CM = \langle D, M \rangle$ with $D$ detection event and $M$ mitigation event), create a binary decision node $X_{CM}$ with values active (attack detected and mitigated) and inactive;
- for each attack event $A$ output of a gate $G$ (representing the Boolean function $g$) with inputs attack events $A_1, \ldots A_k$, create a binary deterministic node $X_E$ (double-boarded oval in the figure), set $X_{A_1} \ldots X_{A_k}$ as parent of $X_E$ and set the deterministic function of $X_E$ according to $g$;
- for each attack event $A$ output of a gate $G$ (Boolean function $g$) with inputs attack events $A_1, \ldots A_k$ and input countermeasure $CM = \langle D, M \rangle$ (with probability of detection $p_D$ and probability of mitigation $p_M$), create a binary chance node $X_E$, set $X_{A_1} \ldots X_{A_k}, X_{CM}$ as parent of $X_E$ and set the CPT for $X_E =$ true in the following way:
  - entries corresponding to $X_{CM} =$ inactive are set according to the truth value of $g(X_{A_1}, \ldots X_{A_k})$ i.e. either 1 when true or 0 when false;
  - entries corresponding to $X_{CM} =$ active are set as $g(X_{A_1}, \ldots X_{A_k})\ (1 - p_D\ p_M)$.

Concerning the last point, if the coutermeasure in inactive, then the state
of $A$ will be set by the logical function of its input events; on the contrary,
if the countermeasure is active, then the behavior of the corresponding
logical function will be modified in such a way that, if the inputs "predict"
the **true** state of $A$, then such a state will be set only with probability
$(1 - p_D p_M)$, i.e., the probability that countermeasure has no effect.

#### 9.3.1.4   *Decision Network model*

The DN corresponding to the ACT of Figure 9.2 is reported in Figure 9.3,
where also some value/utility nodes (diamonds) are added to the DN as
we will explain in the following. Model construction and inference, i.e,
probabilistic and decision-theoretic computations as reported hereinafter,
refer to the GENIE tool [Druzdzel (1999); Druzdel (2005)]; probability of
attacks are annotated near chance nodes representing basic attacks, while
probability of success of countermeasures (separated as probability of attack
detection and attack mitigation) are near decision nodes. Deterministic
variable nodes have the corresponding Boolean function reported by the
node itself. As an example, Table 9.1 reports the CPT for Node $TSNAS$
given the parents $TSNA$ and $DDRR$. Given that countermeasure $DDRR$
is composed by the detection event **Detect Duplicate Packets** and by
the mitigation event **TCP reset and different route to destination**
(Figure 9.2), with probability of detection $p_D = 0.8$ and probability of
mitigation $p_M = 0.5$ respectively, the probability of countermeasure success
is $p_{DDRR} = 0.8 \cdot 0.5 = 0.4$; thus, when the attack occurs ($TSNA = $ **true**), if
the countermeasure is activated ($DDRR = $ **active**) there is a 60% chance
of having the attack unmitigated and successful (as the CPT in Table 9.1
reports).

The above procedure does not create any value or utility node in the
DN; the reason is that, the structure created with this method represents
a main skeleton over which more features can be added or modified, ac-
cordingly to the analysis goals, as well as to more specific modeling issues.
For example, as we mentioned before, in case of "noisy gates" (which are
not representable in the ACT), we can adapt the corresponding CPT to account for this additional uncertainty. For example, consider the attacker's
goal of the BGP scenario (BGP session reset): it may be the case that
sending a spoofed reset message to the router is not always a guarantee,
for the attacker, of having the BGP session reset, because there is a small
percentage of cases in which the spoofed message does not actually reach

the router; a noisy-OR interaction model can then be adopted to this end, to reflect such possibility.

### 9.3.1.5 *Example*

Consider the case where there is a 2% probability that a spoofed malicious message does not reach the router; in addition, suppose we want to model additional uncertainty, by introducing also a small chance (e.g. 1% probability) of the router being reset for some unmodeled causes in the attack/defense scenario. In such a case the type of node *ResetBGP* can be changed from deterministic to a noisy-OR chance node with leak (see Chapter 1, Section 2.1.2); the noisy-OR parameters are then

$p_1 = Pr\{Goal = \texttt{true}|RRS = \texttt{true}, CRS = \texttt{false}\} = 0.98$
$p_2 = Pr\{Goal = \texttt{true}|CRS = \texttt{true}, RRS = \texttt{false}\} = 1$
$p_{leak} = Pr\{Goal = \texttt{true}|RRS = \texttt{false}, CRS = \texttt{false}\} = 0.01$

and the resulting CPT is shown in Table 9.2. Of course, in case of more sophisticated dependencies violating the noisy-OR assumptions, a complete CPT similar to the one in Table 9.2 can be manually provided.

### 9.3.2 *Quantitative analysis*

#### 9.3.2.1 *Probability of attacker's goal success*

This corresponds to the computation of the probability that an attacker will actually pursue the goal, given some initial specification in terms of probability of basic attacks and of presence of countermeasures. This is a probabilistic inference task that can be performed on the DN through a standard posterior probability computation $P[Goal|Evidence]$, where *Evidence* is a state assignment to decision nodes representing countermeasures.

#### 9.3.2.2 *Example*

In the BGP scenario modeled by the DN of Figure 9.3, we can compute the probability of a successful attack given that we implemented only the IDPF detection with MD5 authentication (i.e. evidence inserted as $IDMD5 = \texttt{active}$ and other countermeasures set to $\texttt{inactive}$), by performing the query
  $Pr\{Goal|IDMD5 = \texttt{active}, DDRR = \texttt{inactive}, FSR = \texttt{inactive}\} = 0.418;$

this results in more than 40% probability of being vulnerable to the attack. We can notice that, given that countermeasure are not 100% effective, the attacker can reach his/her goal (with about 27% of probability) even in presence of all the possible countermeasures, since

$P\{Goal|IDMD5 = \texttt{active}, DDRR = \texttt{active}, FSR = \texttt{active}\} = 0.274.$

### 9.3.2.3  *Importance measures of attack events*

Such quantities can be defined in different ways and are usually identified with the aim of prioritizing defense mechanisms (i.e. countermeasures) to counteract attack events. There are two main importance measures that can be adapted from reliability theory: *Birnbaum Importance (BI)* and *Fussell-Vesely Importance (FVI)*. In reliability theory, both indices are defined with respect to a specific component of a system[1], while in attack/defense scenarios they can be associated with attack events. BI measures the change in the probability of the attacker's goal caused by a change in the probability of the attack of interest; this means that

$BI(A_i) = Pr\{[Goal = \texttt{true}|A_i = \texttt{true}\} - Pr\{Goal = \texttt{true}|A_i = \texttt{false}\}.$

The BI measure of every attack can then be easily computed through a posterior probability inference on the DN. The same holds for FVI, since, given an attack $A_i$ we have that

$FVI(A_i) = Pr\{A_i = \texttt{true}|Goal = \texttt{true}\}.$

### 9.3.2.4  *Example*

Consider again the DN in Figure 9.3. Figure 9.4 and 9.5 show the importance measures BI and FVI respectively, under different set of countermeasures of the six basic attacks of the modeled BGP scenario. We noticed that both indices point out that compromising the router (attack $CR$) is the most important attack. This is due to the fact that unmitigating the attack will definitely cause the occurrence of the goal; moreover, BI measure puts in evidence (more than FVI) the fact that such an attack is more important in case it is not defended by the suitable countermeasure.

---

[1] As we have already reported, BI of component $c$ is the change in the system unavailability given that $c$ goes down, while FVI of $c$ is the probability of $c$ down, given that the system failure has occurred [Langseth and Portinale (2007); Meng (2000); Borgonovo (2007)]

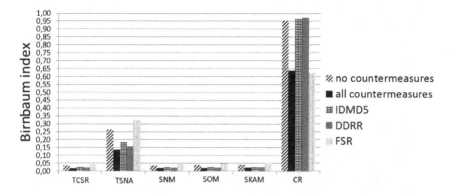

Fig. 9.4    BI measure of basic attacks.

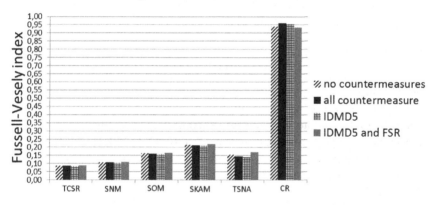

Fig. 9.5    FVI measure of basic attacks.

### 9.3.2.5    *Risk and Impact Computation*

This corresponds to compute the expected impact of a particular attack/defense scenario. Since the impact $I_{Goal}$ is measured as the amount of damage provided by the success of the attacker's goal, the risk is defined as $R = p_{Goal}I_{Goal}$ (being $p_{Goal}$ the probability of success of the goal [Roy *et al.* (2011)]). As for the probability of success of the goal, the risk is computed relatively to a particular context, usually a specific set of active countermeasures. In the DN framework, the risk can be computed through belief propagation, by adding a value node to the goal node and setting the active and inactive countermeasures as evidence to decision nodes (see *Impact* node in Figure 9.3). The value function on the *Impact* node can

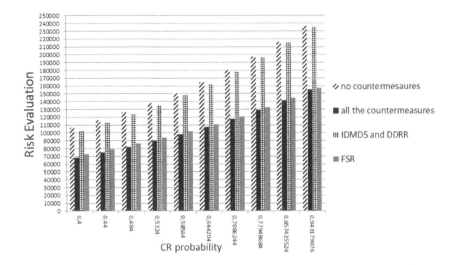

Fig. 9.6    Risk evaluation w.r.t. probability of $CR$ attack.

be determined either by a direct estimation of the damage of a successful attack (occurrence of the goal) or by exploiting some heuristic approach synthesizing the impact on the goal, starting from local impact estimation of each basic attack's impact (see [Roy *et al.* (2011)] for an example). Since the goal's impact represents a damage (i.e. a cost) to the system under defense, a negative utility can be used in the corresponding value node.

### 9.3.2.6 *Example*

Figure 9.6 reports the risk value (expected impact) of the scenario with respect to different set of active countermeasures, by varying the probability of $CR$ attack (the most important one as noticed before) from the initial value 0.4 to about 0.94, with a step increment of 10% of the previous value. The goal impact value is computed as $I_{Goal} = 250000$ using the procedure in [Roy *et al.* (2011)]. We confirm also from risk evaluation that activating countermeasures not related to a router hijacking attack is not useful at reducing the global risk of the scenario, while the presence of an active firewall and of an alternative routing strategy can provide a risk reduction.

### 9.3.2.7 *Investment*

When measuring the impact deriving from a set of countermeasures, the investment cost in setting up such defense mechanisms should be taken into

Table 9.3   Expected Cost Computation.

| IDMD5 | DDRR | FSR | Expected Cost |
|---|---|---|---|
| inactive | inactive | inactive | 106554 |
| inactive | inactive | active | 73133.8 |
| inactive | active | inactive | 103963 |
| inactive | active | active | 69930.3 |
| active | inactive | inactive | 104628 |
| active | inactive | active | 70748.6 |
| active | active | inactive | 102823 |
| active | active | active | 68515.2 |

Table 9.4   Best set of countermeasures for BGP scenario.

| Obs. Att. | IDMD5 | DDRR | FSR | Exp. Cost |
|---|---|---|---|---|
| None | ✓ | ✓ | ✓ | 68515.179 |
| CR=false | ✓ | ✓ | | 4658.08 |
| CR=true | ✓ | ✓ | ✓ | 164225.83 |
| TSNA=true | ✓ | ✓ | ✓ | 99071.792 |
| TSNA=false | | | ✓ | 65050 |
| TCSR=true | ✓ | ✓ | ✓ | 72890 |
| TCSR=false | ✓ | ✓ | ✓ | 68134.76 |

account as well. In order to consider also investment costs, value nodes corresponding to such costs (i.e. with negative utility values) can be added in the DN to decision nodes (see value nodes $IC1, IC2, IC3$ in Figure 9.3). Total expected cost can then be computed by considering a cost function which is the sum of value nodes (countermeasure cost nodes, as well as goal impact node).

### 9.3.2.8   *Example*

Considering a cost of $40, 30$ and $50$ units for activating countermeasures $IDMD5, DDRR$ and $FSR$ respectively, and a goal impact $I_{goal} = 250,000$ units as before, Table 9.3 reports the total expected cost for the sets of possible activation of countermeasures.

### 9.3.2.9   *Best set of countermeasures*

The definition of a suitable cost function is also the basis to define the following decision problem: *given a (possibly empty) set of observed attacks, what is the best (in terms of minimal expected cost) set of countermeasures to activate?* The solution to such a problem can then be obtained by solving the DN for the optimal set of decisions with respect to the objective function determined by the value nodes (i.e., by computing the optimal strategy for the DN, as discussed in Chapter 1).

**Example.** Table 9.4 reports the results of the computation (on DN of Figure 9.3 without considering the dashed area) of the best set of counter-measure to activate, depending on some possible observed attacks in the BGP scenario concerning nodes $CR, TSNA$ and $TCSR$. We can notice again that having countermeasure $FSR$ inactive is a good option (the best one), only when we are sure that the $CR$ attack has not occurred.

### 9.3.2.10  *Influence Diagrams vs LIMIDs*

As we have discussed in Chapter 1, solving the DN requires to make assumptions about the order of decisions; if we impose a sequence order to the countermeasures (regularity assumption), then the DN is an *Influence Diagram* (ID). However, since decisions corresponding to countermeasures do not depend on other variables and there is usually no domain constraint on the order on which to consider them, any arbitrary sequence ordering can be used to solve the DN using an ID-based algorithm. Of course, if some order constraints are imposed at the domain level, they can be captured by imposing such an order in the model. Alternatively, we could consider the DN not obeying the regularity assumption; in such a case the model is a LIMID, and it can be solved, with no explicit order of countermeasures, using either single policy updating (SPU) to get an approximate solution or variable elimination for an exact solution [Maua *et al.* (2012)].

### 9.3.2.11  *ROI*

Finally, as in the case of decision-theoretic dependability discussed in Chapter 5, an interesting aspect related to the selection of the best countermeasures concerns the called *Return on Investment* (ROI) index [Roy *et al.* (2011)]. We already know that it represents the percentage of investment gain with respect to the investment cost, and it is defined by comparing a status-quo situation (in this framework a set of countermeasures $CM_{i-1}$) and a target one (in this framework another set of countermeasures $CM_i$), differing from the status-quo in terms of a set of investments . By denoting with $R_i$ the risk associated with set $CM_i$ and by $C_i$ the cost of implementing countermeasure set $CM_i$ from $CM_{i-1}$, then the ROI index can be defined as:

$$ROI(i) = \frac{R_{i-1} - R_i - C_i}{C_i} \tag{9.1}$$

### 9.3.2.12 *Example*

Consider the situation corresponding to the first row of Table 9.3 ($CM_0$: "no countermeasure active") corresponding to a risk (expected cost) of 106554; in case we do not have any evidence about attacks, solving the DN suggests that the best (in terms of expected cost) decision is $CM_1$: "activate all the countermeasures", corresponding to a risk of 68395.18 (first row of Table 9.4). Since implementing $CM_1$ has an investment cost $C_1 = 120$ we compute the ROI as

$$\frac{R_0 - R_1 - C_1}{C_1} = \frac{106554 - 68515.79 - 120}{120} = 316.99$$

meaning that for each unit of investment, we get back about 317 units. However, as also noticed in Chapter 5, optimizing the set of countermeasures with respect to ROI is in general different that optimizing them with respect to risk. This can be shown here by computing the best set of countermeasures, in terms of ROI, directly on the DN; what we have to do is to add to the DN of our example the dashed part in Figure 9.3, and to solve the model. Value node $Ip$ represents the expected cost computed at the previous step (i.e. the risk of the defense situation $CM_{i-1}$, against which we are currently evaluating the ROI of a new defense situation $CM_i$); value node $ROI$ contains ROI index definition (i.e., Equation 9.1) and becomes the objective function for the decision problem. If we consider again situation $CM_0$ with no evidence about attacks, and we solve the model optimizing the ROI, we get that the best decision is to activate only $FSR$, resulting in a $ROI = 668.4$ (that is greater than the ROI of $CM_1$ above), but in a risk of 73083.8 (which is also greater than the risk of $CM_1$ above).

In conclusion, the present case study suitably supports the idea of DN as a reference model for the analysis of attack/defense scenarios in critical infrastructures (such as those represented by the BGP case study itself). The advantages can be considered from both the modeling and the analysis point of view; uncertainty at every level of the scenario can be captured, probabilistic indices can be computed through standard inference, and a decision theoretic approach can be exploited to select the best set of countermeasures to activate.

Chapter 10

# Case Study 4: Dynamic Reliability

## 10.1 Problem Introduction

Dynamic reliability is a concept adopted when the reliability parameters of the system change according to the current configuration or state of the system [Marseguerra and Zio (1996)]. For example, the failure rate of a pump may be expressed as a function of the liquid's temperature. In dynamic reliability, we actually have to consider the whole system behavior. This means modeling the normal functioning of the system, the occurrence of component failure events and their effect on the system functioning. The use of combinatorial models such as Fault Trees and Reliability Block Diagrams is not enough to deal with cases of dynamic reliability, because such kinds of model can only represent combinations of independent failure events. Their extensions such as Dynamic Fault Trees (DFT) and Dynamic Reliability Block Diagrams (DRBD) [Distefano and Puliafito (2009)] introduce the possibility to represent dependencies among the failure events, but they still only focus on the failure propagation, ignoring the other aspects of the system behavior. Of course, the complete system behaviour can be represented by means of state space based models, such as Markov Chains or Petri Nets, since they rely on the specification of the whole set of the possible system states, so that the stochastic behavior of each component may depend on the state of all the other components. However, we already know that their use may determine a state space explosion, making the model analysis impractical because of the high computational cost. If so, Petri Nets can undergo simulation, with a consequent approximation of the results with respect to the model analysis.

In such situations, PGMs can then be considered as a valuable alternative. In this chapter, we present a case study on dynamic reliability

Table 10.1  The effect on H in each state configuration. The symbols =, ↓, ↑, ↑↑ mean steady, decreasing by 0.6 *m/h*, increasing by 0.6 *m/h*, and increasing by 1.2 *m/h*, respectively.

| Conf. | P1 | P2 | V | effect | Conf. | P1 | P2 | V | effect |
|-------|-----|-----|-----|--------|-------|-----|-----|-----|--------|
| 1 | OFF | OFF | OFF | = | 5 | ON | OFF | OFF | ↑ |
| 2 | OFF | OFF | ON | ↓ | 6 | ON | OFF | ON | = |
| 3 | OFF | ON | OFF | ↑ | 7 | ON | ON | OFF | ↑↑ |
| 4 | OFF | ON | ON | = | 8 | ON | ON | ON | ↑ |

based on the exploitation of DBN formalism and of the RADYBAN tool (a more detailed discussion can also be found in [Codetta-Raiteri and Portinale (2014)]). In particular, we consider a specific benchmark taken from the literature [Marseguerra and Zio (1996)] and described in the following in Section 10.2. In the past, such a benchmark was evaluated by means of Monte Carlo simulation and Petri Nets. In Section 10.4, the system is modeled as a DBN by means of RADYBAN, with the purpose of computing both the system unreliability (the original goal of the benchmark [Marseguerra and Zio (1996)]), and diagnostic indices, which are an additional and very interesting possibility offered by DBN modeling.

## 10.2   The Benchmark

### 10.2.1   *Version 1: basic system*

The system (Figure 10.1.a) is composed by a tank, two pumps (P1 and P2) to inject liquid, one valve (V) to remove liquid, and the controller (C) monitoring the liquid level (H). The state of P1, P2, V can be ON, OFF, Stuck ON (S_ON), or Stuck OFF (S_OFF). Initially H is 0, with P1 and V in state ON, and P2 in state OFF; since P1, P2 and V have the same level variation rate (Q=0.6 *meter/hour* (*m/h*)), H does not change while the initial configuration holds. A variation of H is caused by a component failure during the ON or OFF state. The failure probability obeys the negative exponential distribution ruled by the failure rate $\lambda$, which is the inverse of the mean time to failure. The values of $\lambda$ for P1, P2 and V are 0.004566 $h^{-1}$, 0.005714 $h^{-1}$ and 0.003124 $h^{-1}$, respectively. The effect of the failure is the stuck condition, while the state transitions toward S_ON and S_OFF, are uniformly distributed (Figure 10.1.b).

Table 10.1 shows how H changes with respect to the current states of components; C believes that the system is correctly functioning while H is inside the region between the levels denoted by HLA (-1 *m*) and HLB

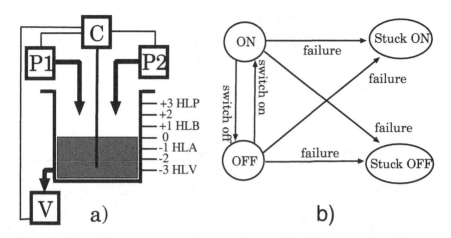

Fig. 10.1   The system scheme (a) and the possible states of P1, P2 and V (b) in Versions 1, 2, 3.

Table 10.2   State dependent failure rates for each component, in Version 2. The values of $\lambda$ are reported in Section 10.2.

| Comp. | from | to | rate | Comp. | from | to | rate |
|---|---|---|---|---|---|---|---|
| P1 | OFF | S_OFF | 100$\lambda$ | P2 | ON | S_ON | 10$\lambda$ |
| P1 | OFF | S_ON | 10$\lambda$ | V | OFF | S_OFF | 100$\lambda$ |
| P1 | ON | S_ON or S_OFF | $\lambda$ | V | OFF | S_ON | 10$\lambda$ |
| P2 | OFF | S_ON or S_OFF | $\lambda$ | V | ON | S_ON or S_OFF | $\lambda$ |
| P2 | ON | S_OFF | 100$\lambda$ | | | | |

(+1 $m$) shown in Figure 10.1.a. If H reaches HLA, then C orders P1 and P2 to switch on, and V to switch off (**order n. 1**), with the aim of increasing H and avoiding the dry out; this event occurs when H reaches the level denoted as HLV (-3 $m$). If a component is stuck, it does not obey the order and maintains its state. The other undesired situation is the overflow; this happens when H reaches HLP (+3 $m$). If H becomes equal to HLB, C orders P1 and P2 to switch off, and V to switch on (**order n. 2**), with the aim of increasing H and avoiding the overflow.

## 10.2.2   *Version 2: state dependent failure rates*

The failure rate of a component changes according to both its current state and the state reached as a consequence of the failure, as shown in Table 10.2.

### 10.2.3   *Version 3: controller failure on demand*

C has a 0.1 probability of failure on demand. This means that each
time H reaches HLA or HLB, C may generate no commands, with 0.1
probability.

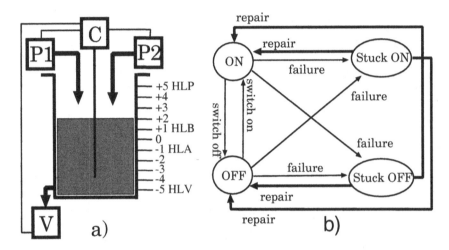

Fig. 10.2   The system scheme (a) and the possible states of P1, P2 and V (b) in
Version 4.

### 10.2.4   *Version 4: repairable components*

Failed (stuck) components can be repaired during the grace period which
begins when H goes outside the region of correct functioning for the first
time, and ends when the system failure (dry out or overflow) occurs. The
time to repair a component is a random variable obeying the negative exponential distribution ruled by the repair rate $\mu$=0.2 $h^{-1}$ which is the
inverse of the mean time to repair (5 $h$). The effect of the repair consists of removing the stuck condition of the component and setting its
state to ON or OFF (Figure 10.2.b) according to the current H. The repaired component can respond to future orders, but it may fail and undergo repair again. HLV and HLP are set to -5 $m$ and +5 $m$ respectively
(Figure 10.2.a).

## 10.3 Related Work

The benchmark is specified in [Marseguerra and Zio (1996)] where the unreliability of the system is first evaluated in analytical way by computing the probabilities of the *minimal cut sets* (MCS) (Section 1.2.1.2) which are the minimal combinations of component failure events leading to the system failure (dry out or overflow). Then, the system unreliability is evaluated by means of the Monte Carlo simulation of the complete behaviour of the system. The relevant difference between the unreliability values returned by the two techniques puts in evidence the necessity to consider the complete system behavior in order to evaluate the system in an accurate way.

In [Codetta-Raiteri and Bobbio (2005)] the benchmark has been modeled as a GSPN (Section 1.3.2). The GSPN model can undergo analysis, but this requires the liquid level in the tank to be discretized into several intermediate integer levels, because only discrete variables can be represented as the number of tokens (marking) inside places. The number of intermediate levels has to be low, otherwise the state space dimensions may explode. Moreover, some deterministic timed events such as the action of the pumps on the liquid level, have to be approximated to stochastic events, in order to allow the model analysis. So, despite of the advantages given by the model analysis instead of simulation, the GSPN model suffers from some approximation about the liquid level and its variations during the time. The GSPN analysis is actually performed on the CTMC (Section 1.3.1) generated from the reachability graph of the GSPN.

Still in [Codetta-Raiteri and Bobbio (2005)], the benchmark is modeled and simulated as a *Fluid Stochastic Petri Net* (FSPN) [Gribaudo *et al.* (2001)], a particular form of Petri Net including fluid places containing a continuous amount of fluid instead of a discrete number of tokens. Fluid places directly represent continuous variables describing the current state of the system, such as the liquid level in the tank. In [Codetta-Raiteri (2011)] *Stochastic Activity Networks* (SAN) [Sanders and Meyer (2001)] have been applied in order to model the benchmark. SAN extend Petri Nets introducing input or output gates able to express complex conditions and effects about the firing of transitions, compacting the model as a consequence. Moreover, SAN can represent float variables by means of extended places and include both deterministic and stochastic transitions. The simulation of the SAN models returned unreliability values coherent with those obtained by FSPN simulation, GSPN analysis and Monte Carlo simulation. However, none of the Petri Net based approaches applied in the past, gives

Table 10.3    The CPT of $P1\#$ (or $P2\#$) in Versions 1 and 3. The value of $\lambda$ is reported in Section 10.2. $\Delta$ is set to 0.8333 $h$.

| n. | P1 | com.# | **P1#** | prob. | n. | P1 | com.# | **P1#** | prob. |
|----|----|-------|---------|-------|----|----|-------|---------|-------|
| | 0 | 0 | 0 | 0 | | 2 | 0 | 0 | 0 |
| 1 | 0 | 0 | 1 | $1-(1-e^{-\lambda\Delta})$ | 7 | 2 | 0 | 1 | 0 |
| | 0 | 0 | 2 | $(1-e^{-\lambda\Delta})/2$ | | 2 | 0 | 2 | 1 |
| | 0 | 0 | 3 | $(1-e^{-\lambda\Delta})/2$ | | 2 | 0 | 3 | 0 |
| | 0 | 1 | 0 | $1-(1-e^{-\lambda\Delta})$ | | 2 | 1 | 0 | 0 |
| 2 | 0 | 1 | 1 | 0 | 8 | 2 | 1 | 1 | 0 |
| | 0 | 1 | 2 | $(1-e^{-\lambda\Delta})/2$ | | 2 | 1 | 2 | 1 |
| | 0 | 1 | 3 | $(1-e^{-\lambda\Delta})/2$ | | 2 | 1 | 3 | 0 |
| | 0 | 2 | 0 | $1-(1-e^{-\lambda\Delta})$ | | 2 | 2 | 0 | 0 |
| 3 | 0 | 2 | 1 | 0 | 9 | 2 | 2 | 1 | 0 |
| | 0 | 2 | 2 | $(1-e^{-\lambda\Delta})/2$ | | 2 | 2 | 2 | 1 |
| | 0 | 2 | 3 | $(1-e^{-\lambda\Delta})/2$ | | 2 | 2 | 3 | 0 |
| | 1 | 0 | 0 | 0 | | 3 | 0 | 0 | 0 |
| 4 | 1 | 0 | 1 | $1-(1-e^{-\lambda\Delta})$ | 10 | 3 | 0 | 1 | 0 |
| | 1 | 0 | 2 | $(1-e^{-\lambda\Delta})/2$ | | 3 | 0 | 2 | 0 |
| | 1 | 0 | 3 | $(1-e^{-\lambda\Delta})/2$ | | 3 | 0 | 3 | 1 |
| | 1 | 1 | 0 | 0 | | 3 | 1 | 0 | 0 |
| 5 | 1 | 1 | 1 | $1-(1-e^{-\lambda\Delta})$ | 11 | 3 | 1 | 1 | 0 |
| | 1 | 1 | 2 | $(1-e^{-\lambda\Delta})/2$ | | 3 | 1 | 2 | 0 |
| | 1 | 1 | 3 | $(1-e^{-\lambda\Delta})/2$ | | 3 | 1 | 3 | 1 |
| | 1 | 2 | 0 | $1-(1-e^{-\lambda\Delta})$ | | 3 | 2 | 0 | 0 |
| 6 | 1 | 2 | 1 | 0 | 12 | 3 | 2 | 1 | 0 |
| | 1 | 2 | 2 | $(1-e^{-\lambda\Delta})/2$ | | 3 | 2 | 2 | 0 |
| | 1 | 2 | 3 | $(1-e^{-\lambda\Delta})/2$ | | 3 | 2 | 3 | 1 |

the possibility to compute probability measures conditioned by the observation of specific variables. This is an added value given by DBN.

## 10.4   DBN Models of the Benchmark

### 10.4.1   *Modelling Version 1*

The DBN model of Version 1 designed by means of RADyBaN, is shown in Figure 10.3. The variables characterized by a temporal evolution have two instances, one for each time slice, connected by a temporal arc graphically appearing as a thick line. For instance, $P1$ and $P1\#$ are present at $t$ and $t + \Delta$ respectively, and are connected by the arc $(P1, P1\#)$. This means that P1 may change its state during the interval $\Delta$ between two consecutive time steps.

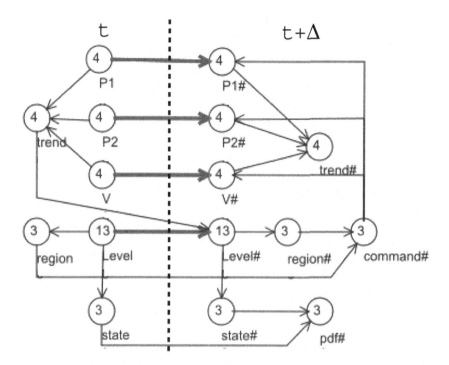

Fig. 10.3 The graph of the DBN model (in canonical form) of Versions 1, 2, 3. The numbers inside the nodes indicate the size (quantity of possible values) of the variables. The symbol # completes the names of the variables in the time slice $t + \Delta$. Temporal arcs are shown as bold lines.

### 10.4.1.1 *State of components*

The value of $P1$ and $P1\#$ can be 0, 1, 2, or 3, in order to represent OFF, ON, S_OFF, S_ON, respectively. $P1$ at $t$ does not depend on any other variable ($P1$ is a root node). Therefore its CPT simply provides its initial probability distribution. In particular, the value 1 has probability 1 in order to express that the initial state of P1 is ON. $P1\#$ at $t + \Delta$ depends on $P1$ and *command#* because the current state depends on the state in the previous time step, and on the command currently provided by C. *command#* is ternary: the values 0 and 2 corresponds to the orders n. 1 and 2 respectively (Section 10.2), while 1 represents the absence of orders. The CPT of $P1\#$ (Table 10.3) contains the probability distribution of $P1\#$ given all the possible combinations of $P1$ and *command#*. Let us consider the entries of this CPT:

- the **entry n. 1** is the case where $P1 = 0$ and $command\# = 0$; this means that P1 was OFF in the previous time step and C orders the pumps to switch on in the current time. So, the probability that $P1\# = 0$ (P1 is currently OFF) is null because P1 executes the order. The probability that $P1\# = 1$ (P1 is currently ON) is the probability that P1 does not fail (*reliability* of P1) during the transition between $t$ and $t+\Delta$, according to the negative exponential distribution, $\lambda$ (Section 10.2) and $\Delta$ (its value will be specified in the following). The probability that $P1\# = 2$ (P1 is currently S_OFF) is half of the probability of failure, because the probability to turn S_ON or S_OFF after the failure, is uniformly distributed (Section 10.2). The probability that $P1\# = 3$ (P1 is currently S_ON) is computed in the same way. The sum of the probabilities in each entry has to be 1.

- The **entry n. 2** is the case where P1 was OFF and C provides no order. Therefore $Pr\{P1\# = 1\}$ is null, while $Pr\{P1\# = 0\}$ is the reliability of P1 during $\Delta$. $Pr\{P1\# = 2\}$ and $Pr\{P1\# = 3\}$ are computed in the same way as in the entry n. 1 and the following ones, up to entry n. 6.

- In the **entry n. 3** P1 was OFF and C orders the pumps to switch off. So, $Pr\{P1\# = 0\}$ is the reliability of P1, while $Pr\{P1\# = 1\}$ is null because of the order from C.

- In the **entry n. 4**, P1 was ON and the command is to turn ON. Therefore $Pr\{P1\# = 0\}$ is null, while $Pr\{P1\# = 1\}$ is reliability of P1.

- In the **entry n. 5**, P1 was ON and no commands are provided, so the same probability distribution as in the entry n. 4, holds.

- The **entry n. 6** is the case where P1 was ON and C orders the pumps to switch off. Therefore $Pr\{P1\# = 0\}$ is the component reliability, while $Pr\{P1\# = 1\}$ is equal to 0.

- In the **entries n. 7, 8, 9**, P1 was in the S_OFF state ($P1 = 2$) in the previous time step. Since P1 is not repairable, P1 maintains such state in the current time step, ignoring any command from C. Therefore $Pr\{P1\# = 2\}$ is equal to 1 in all the entries.

- In the **entries n. 10, 11, 12**, P1 was S_ON ($P1 = 3$), so $Pr\{P1\# = 3\}$ is equal to 1.

The states of P2 are modelled in the same way by $P2\#$ depending on P2 and $command\#$. The CPT of $P2\#$ has the same entries of the CPT of $P1\#$ because P2 has the same failure mode and the same behaviour of P1 with respect to the orders sent by C. The states of V are represented by $V\#$ influenced by V and $command\#$. The CPT of $V\#$ takes into account the opposite reactions of V to the orders (Section 10.2).

Table 10.4    The values of *Level* and the corresponding intermediate liquid
levels (Figure 10.1.a), in Versions 1, 2, 3.

| Level | actual level | boundary | Level | actual level | boundary |
|---|---|---|---|---|---|
| 12 | +3.0 $m$ | HLP | 5 | -0.5 $m$ | |
| 11 | +2.5 $m$ | | 4 | -1.0 $m$ | HLA |
| 10 | +2.0 $m$ | | 3 | -1.5 $m$ | |
| 9 | +1.5 $m$ | | 2 | -2.0 $m$ | |
| 8 | +1.0 $m$ | HLB | 1 | -2.5 $m$ | |
| 7 | +0.5 $m$ | | 0 | -3.0 $m$ | HLV |
| 6 | +0.0 $m$ | | | | |

### 10.4.1.2    *Variations to H*

Node *trend* depends on $P1$, $P2$ and $V$, and represents the four possible
effects on H according to the current state of P1, P2 and V. In particular,
the value 0 represents the decrease, 1 represents the steadiness, 2 models
the slow growth, 3 models the quick growth of H. The CPT of *trend* reflects
the content of Table 10.1.

A DBN can represent discrete quantities in terms of the values of variables. H is a continuous measure, so it needs to be discretized. On one
hand, a low number of discrete intermediate levels may lead to some approximation of the inference results. On the other hand, a high number may
increase in a relevant way the size of several CPTs and as a consequence,
the complexity of the model analysis. In order to achieve a good trade-off
between accuracy and complexity, in the DBN we discretize H into 13 intermediate levels. To this aim, we exploit *Level* whose value can vary between
0 and 12. This means that the distance between an intermediate level and
the following one is 0.5 $m$: Table 10.4 defines the correspondence between
the 13 values of *Level* and the effective liquid level in the tank. Given that
two consecutive intermediate values differ by 0.5 $m$, in the DBN we can
represent the variation of H for the same quantity by increasing or decreasing *Level* by one unit. If the variation rate for P1, P2 and V is Q=0.6 $m/h$
(Section 10.2), then a variation of H by 0.5 $m$ (1 unit for *Level*) due to
the action of a single component, takes 0.8333 $h$ of time. We set $\Delta$ to this
value, so that *Level* may change by 1 during one time step.

*Level#* (current H) depends on *Level* (H in the previous time step)
and on *trend*. In particular, the value of *Level#* is the same of *Level* if
*trend* = 1, is decreased by 1 if *trend* = 0, is increased by 1 if *trend* = 2, or
by 2 if *trend* = 3. All of this is specified in the CPT of *Level#* where we
assume that H does not change any more if the dry out or the overflow is
reached.

Table 10.5　The CPT of *command#* and *pdf#* (the symbol / means any value). In the CPT of *command#*, $p = 0$ in Versions 1 and 3; $p = 0.1$ in Version 2. For the sake of brevity, the lines with null probability are omitted in these CPTs and in the following ones.

**CPT of *command#*** (Versions 1, 2, 3)

| n. | region | region# | com.# | prob. |
|----|--------|---------|-------|-------|
| 1 | 0 | / | 1 | 1 |
| 2 | 1 | 0 | 0 | 1 - p |
|   | 1 | 0 | 1 | p |
| 3 | 1 | 1 | 1 | 1 |
| 4 | 1 | 2 | 1 | p |
|   | 1 | 2 | 2 | 1 - p |
| 5 | 2 | / | 1 | 1 |

**CPT of *pdf#*** (Versions 1, 2, 3, 4)

| state | state# | pdf# | prob. |
|-------|--------|------|-------|
| 0 | / | 1 | 1 |
| 1 | 0 | 0 | 1 |
| 1 | 1 | 1 | 1 |
| 1 | 2 | 2 | 1 |
| 2 | / | 1 | 1 |

Table 10.6　The CPT of *grace#*

| grace | Level# | grace# | prob. |
|-------|--------|--------|-------|
| 0 | 0 | 0 | 1 |
| 0 | 1..8 | 1 | 1 |
| 0 | 9..11 | 0 | 1 |
| 0 | 12..19 | 1 | 1 |
| 0 | 20 | 0 | 1 |
| 1 | 0 | 0 | 1 |
| 1 | 1..19 | 1 | 1 |
| 1 | 20 | 0 | 1 |

H can be inside one of three regions: H≤HLA, HLA<H<HLB, H≥HLB (Section 10.2). *region* can be equal to 0, 1, or 2 in order to model the above three regions respectively. Its CPT maps the values of *Level* into the corresponding value of *region*. In the same way, *Level#* influences *region#*.

### 10.4.1.3　*Orders from C*

*command#* depends on both *region* (region in the previous time step) and *region#* (current region), because C generates an order (*command#* = 0 or *command#* = 2) when the H moves from the correct region (*region* = 1) to another one (*region#* = 0 or *region#* = 2, respectively). In the other cases, the value of *command#* is set to 1. This is incorporated by the CPT of *command#* (Table 10.5): the **entries n. 2 and 4** are the situations where C generates a command; the parameter *p* is the probability that C does not act when necessary (failure on demand); in Version 1, *p* is set to 0.

Table 10.7   The CPT of $P1\#$ in Version 2.

| n. | $P1$ | $command\#$ | $P1\#$ | prob. |
|---|---|---|---|---|
| | 0 | 0 | 1 | $1 - ((1 - e^{100\lambda\Delta}) + (1 - e^{10\lambda\Delta}))$ |
| 1 | 0 | 0 | 2 | $1 - e^{100\lambda\Delta}$ |
| | 0 | 0 | 3 | $1 - e^{10\lambda\Delta}$ |
| | 0 | 1 | 0 | $1 - ((1 - e^{100\lambda\Delta}) + (1 - e^{10\lambda\Delta}))$ |
| 2 | 0 | 1 | 2 | $1 - e^{100\lambda\Delta}$ |
| | 0 | 1 | 3 | $1 - e^{10\lambda\Delta}$ |
| | 0 | 2 | 0 | $1 - ((1 - e^{100\lambda\Delta}) + (1 - e^{10\lambda\Delta}))$ |
| 3 | 0 | 2 | 2 | $1 - e^{100\lambda\Delta}$ |
| | 0 | 2 | 3 | $1 - e^{10\lambda\Delta}$ |
| | 1 | 0 | 1 | $1 - (1 - e^{-\lambda\Delta})$ |
| 4 | 1 | 0 | 2 | $(1 - e^{-\lambda\Delta})/2$ |
| | 1 | 0 | 3 | $(1 - e^{-\lambda\Delta})/2$ |
| | 1 | 1 | 1 | $1 - (1 - e^{-\lambda\Delta})$ |
| 5 | 1 | 1 | 2 | $(1 - e^{-\lambda\Delta})/2$ |
| | 1 | 1 | 3 | $(1 - e^{-\lambda\Delta})/2$ |
| | 1 | 2 | 0 | $1 - (1 - e^{-\lambda\Delta})$ |
| 6 | 1 | 2 | 2 | $(1 - e^{-\lambda\Delta})/2$ |
| | 1 | 2 | 3 | $(1 - e^{-\lambda\Delta})/2$ |
| 7 | 2 | 0 | 2 | 1 |
| 8 | 2 | 1 | 2 | 1 |
| 9 | 2 | 2 | 2 | 1 |
| 10 | 3 | 0 | 3 | 1 |
| 11 | 3 | 1 | 3 | 1 |
| 12 | 3 | 2 | 3 | 1 |

#### 10.4.1.4   *System states*

*state#* and *pdf#* will facilitate the computation of predictive measures in Section 10.5. We need the ternary variable *state#* to model the three possible states of the system: working (value 1), dry out (value 0) or overflow (value 2). In particular, the working state is any situation where the dry out or the overflow has not occurred yet. These states are determined by H, so *state#* is influenced by *Level#*. In the CPT of *state#* we set this variable to 0 only when *Level* = 0, and we set it to 2 only when *Level* = 12, according to Table 10.4. Since *Level#* does not change any more its value in case of dry out or overflow (as described above), *state#* maintains its value if set to 0 or 2. *state* at $t - \Delta$ has the same role of *state#*.

*pdf#* is set to 0 or 2 only in the time step where the system turns from working to failed, while in any other time step *pdf#* is set to 1. Therefore *pdf#* depends on *state* and *state#*, as specified in the CPT (Table 10.5): *pdf#* is equal to: 0 (dry out) if *state* = 1 and *state#* = 0; 2 (overflow) if *state* = 1 and *state#* = 2; 1 in any other case.

## 10.4.2   *Modelling Versions 2 and 3*

In terms of graph, the DBN models of Versions 1, 2, and 3 are equivalent (Figure 10.3), but they differ in the content of specific CPTs.

### 10.4.2.1   *Version 2*

In the DBN of Version 2, the CPTs of $P1\#$, $P2\#$ and $V\#$ are modified in order to consider the state dependent failure rates reported in Table 1.2. In the CPT of $P1\#$ (Table 10.7), with respect to Version 1, we have modified the entries n. 1, 2, 3.

### 10.4.2.2   *Version 3*

The DBN of Version 3 differs from the model of Version 1, only for one aspect: the parameter $p$ in the CPT of *command#* (Table 10.5) is set to 0.1 instead of 0, in order to take into account the possibility of failure on demand by C (Section 10.2).

## 10.4.3   *Modelling Version 4*

### 10.4.3.1   *Variations to H*

In Version 4, HLV and HLP have different values (-5 $m$ and +5 $m$ respectively, as shown in Figure 10.2.a). Because of this, the value of *Level* and *Level#* varies between 0 and 20, in order to represent 21 discrete intermediate levels. In this way, we still can represent variation of H by 0.5 $m$, during the transition from a time step to the next one, confirming $\Delta$=0.8333. The CPTs of *Level*, *Level#*, *region*, *region#*, *state* and *state#* have the same roles as in the previous models, but they take into account the 21 (instead of 13) intermediate levels.

### 10.4.3.2   *Grace period*

Version 4 is characterized by the grace period (Section 10.2). In the DBN of Version 4 (Figure 10.4), we introduce the binary variables *grace* and *grace#*. In particular, *grace#* depends on *Level#* because of the activation or deactivation of the grace period, and on *grace* because the value 1 (active) has to be maintained until the system failure. This is reflected in the CPT of *grace#* (Table 10.6).

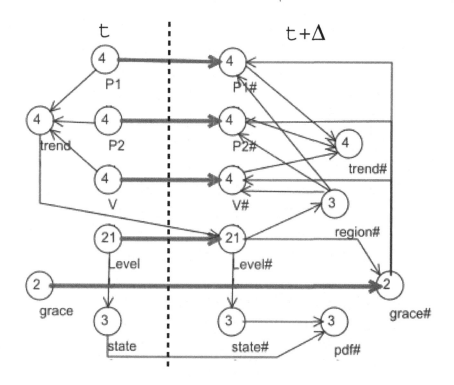

Fig. 10.4    The graph of the DBN model (in canonical form) of Version 4.

### 10.4.3.3  *Repair*

*grace#* influences *P1#*, *P2#* and *V#* because the grace period allows the repair of components. In Version 4, C gives an order to components when H goes out of the correct region and confirms the order when a component is repaired. Therefore the current order corresponds to the current region where H is located. So, in the DBN of Version 4 (Figure 10.4), *P1#*, *P2#* and *V#* depend on *region#*. Let us consider the CPT of *P1#* (Table 10.8):
- the **entries n. 10, 11, 12, 16, 17, 18** are the cases where the repair is allowed. In particular, in the entry n. 10, P1 was S_OFF in the previous time step ($P2 = 2$), the grace period is currently active (*grace#* $= 1$), and H≤HLA (*region#* $= 0$). In this situation, the probability that P1 is recovered during $\Delta$ is $1 - e^{-\mu\Delta}$ (negative exponential distribution), where $\mu$ is the repair rate (Section 10.2). Such probability is associated with *P1#* $= 1$ because in case of repair, P1 will turn to ON, due to H≤HLA. The

Table 10.8    The CPT of $P1\#$ (or $P2\#$) in Version 4. $\mu$ is equal to $0.2\ h^{-1}$.

| n. | P1 | grace# | region# | P1# | prob. |
|---|---|---|---|---|---|
|   | 0 | / | 0 | 1 | $1-(1-e^{-\lambda\Delta})$ |
| 1 | 0 | / | 0 | 2 | $(1-e^{-\lambda\Delta})/2$ |
|   | 0 | / | 0 | 3 | $(1-e^{-\lambda\Delta})/2$ |
|   | 0 | / | 1 | 0 | $1-(1-e^{-\lambda\Delta})$ |
| 2 | 0 | / | 1 | 2 | $(1-e^{-\lambda\Delta})/2$ |
|   | 0 | / | 1 | 3 | $(1-e^{-\lambda\Delta})/2$ |
|   | 0 | / | 2 | 0 | $1-(1-e^{-\lambda\Delta})$ |
| 3 | 0 | / | 2 | 2 | $(1-e^{-\lambda\Delta})/2$ |
|   | 0 | / | 2 | 3 | $(1-e^{-\lambda\Delta})/2$ |
|   | 1 | / | 0 | 1 | $1-(1-e^{-\lambda\Delta})$ |
| 4 | 1 | / | 0 | 2 | $(1-e^{-\lambda\Delta})/2$ |
|   | 1 | / | 0 | 3 | $(1-e^{-\lambda\Delta})/2$ |
|   | 1 | / | 1 | 1 | $1-(1-e^{-\lambda\Delta})$ |
| 5 | 1 | / | 1 | 2 | $(1-e^{-\lambda\Delta})/2$ |
|   | 1 | / | 1 | 3 | $(1-e^{-\lambda\Delta})/2$ |
|   | 1 | / | 2 | 0 | $1-(1-e^{-\lambda\Delta})$ |
| 6 | 1 | / | 2 | 2 | $(1-e^{-\lambda\Delta})/2$ |
|   | 1 | / | 2 | 3 | $(1-e^{-\lambda\Delta})/2$ |
| 7 | 2 | 0 | 0 | 2 | 1 |
| 8 | 2 | 0 | 1 | 2 | 1 |
| 9 | 2 | 0 | 2 | 2 | 1 |
| 10 | 2 | 1 | 0 | 1 | $1-e^{-\mu\Delta}$ |
|   | 2 | 1 | 0 | 2 | $1-(1-e^{-\mu\Delta})$ |
| 11 | 2 | 1 | 1 | 0 | $1-e^{-\mu\Delta}$ |
|   | 2 | 1 | 1 | 2 | $1-(1-e^{-\mu\Delta})$ |
| 12 | 2 | 1 | 2 | 0 | $1-e^{-\mu\Delta}$ |
|   | 2 | 1 | 2 | 2 | $1-(1-e^{-\mu\Delta})$ |
| 13 | 3 | 0 | 0 | 3 | 1 |
| 14 | 3 | 0 | 1 | 3 | 1 |
| 15 | 3 | 0 | 2 | 3 | 1 |
| 16 | 3 | 1 | 0 | 1 | $1-e^{-\mu\Delta}$ |
|   | 3 | 1 | 0 | 3 | $1-(1-e^{-\mu\Delta})$ |
| 17 | 3 | 1 | 1 | 1 | $1-e^{-\mu\Delta}$ |
|   | 3 | 1 | 1 | 3 | $1-(1-e^{-\mu\Delta})$ |
| 18 | 3 | 1 | 2 | 0 | $1-e^{-\mu\Delta}$ |
|   | 3 | 1 | 2 | 3 | $1-(1-e^{-\mu\Delta})$ |

probability that $P1\# = 2$ (P1 maintains the S_OFF state) is $1-(1-e^{-\mu\Delta})$.

- In the **entry n. 11**, H is in the region of correct functioning ($region\# = 1$); therefore the probability of repair is associated with $P1\# = 0$ because in case of repair, P1 will turn from S_OFF to OFF.

- In the **entry n. 12**, there is the necessity to switch off the pumps ($region\# = 2$), so the repair probability is assigned to $P1\# = 0$.

- In the **entries n. 16, 17, 18**, P1 was S_ON in the previous time step

($P1 = 3$). The probability of repair is assigned to $P1\# = 0$ or $P1\# = 1$ according to the value of $region\#$. The probability that P1 is not repaired is always associated with $P1\# = 3$ (P1 maintains the S_ON state).

## 10.5   DBN Analysis Results

The DBN models have been designed and analyzed by means of RADY-BAN, with the purpose of predicting the system unreliability due to the dry out or the overflow. This is the original goal of the benchmark [Marseguerra and Zio (1996)] and is performed for all Versions. However, in order to show the capability of DBN and RADyBaN to compute measures conditioned by observations, let us consider the DBN model of Version 1, in order to diagnose the state of the components P1, P2 and V at each time step assuming that H is monitored.

### 10.5.1   *Predictive analysis*

We can compute the *probability density function* (pdf) and the *cumulative distribution function* (cdf) for the dry out and the overflow. The pdf at time $t$ provides the probability that the system fails exactly at time $t$. The cdf provides the system unreliability as a consequence of dry out or overflow. For instance, the value of the dry out cdf at time $t$ is the probability that the system has failed because of the dry out, during the time period $(0, t)$. Since DBN are discrete models, we actually compute a *probability mass function*.

These measures can be computed by means of the filtering algorithm of RADyBaN (1.5JT algorithm) with an empty stream of observations. In particular, during the inference process, $pdf\#$ is queried in order to obtain the pdf, while $state\#$ is queried to obtain the cdf. In this way, the inference returns the probability distribution of the values 0, 1, 2, corresponding to the dry out, working, and overflow condition, respectively (Section 10.4). For instance, the probability that $state\#$ is equal to 0 at time $t$, provides the dry out cdf at that time, while the overflow pdf is instead given by the probability that $pdf\#$ is equal to 2.

As in [Marseguerra and Zio (1996)], the system is evaluated for a mission time varying between 0 and 1000 $h$ in Versions 1, 2, 3, and between 0 and 500 $h$ in Version 4. The time is discrete in DBN, and two consecutive time steps differ by the interval $\Delta$ which is set to 0.8333 $h$ in the DBN models

Table 10.9   The cdf values for the **dry out** condition in **Version 1**.

| time | step | DBN an. | SAN sim. | GSPN an. | FSPN sim. |
|------|------|---------|----------|----------|-----------|
| 200 $h$ | 240 | 2.2789E-2 | 2.2390E-2 | 2.2077E-2 | 2.400E-2 |
| 400 $h$ | 480 | 6.6455E-2 | 6.5990E-2 | 6.5827E-2 | 6.730E-2 |
| 600 $h$ | 720 | 9.5366E-2 | 9.5290E-2 | 9.5014E-2 | 9.360E-2 |
| 800 $h$ | 960 | 1.1040E-1 | 1.1003E-1 | 1.1022E-2 | 1.084E-1 |
| 1000 $h$ | 1200 | 1.1777E-1 | 1.1747E-1 | 1.1768E-2 | 1.165E-1 |

Table 10.10   The cdf values for the **overflow** condition in **Version 1**.

| time | step | DBN an. | SAN sim. | GSPN an. | FSPN sim. |
|------|------|---------|----------|----------|-----------|
| 200 $h$ | 240 | 1.9890E-1 | 1.9914E-1 | 1.9518E-1 | 2.0050E-1 |
| 400 $h$ | 480 | 3.6172E-1 | 3.6207E-1 | 3.5987E-1 | 3.6220E-1 |
| 600 $h$ | 720 | 4.3652E-1 | 4.3665E-1 | 4.3568E-1 | 4.4160E-1 |
| 800 $h$ | 960 | 4.6997E-1 | 4.7063E-1 | 4.6959E-1 | 4.7630E-1 |
| 1000 $h$ | 1200 | 4.8538E-1 | 4.8572E-1 | 4.8520E-1 | 4.9100E-1 |

of the benchmark (Section 10.4). So, in order to evaluate the system from 0 to 500 $h$ or 1000 $h$, we have to inference the models from 0 to 600 or 1200 time steps, respectively. For example, the system evaluation at 400 $h$ is given by the DBN analysis at 480 time steps (480 = 400 $h$ / 0.8333 $h$).

The results for Versions 1, 2, 3 returned by DBN analysis are graphically compared in Figures 10.5, 10.6, 10.7, 10.8. The results for Version 4 are separately depicted in Figures 10.9, 10.10, 10.11, 10.12 because of the different mission time and thresholds for the dry out and the overflow (Section 10.2). The cdf and pdf values are quite similar to those obtained by Monte Carlo simulation [Marseguerra and Zio (1996)], GSPN analysis [Codetta-Raiteri and Bobbio (2005)], FSPN simulation [Codetta-Raiteri and Bobbio (2005)], and SAN simulation [Codetta-Raiteri (2011)], as shown in Table 10.9 and Table 10.10 for Version 1. In particular, the DBN, the GSPN, and the SAN model capture variations of H by 0.5 $m$, 1 $m$ and 0.01 $m$ respectively, while the FSPN model simulates H as a continuous variable. This verifies that DBN analysis generates results with a good degree of accuracy. For the sake of brevity, for Versions 2, 3 and 4, we compare only the results of DBN analysis and SAN simulation in Table 10.11, Table 10.12, Table 10.13.

## 10.5.2   *Diagnostic analysis*

The original goal of the benchmark is the computation of the system unreliability in a predictive way (prognosis). However, DBN can be exploited to compute measures conditioned by observations. In this case, the difference between a filtering and a smoothing inference relies on the fact that in the former case, while computing the probability at time $t$, only the evidence

Table 10.11   The cdf values for the **dry out** condition in **Versions 2 and 3**.

| time | step | Version 2 | | Version 3 | |
|---|---|---|---|---|---|
| | | **DBN an.** | SAN sim. | **DBN an.** | SAN sim. |
| 200 h | 240 | 4.0657E-2 | 4.0400E-2 | 8.6288E-2 | 8.6710E-2 |
| 400 h | 480 | 6.4539E-2 | 6.3360E-2 | 1.2659E-1 | 1.2664E-1 |
| 600 h | 720 | 7.5211E-2 | 7.3750E-2 | 1.4738E-1 | 1.4707E-1 |
| 800 h | 960 | 7.9762E-2 | 7.8340E-2 | 1.5762E-1 | 1.5739E-1 |
| 1000 h | 1200 | 8.1656E-2 | 8.0240E-2 | 1.6251E-1 | 1.6220E-1 |

Table 10.12   The cdf values for the **overflow** condition in **Versions 2 and 3**.

| time | step | Version 2 | | Version 3 | |
|---|---|---|---|---|---|
| | | **DBN an.** | SAN sim. | **DBN an.** | SAN sim. |
| 200 h | 240 | 1.7508E-1 | 1.6852E-1 | 2.7222E-1 | 2.7244E-1 |
| 400 h | 480 | 2.8591E-1 | 2.7882E-1 | 4.2515E-1 | 4.2492E-1 |
| 600 h | 720 | 3.3635E-1 | 3.2938E-1 | 4.8892E-1 | 4.8808E-1 |
| 800 h | 960 | 3.5979E-1 | 3.5284E-1 | 5.1649E-1 | 5.1537E-1 |
| 1000 h | 1200 | 3.7120E-1 | 3.6500E-1 | 5.2900E-1 | 5.2797E-1 |

Table 10.13   The cdf values for the **dry out** condition in **Version 4**.

| time | step | dry out | | overflow | |
|---|---|---|---|---|---|
| | | **DBN an.** | SAN sim. | **DBN an.** | SAN sim. |
| 100 h | 120 | 3.133E-5 | 6.000E-5 | 2.686E-3 | 2.430E-3 |
| 200 h | 240 | 1.454E-4 | 2.200E-4 | 6.603E-3 | 6.090E-3 |
| 300 h | 360 | 2.882E-4 | 3.700E-4 | 9.889E-3 | 9.460E-3 |
| 400 h | 480 | 4.166E-4 | 4.500E-4 | 1.245E-2 | 1.197E-2 |
| 500 h | 600 | 5.163E-4 | 5.100E-4 | 1.447E-2 | 1.363E-2 |

(observations) gathered up to time $t$ is considered; on the contrary, in the case of smoothing the whole evidence stream is always considered in the posterior probability computation. For diagnostic purposes, filtering can be exploited to perform the on line diagnosis of the system. This means evaluating the state of components during the monitoring of the system behaviour. For instance, in the present case study, we assume that the value of H is observable at each time step $t$, so we can compute the probability of each possible state of P1, P2 and V at $t$. In this way, we can estimate the causes of the current value of H. Smoothing instead, may be exploited in order to reconstruct the history of the system components for a kind of temporal diagnosis. For instance, we may be interested in evaluating the probability of each state of P1, P2 and V at each time step, based on the observations about H, collected during all the system mission time. These kinds of measures were not computed in the previous works about

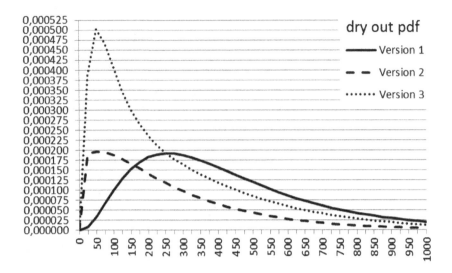

Fig. 10.5   pdf for the dry out in Versions 1, 2, 3.

the benchmark (Section 10.3). They are an additional value given by DBN.

In order to clarify these concepts, we provide an example of filtering and smoothing applied to the DBN of Version 1, assuming to observe the value of *Level* at each time step; *Level* represents H in the model (Table 10.4). The progress of *Level* during the time is depicted in Figure 10.13. In order to detect if current H is due to a particular state of P1, P2 or V, we can perform a filtering task, 5on the DBN model still by means of RADYBAN, querying $P1\#$, $P2\#$ and $V\#$, with the aim of computing the probabilities of their possible values (0, 1, 2, 3) corresponding to the possible states (OFF, ON, S_OFF, S_ON, respectively) of the components (Section 10.4).

The **filtering** results are depicted in Figures 10.14, 10.15, 10.16: at time step 0, the initial configuration holds: P1 is ON, P2 is OFF, V is ON with probability 1. From 1 to 199, P1 may be ON or S_ON, P2 may be OFF or S_OFF, and V may be ON or S_OFF. This means that P1 is injecting liquid, P2 is inactive and V is removing liquid during that period of time, maintaining *Level* steady to 6 as observed. The growth of the probability of the state S_ON (S_OFF), with the consequent decrease of the probability of ON (OFF) is due to the failure rate of the component.

At time step 200, *Level* grows to 7. According to the filtering results, this is due to two alternative causes, with different probabilities: P2 is

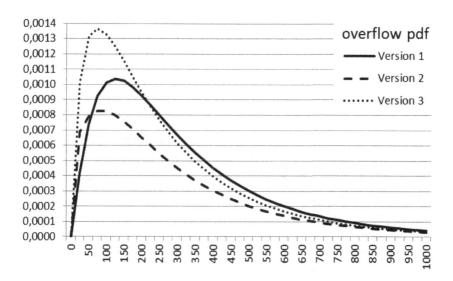

Fig. 10.6   pdf for the overflow in Versions 1, 2, 3.

S_ON or V is S_OFF. At 201, *Level* becomes 8 (H=HLB), so we expect C to provide the order to switch off the pumps and switch on V. Actually in this time step, the probability of P1 to be OFF is 1 (P1 certainly executes the command), while P2 may be OFF (because of the command) or S_ON (as a cause of *Level* = 8), and V may be ON (because of the command) or S_OFF (as a cause of *Level* = 8), with different probabilities. In other words, if the cause of the growth of *Level* is P2, then P2 keeps the S_ON state, while V is switched on by C; if instead the cause is V, then V is S_OFF and P2 is set OFF by C. From 201 to 295, P1 may be OFF or S_OFF because of the failure rate of P1 and the constant value 8 of *Level* during that period. P2 may be S_ON or OFF, but also S_OFF because of the failure rate. V may be S_OFF or ON, but also S_ON.

At time step 296, *Level* grows again and becomes 9; this determines an increase of the probabilities that P1 is S_ON, P2 is S_ON, and V is S_OFF. All these conditions may be the reason of the growth of *Level*. The probabilities of the other possible states are instead decreased. This trend is confirmed in the following time steps leading to the overflow.

If we perform the **smoothing** task, we obtain the results shown in Figures 10.17, 10.18, 10.19; they differ from the filtering results because they are influenced by the knowledge of all the observations. For instance,

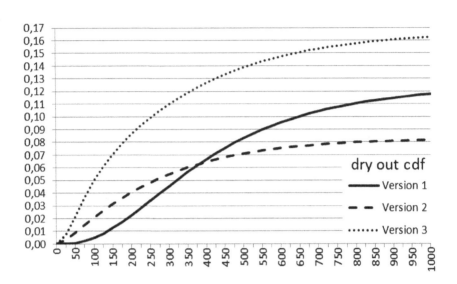

Fig. 10.7    cdf for the dry out in Versions 1, 2, 3.

from 0 to 199, the probability that P1 is S_ON is null because we know in advance that P1 will respond to the order from C at 201, so P1 can not be stuck.

### 10.5.2.1    *Minimal cut sets*

In [Marseguerra and Zio (1996)], the MCSs of the system (Table 10.14) were identified for a preliminary analytical evaluation of the dry out and overflow probabilities (Section 10.3). They provide the states of components leading to the failure. In particular, $m_1$, $m_2$, $m_3$ lead to overflow, $m_4$ to dry out. We can exploit DBN analysis to compute the probability of each MCS given the observation of *Level*. This can be done by computing the conjunctive probability of the component states composing each MCS, by means of RADYBAN. The results of the **filtering** task are reported in Table 10.15: from time step 0 to time step 199, *Level* is equal to 6 (Figure 10.13), so the probabilities of $m_1$, $m_2$, $m_3$, $m_4$ are steady in terms of order of magnitude. At time steps 200 and 201, *Level* grows to 7 and 8 respectively. This event may lead to overflow, so we can notice an evident increase of the probabilities of $m_1$, $m_2$ and $m_3$, while the probability of $m_4$ becomes null. However, from time step 202, *Level* becomes steady to 8 and this determines a relevant decrease of the probabilities of $m_1$, $m_2$ and

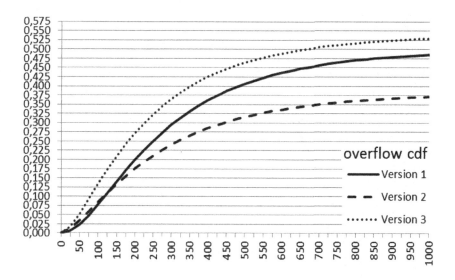

Fig. 10.8 cdf for the overflow in Versions 1, 2, 3.

$m_3$, because the overflow is not actually occurring. At time step 296, *Level* grows again and causes again the increase of the probabilities of $m_1$, $m_2$ and $m_3$. According to the results of the **smoothing** task, all the MCSs have a null probability until time step 294 because only from the following time step we have a growth of *Level* actually leading to overflow. So, from time step 295 to 300 the probabilities of $m_1$, $m_2$, $m_3$, $m_4$ are 37%, 27%, 36%, 0, respectively.

In conclusion, by means of DBN and RADyBaN, we have evaluated several versions of a benchmark on dynamic reliability taken from the literature [Marseguerra and Zio (1996)]. Each version focused on a particular aspect of the system behavior, such as state dependent failure rates, repairable components, failures on demand. The predictive results about the system unreliability that are obtained, are in general quite similar to those computed by means of other techniques. This suggests that DBN modeling and tools like RADyBaN can be suitable means to deal with dynamic reliability cases. However, only discrete quantities can be represented; therefore the liquid level had to be discretized into several intermediate levels. Moreover, the time is discrete. All of this leads to some approximation in the results. This is compensated by two main advantages:

(1) With respect to state space based models, the use of a DBN takes ad-

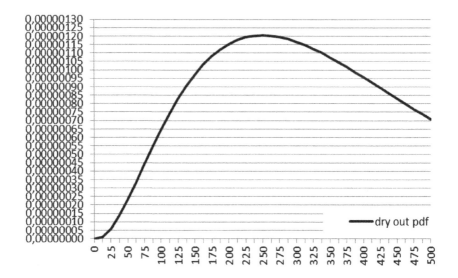

Fig. 10.9    pdf for the dry out in Version 4.

vantage of factorization: the conditional independence assumptions enable a compact representation of the system, by factorizing the system states into the model variables. In this way, we avoid the complexity of specifying and analyzing a global-state model where all the possible system states must be enumerated (as in Markov Chains) or generated (as in Petri Nets). Moreover, in order to model Versions 2 and 3, we had only to modify the CPT of specific variables, while the graph of the model has not changed with respect to Version 1. Few changes have been required to model Version 4.

(2) DBN allow computing measures conditioned by observations at specific times. This has been applied in order to compute diagnostic measures about the state of components, based on the observation of current liquid level during the mission time. This possibility is not available in the Petri Net based approaches, and can be exploited to compute other conditioned measures, since in general, each variable of the DBN can be queried given the observation of any other variable.

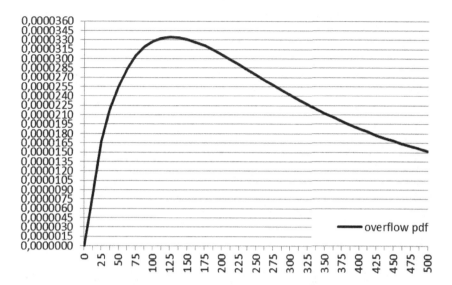

Fig. 10.10   pdf for the overflow in Version 4.

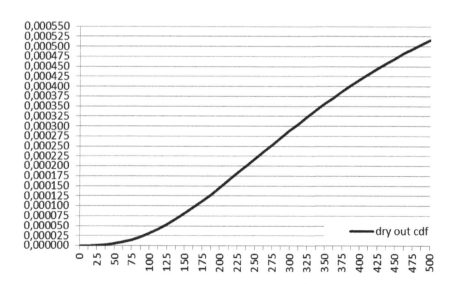

Fig. 10.11   cdf for the dry out in Version 4.

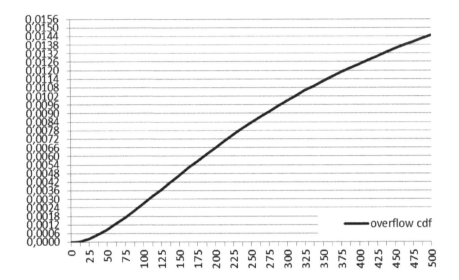

Fig. 10.12    cdf for the overflow in Version 4.

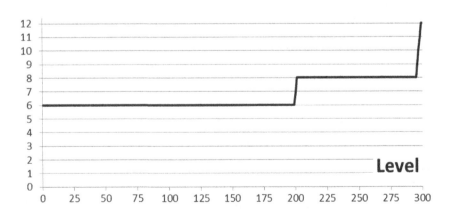

Fig. 10.13    The observations about *Level*.

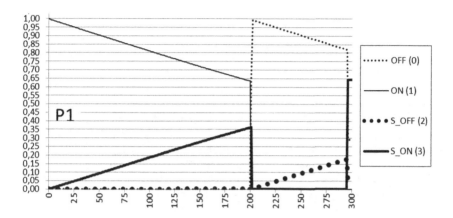

Fig. 10.14    The diagnosis results given by the **filtering** task for P1.

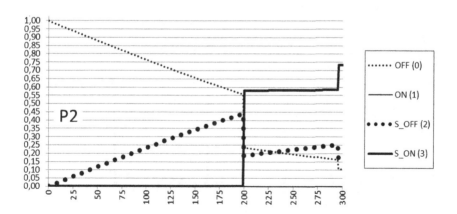

Fig. 10.15    The diagnosis results given by the **filtering** task for P2.

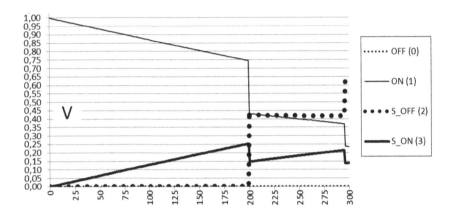

Fig. 10.16   The diagnosis results given by the **filtering** task for V.

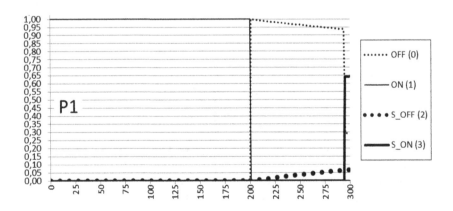

Fig. 10.17   The diagnosis results given by the **smoothing** task for P1.

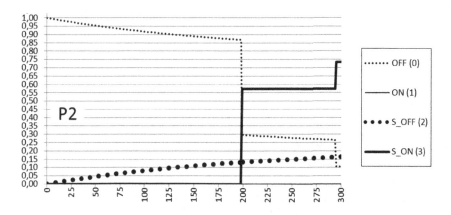

Fig. 10.18   The diagnosis results given by the **smoothing** task for P2.

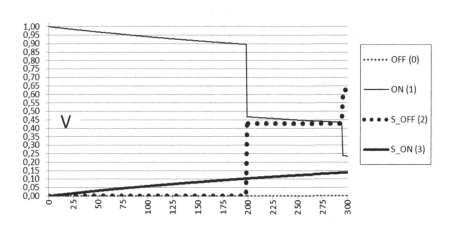

Fig. 10.19   The diagnosis results given by the **smoothing** task for V.

Table 10.14   The minimal cut sets (MCS) of the
system [Marseguerra and Zio (1996)].

| MCS | P1 | P2 | V | Failure |
|------|------|------|------|---------|
| $m_1$ | S_ON | S_ON | any | overflow |
| $m_2$ | S_ON | any | S_OFF | overflow |
| $m_3$ | any | S_ON | S_OFF | overflow |
| $m_4$ | S_OFF | S_OFF | S_ON | dry out |

Table 10.15   The probabilities of the MCSs given the observation of
*Level*, returned by the filtering task.

| step | *Level* | $m_1$ | $m_2$ | $m_3$ | $m_4$ |
|------|---------|----------|----------|----------|----------|
| 50 | 6 | 1.987E-4 | 1.152E-4 | 3.078E-6 | 1,321E-5 |
| 100 | 6 | 3.424E-4 | 2.126E-4 | 3.011E-6 | 4,659E-5 |
| 150 | 6 | 4.342E-4 | 2.914E-4 | 2.895E-6 | 9,052E-5 |
| 199 | 6 | 4.801E-4 | 3.506E-4 | 2.743E-6 | 1.354E-4 |
| **200** | **7** | **2.097E-1** | **1.531E-1** | **1.752E-3** | **0** |
| **201** | **8** | **2.107E-1** | **1.538E-1** | **1.752E-3** | **0** |
| 202 | 8 | 1.097E-3 | 8.004E-4 | 1.115E-3 | 0 |
| 250 | 8 | 1.002E-3 | 7.216E-4 | 9.845E-4 | 0 |
| 295 | 8 | 9.124E-4 | 6.518E-4 | 8.731E-4 | 0 |
| **296** | **9** | **3.752E-1** | **2.682E-1** | **3.588E-1** | **0** |
| **297** | **10** | **3.753E-1** | **2.682E-1** | **3.586E-1** | **0** |
| **298** | **11** | **3.754E-1** | **2.683E-1** | **3.584E-1** | **0** |
| **299** | **12** | **3.762E-1** | **2.691E-1** | **3.590E-1** | **0** |
| **300** | **12** | **3.770E-1** | **2.700E-1** | **3.596E-1** | **0** |

# Appendix A

# The Junction Tree Algorithms

In this appendix we recall the Junction Tree algorithm for inference in Bayesian Networks; in particular, we present the version for static BNs in Section A.1 and the version for DBNs in Section A.2.

## A.1 JT Algorithm for Static Bayesian Networks

An important class of exact inference algorithms for BNs is the class based on the method denoted as **PPTC: Probability Propagation in Trees of Clusters** [Lauritzen and Spiegelhalter (1988); Jensen *et al.* (1990); Shafer and Shenoy (1990); Huang and Darwiche (1996)]; the approach is based on the transformation of the original BN into a secondary structure called *Junction* or *Join Tree*, which is a tree whose nodes are clusters (i.e., groups) of variable nodes of the original BN. The method is well suited when the exact posterior probability of each variable of the net is required. The general idea is to enter the evidence information into the structure, and then to "propagate" the probabilistic information among the clusters, until a sort of quiescence in obtained; at this point each cluster contains the posterior joint probability distribution of the associated variables, and the posterior of each variable contained in a cluster is just a matter of marginalization.

Thus, the first step of the PPTC method is to transform the original BN into a Junction/Join Tree (JT); next section will describe how to do it.

### A.1.1 *Constructing the Junction/Join Tree*

Given a graph $\mathcal{G}$, a Junction Tree of $\mathcal{G}$ is an undirected tree $\mathcal{T}$ having the following properties (recall that in a tree there exists only one path between two given nodes):

- nodes of $\mathcal{T}$ are clusters of nodes of $\mathcal{G}$
- edges in $\mathcal{T}$ are labeled with the intersection of connected clusters: this intersection is called **sepset**
- the **running intersection property** (also called *join tree property*) holds: given two clusters $X, Y$ (nodes of $\mathcal{T}$), then any cluster in the path between $X$ and $Y$ contains $X \cap Y$.

In order to construct the JT $\mathcal{T}$ from the DAG $\mathcal{G}$ corresponding to a BN, the following procedure can be adopted:

(1) make $\mathcal{G}$ undirected by removing arrows from the edges;
(2) *moralize* the graph, that is add an edge between two nodes that have a common child in $\mathcal{G}$, if such an edge does not exist; the resulting graph is called the *moral graph*;
(3) *triangulate* the moral graph, that is add edges in such a way that the resulting graph is triangulated: this means that every cycle of length four or greater contains an edge that connects two nonadjacent nodes in the cycle (i.e., a *chord*) [Bondy and Murty (2008)];
(4) identify the *cliques* of the triangulated graph; a *clique* is a subgraph that is *complete* (every pair of distinct nodes is connected by an edge) and *maximal* (it is not properly contained in a larger, complete subgraph) [Bondy and Murty (2008)];
(5) identify a partial order of the cliques, that is form a a tree of cliques by iteratively inserting edges between pairs of cliques, until the cliques are connected by $n - 1$ edges: the resulting tree is a Junction/Join Tree of the original BN.

Figure A.1 shows an example of the execution of steps (1) and (2) (the constriction of the moral graph from the BN) taken from [Huang and Darwiche (1996)].

Concerning steps (3) ad (4), they can be done at the same time; in particular, the algorithm presented in [Huang and Darwiche (1996)] performs the triangulation of the graph through the iterated elimination of the vertices of the graph, by identifying, at each elimination step, the clique composed by the eliminated vertex and its adjacent nodes.

Let us introduce the following definition: given a node $V$, the *weight* of $V$, denoted as $w(V)$, is the cardinality of the random variable corresponding to $V$ (i.e., the number of states/values of the variable); the weight of a cluster $C$ is the product of the weights of the nodes contained in the cluster, i.e., $w(C) = \prod_{V \in C} w(V)$.

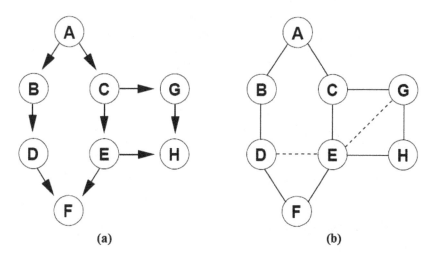

**(a)**                                                    **(b)**

Fig. A.1    Construction of the moral graph (from [Huang and Darwiche (1996)]): (a) the Bayesian Network; (b) the Moral Graph.

The procedure for graph triangulation and clique identification can be described as follows

- make a copy of the moral graph $\mathcal{G}_M$ of $\mathcal{G}$ and call it $\mathcal{G}'_M$;
- while $\mathcal{G}'_M$ is not empty repeat the following
  - select a node $V$ from $\mathcal{G}'_M$ such that $V$ causes the least number of edges to be added in the next step, breaking ties by choosing the node that induces the cluster with the smallest weight;
  - form a *cluster* with the selected node $V$ and the nodes adjacent to $V$ : connect all the nodes in the cluster and, for each added edge in $\mathcal{G}'_M$, add the same edge in $\mathcal{G}_M$
  - remove $V$ from $\mathcal{G}'_M$

At the end of this procedure we obtain the following:

(1) the graph $\mathcal{G}_M$ is triangulated;
(2) each cluster that is not a subset of any previously induced cluster is a clique.

Figure A.2 shows the results of the above steps on the BN of Figure A.1(a).

Once we have obtained the set of cliques, we have to build the JT out of them. We recall that in a JT, each edge is labeled with a sepset,

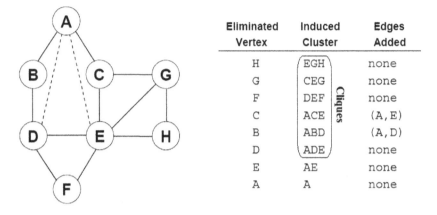

| Eliminated Vertex | Induced Cluster | Edges Added |
|:---:|:---:|:---:|
| H | EGH | none |
| G | CEG | none |
| F | DEF | none |
| C | ACE | (A, E) |
| B | ABD | (A, D) |
| D | ADE | none |
| E | AE | none |
| A | A | none |

**Triangulated Graph**          **Elimination Ordering**

Fig. A.2   Triangulation and identification of cliques (from [Huang and Darwiche (1996)]).

i.e., the set of nodes/variables that are contained in the intersection of the clusters connected by the edge. Let us then introduce the following notions: the *mass* $m(S)$ of a sepset $S$ is the number of variables/nodes it contains; the *cost* $c(S_{XY})$ of a sepset $S_{XY}$ between clusters $X$ and $Y$ is $c(S_{XY}) = w(X) + w(Y)$ (the sum of the weights of the connected clusters).

The following algorithm proposed in [Jensen and Jensen (1994)] iteratively build a JT out of the set of $n$ cliques obtained with the previous triangulation algorithm.

- Let $S = \emptyset$ and $T$ a forest of $n$ degenerated trees composed by one single clique each;
- for each pair of cliques $X, Y$, create a candidate sepset $S_{XY}$ and add it to set $S$;
- repeat the following until $(n - 1)$ sepsets are in $T$:
    - select the sepset $S_{XY}$ from $S$ having the largest mass, breaking ties by selecting the one with minimum cost, finally breaking ties randomly;
    - remove $S_{XY}$ from $S$;
    - if $X$ and $Y$ are in different trees of $T$, say $\tau(X)$ and $\tau(Y)$, then remove $\tau(X)$ and $\tau(Y)$ from $T$, and add the new tree $\tau(X) \cup S_{XY} \cup \tau(Y)$ to $T$.

Table A.1  Candidate sepsets for
the BN in Figure A.3.

| Sepset | | Mass | Cost |
|---|---|---|---|
| $S_{12}$ | $\{C\}$ | 1 | 12 |
| $S_{13}$ | $\{A, C\}$ | 2 | 16 |
| $S_{14}$ | $\{C\}$ | 1 | 16 |
| $S_{23}$ | $\{C\}$ | 1 | 12 |
| $S_{24}$ | $\{C\}$ | 1 | 12 |
| $S_{34}$ | $\{B, C\}$ | 2 | 16 |

In order to illustrate this procedure, let us consider the BN and the moral triangulated graph shown in Figure A.3. Let us suppose that every variable

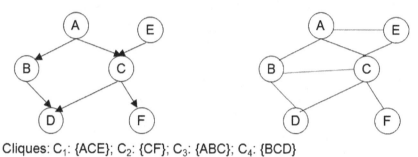

Cliques: $C_1$: {ACE}; $C_2$: {CF}; $C_3$: {ABC}; $C_4$: {BCD}

Fig. A.3    Example of cliques identification for JT construction.

in the BN is binary; the set of cliques from which to build the JT is also shown in the figure. The set of candidate sepsets is reported in Table A.1, together with the indication of the mass and the cost of each sepset. By applying the JT construction algorithm outlined above, we can see that the first two selected sepsets are $S_{34}$ and $S_{13}$ (in arbitrary order since they have the same largest mass and the same cost); the last sepset to be selected (we have to select 3 sepsets, since the number of cliques is $n = 4$) is one among $S_{12}, S_{23}$ and $S_{24}$; the only one that cannot be selected is $S_{14}$ that has mass equal to 1, but a larger cost (16 vs 12). If $S_{12}$ is selected, then the JT is the one depicted in Figure A.4. In the figure, clusters (i.e., cliques) are shown as ovals, while sepsets are shown as rectangles.

## A.1.2    *Belief Propagation on Junction Tree*

Once the JT has been obtained, it must be quantified in order to perform the required probabilistic inference. This is performed through a procedure

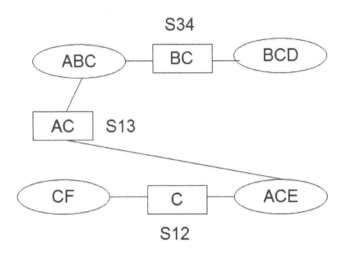

Fig. A.4   A JT finally obtained from the BN of Figure A.3.

called *Belief Propagation* (or *Belief Updating*), based on an exchange of messaged among the clusters and the sepsets of the JT. First of all, we associate with each cluster and sepset a *potential*; given a cluster or sepset $X$, a potential $\phi_X$ is a function mapping instances of $X$ (i.e., t-uples with a value for each variable contained in $X$) into real numbers.

A JT is said to be consistent if, for each cluster $C$ and adjacent sepset $S$ we have that $\sum_{C-S} \phi_C = \phi_S$; this means that the potential of the sepset is exactly the marginalization of the potential of the adjacent clusters on the sepset's variables. If the JT is consistent then the following property holds:

$$Pr\{U\} = \frac{\prod_i \phi_{C_i}}{\prod_j \phi_{S_j}}$$

where $U$ is the set of all the BN's variables, $C_i$ are the clusters (cliques) and $S_j$ the sepsets of the JT respectively. In particular, after the belief propagation phase, the JT is consistent and we have that each cluster (and sepset) potential represents the joint probability of the variables it contains, and thus given a variable $V \in C$, we have that

$$Pr\{V\} = \sum_{C-V} \phi_C$$

The core of the belief propagation scheme is the message passing process between two clusters $X$ and $Y$ through the sepset $S$. Consider the situation

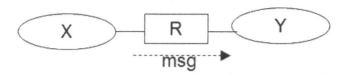

Fig. A.5 Message passing in the JT.

depicted in Figure A.5; When a message is sent from cluster $X$ to cluster $Y$, through sepset $S$, then the potentials of both $S$ and $Y$ are modified, by means of the following rules:

**Projection:** $\phi_S^{old} := \phi_S$; $\phi_S := \sum_{X-S} \phi_X$;

**Absorption:** $\phi_Y := \phi_Y \times \frac{\phi_S}{\phi_S^{old}}$

We can now describe the whole belief propagation algorithm on the JT, to perform posterior probability computation (i.e., inference) on a BN. Let $\Pi_V$ denotes the set of parents of variable $V$ in the BN. Let also $\Lambda_V : V \to [0,1]$ be the *likelihood function* of variable $V$: it maps each value of $V$ into a probability value, the so-called *soft evidence*: it represents the fact that value $v \in V$ has been observed with probability $\Lambda_V(v)$; in the most common case $\Lambda_V(v) = 1$ for exactly one value $v$ and it is 0 for all the others, and in this case we talk about *hard evidence*.

**Initialization:**

- for each cluster and sepset $X$, set $\phi_X(x) = 1$ for every instantiation $x$ of the variables in $X$.
- associate each variable $V$ of the original BN with a cluster containing $V$ and its family (i,e., $V$ and its parents); set $\phi_X := \phi_X \times Pr\{V|\Pi_V\} \times \Lambda_V$;

**Root selection:** select a cluster $R$ as the root of the JT;

**Upward propagation:** unmark all the clusters; call procedure COLLECT-EVIDENCE($R$);

**Downward propagation:** unmark all the clusters; call procedure DISTRIBUTE-EVIDENCE($R$);

**Marginalization:** for each variable $V$ call procedure MARGINALIZE($V$)

At the end, every variable $V$ has a probability distribution associated with its values which is exactly $Pr\{V = v|E\}$, being $E$ the observed (either soft or hard) evidence.

The algorithm calls some sub-routine that are detailed in the following.

COLLECT-EVIDENCE(X)

- mark cluster $X$;
- for each unmarked $Y$ adjacent to $X$:
  - call COLLECT-EVIDENCE(Y);
  - execute **Projection** and **Absorption** from $X$ to the caller of the current sub-routine instance.

DISTRIBUTE-EVIDENCE(X)

- mark cluster $X$;
- for each unmarked $Y$ adjacent to $X$:
  - execute **Projection** and **Absorption** from $X$ to $Y$;
  - call DISTRIBUTE-EVIDENCE(Y).

MARGINALIZE(V)

- select the cluster $X$ associated with variable $V$;
- compute $P(V, E) = \sum_{X-V} \phi_X$
- compute $P(V|E) = \alpha P(V, E)$ being $\alpha = P(E) = \sum_{V'} P(V', E)$ the normalization constant of the posterior distribution.

COLLECT-EVIDENCE(R) is a process that propagate messages from the leaves of the JT to the chosen root $R$, while DISTRIBUTE-EVIDENCE(R) performs the propagation from the root to the leaves; at the end of the process, every node has received a contribution from all the other nodes of the JT. The proof of the correctness of such an algorithm can be found in several books on BNs ([Pearl (1988); Jensen and Nielsen (2007); Koller and Friedman (2009)]).

## A.2   JT Algorithm for Dynamic Bayesian Networks

In case of a DBN, the algorithm described in the previous section can be adapted, by taking into account the markovian assumption, i.e., by considering a 2-TBN model (see Chapter 2).

First of all, let us define the *outgoing interface* $I_t$ of a DBN as the set of nodes in the anterior layer $t$ having a child in the ulterior layer $t + \Delta$. The following property holds ([Murphy (2002)]):

*The outgoing interface $I_t$ d-separates nodes at time $t' < t$ and nodes at time $t$ not in $I_t$, from nodes at time $t'' > t$*

This means that $I_t$ is the sufficient statistics to keep the history of the model evolution until time $t$. For example, consider the DBN in Figure A.6, where nodes with index 1 are at the anterior layer and node with index 2 are at the ulterior layer; We can immediately determine the outgoing

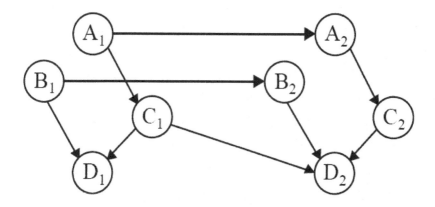

Fig. A.6   A simple DBN (adapted from [Gimpel (2006)]).

interface $I_t = \{A_1, B_1, C_1\}$. Once we know $A_1, B_1$ and $C_1$ at a generic time $t$, all other nodes both at time $t$ ($D_1$ in this case) and at time $t' < t$ are irrelevant to determine the future states of the net's variables at time $t'' > t$. Notice that, the canonical form of the DBN corresponds to showing only the outgoing interface at the anterior layer.

### A.2.1   The 1.5JT algorithm

In [Murphy (2002)], Murphy proposed an exact JT-based algorithm for DBN now called 1.5JT. It can be used for both filtering/prediction and smoothing tasks; however, for the sake of simplicity we present here only the filtering version. The algorithm can be summarized as follows (by convention node $X$ is labeled as $X_1$ if at the anterior layer and $X_2$ if at the ulterior layer); first of all, two different JT are constructed: $J_0$ for the initial time point $t = 0$ and $J_t$ for the time points $t > 0$.

In order to build $J_0$, we consider the (static) BN composed by the nodes of the anterior layer, and we identify the outgoing interface $I_1$ on such a network; the JT $J_0$ is then constructed as described for the static case, with the addition of the following step: after moralization, we also add edges in such a way that nodes contained in $I_1$ become connected to each other. This ensures that $J_0$ has a clique containing the outgoing interface; we then label the cluster corresponding to such a clique as both *in-clique* and *out-clique*. Finally, initialize $J_0$ as in the static case, by incorporating possible evidence observed at time $t = 0$. Figure A.7 shows the construction of $J_0$ for the DBN of Figure A.6.

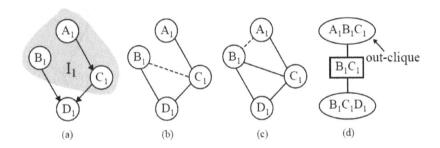

Fig. A.7    Construction of $J_0$: (a) identification outgoing interface; (b) moralization; (c) connecting outgoing interface; (d) resulting JT (adapted from [Gimpel (2006)]).

The second JT to be constructed, $J_t$, is the one to be used for performing a generic step of inference from the anterior to the ulterior layer. To build $J_t$, we first identify the outgoing interfaces of both layers, and we call them $I_1$ and $I_2$ respectively. Then we consider the canonical form of the DBN, and we build the corresponding JT, by adding, as before for $J_0$, the step connecting the nodes in the interfaces, after the moralization step. Such steps, applied to the DBN of Figure A.6 are shown in Figure A.8. After triangulation, cliques identification and JT construction, the resulting JT will have two different clusters, one containing $I_1$ and one containing $I_2$: we call them *in-clique* and *out-clique* respectively. Figure A.9 shows these last steps, again for the DBN of Figure A.6; Figure A.10 finally shows the resulting JT $J_t$.    Once $J_t$ has been constructed, cluster potentials are initialized by considering only the CPTs of nodes at the ulterior layer; moreover, if the current time instant is $t$, then the evidence observed at time $t$ is also incorporated as usual. The initialized JT is then ready to perform an inference step from $t - \Delta$ to $t$.

Inference is then performed step by step (each step counting $\Delta$ time

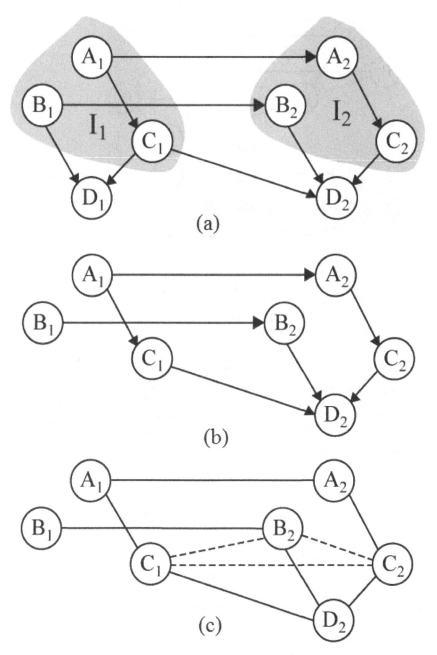

Fig. A.8 Construction of $J_t$: (a) identification of interfaces; (b) canonical form; (c) moralization (adapted from [Gimpel (2006)]).

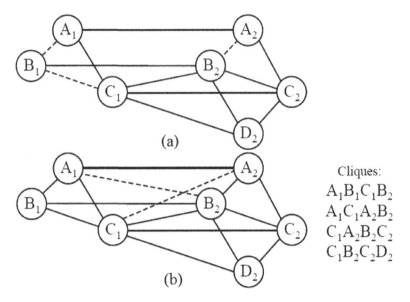

Fig. A.9  Construction of $J_t$: (a) connecting interfaces; (b) triangulation and cliques identification (adapted from [Gimpel (2006)]).

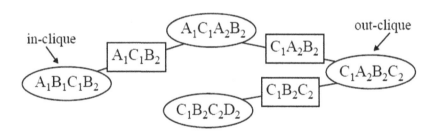

Fig. A.10  Resulting $J_t$ for DBN of Figure A.6 (adapted from [Gimpel (2006)]).

instants), by propagating probabilistic information from the out-clique of the previous step to the in-clique of the next step. Every time, we consider two copies of $J_t$ that we call $J_t$ and $J_{t+1}$ respectively (at time $t = 0$ we just have $J_0$ and $J_t$). Nodes $X_2$ of $J_t$ will correspond to nodes $X_1$ in $J_{t+1}$; an exception is $J_0$, where only nodes $X_1$ are present: they are put in correspondence with the same nodes in $J_t$ for the advancement from $t = 0$ to $t = \Delta$.

Let $I_2$ be the out-clique of $J_t$ and $I_1$ be the in-clique of $J_{t+1}$; the advancement of inference is performed by computing the following factor

$$\alpha_t = \sum_{I_2 - I_1} \phi_{I_2}$$

which is the marginalization over the outgoing interface from one step to the next one. Of course $\alpha_0 = \phi_{I_1} = \phi_{I_2}$.

This factor summarizes all the needed information for the advancement of the inference and can then be incorporated on the next JT. More in details we can describe the algorithm as follows.

### 1.5 JT algorithm

- **Initialization.** Create a JT $J_0$ for the initial time point $t = 0$ and a JT $J_t$ for the time points $t > 0$;
- **Evidence incorporation.** If evidence is at time $t = 0$, then it is incorporated into $J_0$ at time $t = 0$; if evidence is at time $t > 0$, then it is incorporated into $J_t$ at time $t$;
- **Query at time** $t \geq 0$. Execute belief propagation on $J_t$ and marginalize on the queried variables. Consider now the out-clique of $J_t$ and the in-clique of $J_{t+1}$; compute factor $\alpha_t$, increment time to $t + \Delta$, make $J_{t+1}$ the current $J_t$ and update $\phi_{I_1} := \alpha_t \phi_{I_1}$.

Figure A.11 shows an example of advancement from $t = 2$ to $t = 3$ on our example DBN.

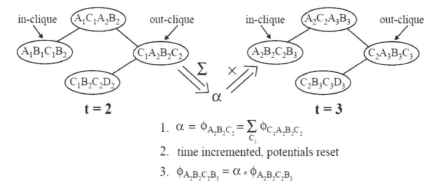

Fig. A.11   DBN inference advancement (adapted from [Gimpel (2006)]).

### A.2.2   *The Boyen-Koller algorithm*

A slight variation of the 1.5JT algorithm has been proposed by Boyen and Koller [Boyen and Koller (1998)] and is now called *BK algorithm*; it encompasses 1.5JT algorithm as a special case, and it is an approximate algorithm for inference on DBNs, based on JT propagation.

Since in Murphy's 1.5JT algorithm the outgoing interface must be contained in a single clique, this can be a major source of complexity when the size of the outgoing interface is huge. The idea behind the BK algorithm is to split the interface into several sets, called *bk-clusters*, and to approximate the joint distribution of the interface as the product of the joint distribution of each bk-cluster. This implies that cliques on the JT can be kept smaller, and thus also the potential tables. The price to be paid is that independence among the bk-clusters is assumed, and this can lead to an approximation of the requited posterior distribution. The most aggressive approximation is provided when each bk-cluster is a singleton, containing a single interface node; this version is called *fully factorized BK*. Murphy's 1.5JT algorithm is obtained when one single bk-cluster containing all the interface is considered, leading to exact inference. Figure A.12 shows the splitting of the outgoing interface $\{A_1, B_1, C_1\}$ of our example DBN into two bk-clusters, one containing only node $B_1$ and one containing nodes $A_1, C_1$. The whole interface potential can be approximated by the product of the (smaller) potentials of the two bk-clusters. The BK algorithm pro-

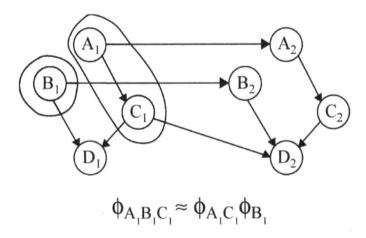

$$\phi_{A_1 B_1 C_1} \approx \phi_{A_1 C_1} \phi_{B_1}$$

Fig. A.12   Example of assignment of bk-clusters (adapted from [Gimpel (2006)]).

ceeds as the 1.5JT one, by keeping multiple in-cliques and out-cliques, one for each bk-cluster, and by computing multiple advancement factors $\alpha_t$ (one for each bk-cluster), as outlined in Figure A.13. The best accuracy in the

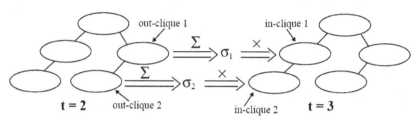

1. $\sigma_1 = \sum \phi_{\text{out-clique 1}}$
   $\sigma_2 = \sum \phi_{\text{out-clique 2}}$

2. time incremented, potentials reset

3. $\phi_{\text{in-clique 1}} = \sigma_1 * \phi_{\text{in-clique 1}}$
   $\phi_{\text{in-clique 2}} = \sigma_2 * \phi_{\text{in-clique 2}}$

Fig. A.13 DBN inference advancement with BK algorithm (adapted from [Gimpel (2006)]).

approximation (in terms of KL divergence [Kullback and Leibler (1951)]) is obtained when no node in any bk-cluster is a parent of a node in a different bk-cluster, within the same time slice.

# Bibliography

Ajmone-Marsan, M., Balbo, G., Conte, G., Donatelli, S. and Franceschinis, G. (1995). *Modelling with Generalized Stochastic Petri Nets* (J. Wiley and Sons).

Almond, R. (1992). An extended example for testing GRAPHICAL-BE,LIEF, Tech. Rep. 6, Statistical Sciences Inc.

Amari, S., Dugan, J. and Misra, R. (1999). A separable method for incorporating imperfect fault-coverage into combinatorial models, *IEEE Transactions on Reliability* **48**, pp. 267–274.

Avizienis, A., Laprie, J. and Randell, B. (2001). Fundamental concepts of dependability, Tech. Rep. UCLA CSD10028, LAAS 01-154, NU CS-TR-739, UCLA, LAAS-CNRS, Newcastle Univ., URL http://citeseerx.ist.psu.edu/viewdoc/summary?doi=10.1.1.24.6074.

Barlow, R. (1988). Using Influence Diagrams, in C. Clarotti and D. Lindley (eds.), *Accelerated life testing and experts opinions in reliability*, pp. 145–157.

Bearfield, G. and Marsh, W. (2005). Generalising event trees using Bayesian networks with a case study of train derailment, in R. Winther, B. Gran and G. Dahll (eds.), *Lecture Notes in Computer Science*, Vol. 3688 (Springer), pp. 52–66.

Bedford, T. and Cooke, R. (2001). *Probabilistic Risk Analysis: Foundations and Methods* (Cambridge University Press).

Birnbaum, Z. W. (1969). On the importance of different components and a multicomponent system, in P. R. Korishnaiah (ed.), *Multivariable analysis II* (Academic Press, New York).

Bobbio, A., Ciancamerla, E., Franceschinis, G., Gaeta, R., Minichino, M. and Portinale, L. (2003a). Sequential application of heterogeneous models for the safety analysis of a control system: a case study, *Reliability Engineering and System Safety* **81**, pp. 269–280.

Bobbio, A., Franceschinis, G., Gaeta, R. and Portinale, L. (2003b). Parametric fault tree for the dependability analysis of redundant systems and its high-level Petri net semantics, *IEEE Transactions on Software Engineering* **29**, 3, pp. 270–287.

Bobbio, A., Portinale, L., Minichino, M. and Ciancamerla, E. (2001). Improving the analysis of dependable systems by mapping fault trees into bayesian networks, *Reliability Engineering and System Safety* **71**, pp. 249–260.

Bondy, A. and Murty, U. (2008). *Graph Theory* (Springer).

Borgonovo, E. (2007). Differential, criticality and birnbaum importance measures: An application to basic event, groups and SSCs in event trees and binary decision diagrams, *Reliability Engineering & System Safety* **92**, 10, pp. 1458–1467.

Boudali, H., Crouzen, P. and Stoelinga, M. (2007). Dynamic Fault Tree analysis using Input/Output Markov Chains, in *Proceedings 37th IEEE/IFIP Conference on Dependable Systems and Networks (DSN'07)*, pp. 708–717.

Boudali, H. and Dugan, J. (2005). A discrete-time Bayesian network reliability modeling and analysis framework, *Reliability Engineering and System Safety* **87**, pp. 337–349.

Boudali, H. and Dugan, J. (2006). A continuous-time Bayesian network reliability modeling and analysis framework, *IEEE Transactions on Reliability* **55**, pp. 86–97.

Bouissou, M. and Bon, J. (2003). A new formalism that combines advantages of fault-trees and Markov models: Boolean logic driven Markov processes, *Reliability Engineering and System Safety* **82**, 2, p. 149163.

Boyen, X. and Koller, D. (1998). Tractable inference for complex stochastic processes, in *Proceedings of the Conference on Uncertainty in Artificial Intelligence*, pp. 33–42, http://www.cs.stanford.edu/~xb/uai98/.

Casella, G. and Robert, C. (1996). Rao-Blackwellisation of sampling schemes, *Biometrika* **83**, 1, pp. 81–94.

Cassandra, A., Kaebling, L. and Littman, M. (1994). Acting optimally in partially observable stochastic domains, in *Proccedings of the 12th National Conference on Artificial Intelligence (AAAI 94)* (Seattle, WA), pp. 1023–1028.

Chan, H. and Darwiche, A. (2004). Sensitivity analysis in Bayesian networks: from single to multiple parameters, in *Proceedings of the 20th Conference on Uncertainty in Artificial Intelligence (UAI-04)* (Banff, AB), pp. 67–75.

Chan, H. and Darwiche, A. (2006). On the robustness of most probable explanations, in *Proceedings of the 22th Conference on Uncertainty in Artificial Intelligence (UAI-06)* (Cambridge, MA), pp. 63–71.

Chowdhury, B. and Baravc, S. (2006). Creating Cascading Failure Scenarios in Interconnected Power Systems, in *Proceedings of the IEEE Power Engineering Society General Meeting*, pp. 18–22.

Codetta-Raiteri, D. (2005). *Extended Fault Trees Analysis supported by Stochastic Petri Nets*, Ph.D. thesis, Dipartimento di Informatica, Università di Torino.

Codetta-Raiteri, D. (2011). Modelling and simulating a benchmark on dynamic reliability, as a Stochastic Activity Network, in *European Modeling & Simulation Symposium* (Rome, Italy), pp. 545–554.

Codetta-Raiteri, D. and Bobbio, A. (2005). Solving Dynamic Reliability Problems by means of Ordinary and Fluid Stochastic Petri Nets, in *European Safety and Reliability Conference* (Gdansk, Poland), pp. 381–389.

Codetta-Raiteri, D., Bobbio, A., Montani, S. and Portinale, L. (2012). A dynamic bayesian network based framework to evaluate cascading effects in a power grid, *Engineering Applications of Artificial Intelligence* **25**, 4, pp. 683–697.

Codetta-Raiteri, D., Franceschinis, G. and Gribaudo, M. (2006). Defining formalisms and models in the Draw-Net Modeling System, in *International Workshop on Modelling of Objects, Components and Agents* (Turku, Finland), pp. 123–144.

Codetta-Raiteri, D., Franceschinis, G., Iacono, M. and Vittorini, V. (2004). Repairable Fault Tree for the automatic evaluation of repair policies, in *International Conference on Dependable Systems and Networks* (IEEE Computer Society, Florence, Italy), pp. 659–668.

Codetta-Raiteri, D. and Portinale, L. (2014). Approaching dynamic reliability with predictive and diagnostic purposes by exploiting dynamic Bayesian networks, *Journal of Risk and Reliability (Proceedings of the Institution of Mechanical Engineers, Part O)* **228**, 5, pp. 488–50.

Codetta-Raiteri, D. and Portinale, L. (2015). Dynamic bayesian networks for fault detection, identification and recovery in autonomous spacecraft, *IEEE Transactions on Systems, Mans and Cybernetics: Systems* **45**, 1, pp. 13–24.

Codetta-Raiteri, D., Portinale, L. and Terruggia, R. (2014a). Decision networks for modeling and analysis of attack/defense scenarios in critical infrastructures, in *Proc. 27th International Florida Artifical Intelligence Research Society Conference(FLAIRS 14)* (Pensacola Beach, FL), pp. 24–27.

Codetta-Raiteri, D., Portinale, L. and Terruggia, R. (2014b). Quantitative evaluation of attack/defense scenarios through decision network modelling and analysis, in *Proc. 48th IEEE Intern. Carnahan Conference on Security Technology (ICCST 2014)* (Rome, Italy), pp. 432–437.

Conrady, S. and Jouffe, L. (2013). Introduction to Bayesian networks and BayesiaLab, Tech. rep., Bayesia Corp., Laval Cedex, France, URL http://library.bayesia.com/display/whitepapers/Introduction+to+Bayesian+Networks+and+BayesiaLab.

Console, L., Portinale, L., Torasso, P. and Theseider Duprè, D. (1992). Diagnosing time-arying misbehavior across different time points, in *Proc. 10th European Conference on Artificial Intelligence (ECAI 92)* (Vienna), pp. 369–373.

Console, L., Portinale, L., Torasso, P. and Theseider Duprè, D. (1994). Diagnosing time-varying misbehavior: an approach based on model decomposition, *Annals of Mathematics and Artificial Intelligence* **11**, 1-4, pp. 381–398.

Contini, S. and Poucet, A. (1990). Advances on fault tree and event tree techniques, in A. Colombo and A. S. de Bustamante (eds.), *System Reliability Assessment* (Kluwer Academic P.G.), pp. 77–102.

Cooper, G. (1988). A method for using belief networks as influence diagrams, pp. 55–63.

Cowell, R. G., Dawid, A. P., Lauritzen, S. L. and Spiegelhalter, D. J. (1999). *Probabilistic Networks and Expert Systems* (Springer).

Crucitti, P., Latora, V. and Marchiori, M. (2004). Model for cascading failures in complex networks, *Physical Review E* **69**, pp. 045104/1–4.

Dagum, P., Galper, A. and Horvitz, E. (1992). Dynamic network models for forecasting, in *Proceedings of the Eighth Conference Annual Conference on*

*Uncertainty in Artificial Intelligence (UAI-92)* (Morgan Kaufmann, San Mateo, CA), pp. 41–48.

D'Ambrosio, B. (1995). Local expression languages for probabilistic dependence, *International Journal for Approximate Reasoning* **13**, 1, pp. 61–81.

Dean, T. and Kanazawa, K. (1990). A model for reasoning about persistence and causation, *Computational Intelligence* **5**, 3, pp. 142–150.

DeMarco, C. (2001). Cascading network failure, *IEEE Control System Magazine*, pp. 40–51.

Diez, F. (1993). Parameter adjustment in bayes networks. the generalized noisy or-gate, in *Proceedings of the Ninth Conference Annual Conference on Uncertainty in Artificial Intelligence (UAI-93)* (Seattle, WA), pp. 99–105.

Distefano, S. and Puliafito, A. (2009). Dependability Evaluation with Dynamic Reliability Block Diagrams and Dynamic Fault Trees, *IEEE Transactions on Dependable and Secure Computing* **6**, 1, pp. 4–17.

Dobson, I., Carreras, B., Lynch, V. and Newmann, D. (2002). Critical points and transitions in an electric power transmission model for cascading failure blackouts, *Chaos* **12**, 4, pp. 985–994.

Dobson, I., Carreras, B., Lynch, V. and Newmann, D. (2004). Complex system analysis of series of blackouts: cascading failures, criticality and self-organization, in *Symposium on Bulk Power System Dynamics and Control* (Cortina d'Ampezzo, Italy).

Dobson, I., Carreras, B., Lynch, V. and Newmann, D. (2005). A loading-dependent model of probabilistic cascading failure, *Probability in the Engineering and Informational Sciences* **19**, pp. 15–32.

Domingos, P. and Pazzani, M. (1997). On the optimality of the simple Bayesian classifier under zero-one loss, *Machine Learning* **29**, pp. 103–137.

Donahoe, D., Zhao, K., Murray, S. and Ray, R. (2008). Accelerated life testing, in *Encyclopedia of Quantitative Risk Analysis and Assessment* (John Wiley & Sons).

Doucet, A., Freitas, N. D., Murphy, K. and Russell, S. (2000). RaoBlackwellised particle filtering for dynamic Bayesian networks, in *Proceedings of the Sixteenth conference on Uncertainty in Artificial Intelligence (UAI 00)* (Stanford, CA), pp. 176–183.

Druzdel, M. J. (1999). GeNIe: A development environment for graphical decision-analytic models, in *Proceedings of the 1999 Annual Symposium of the American Medical Informatics Association (AMIA-1999)* (Washington, DC), p. 1206.

Druzdel, M. J. (2005). Intelligent decision support systems based on SMILE, *Software 2.0* **2**, pp. 26–29.

Druzdzel, M. J. (1999). SMILE: Structural modeling, inference, and learning engine and GeNIe: A development environment for graphical decision-theoretic models, in *Proc. 16th National Conference on Artificial Intelligence (AAAI 99)* (Orlando, FL), pp. 902–903.

Duda, R. O. and Hart, P. E. (1973). *Pattern Classification and Scene Analysis* (J. Wiley).

Dugan, J. and Trivedi, K. (1989). Coverage modeling for dependability analysis of fault-tolerant systems, *IEEE Transactions on Computers* **38**, pp. 775–787.

Dugan, J. B., Bavuso, S. J. and Boyd, M. A. (1992). Dynamic Fault-Tree Models for Fault-Tolerant Computer Systems, *IEEE Transactions on Reliability* **41**, pp. 363–377.

Dugan, J. B., Sullivan, K. J. and Coppit, D. (2000). Developing a Low-Cost High-Quality Software Tool for Dynamic Fault-Tree Analysis, *IEEE Transactions on Reliability* **49**, pp. 49–59.

Dutuit, Y. and Rauzy, A. (1996). A Linear-Time Algorithm to Find Modules of Fault Trees, *IEEE Transactions on Reliability* **45**, pp. 422–425.

Dutuit, Y. and Rauzy, A. (2000). Efficient Algorithms to Assess Components and Gates Importances in Fault Tree Analysis, *Reliability Engineering and System Safety* **72(2)**, pp. 213–222.

Faza, A., Sedigh, S. and McMillin, B. (2007). Reliability Modeling for the Advanced Electric Power Grid, *Lecture Notes in Computer Science* **4680**, pp. 370–383.

Feather, M. S. (2004). Towards a unified approach to the representation of, and reasoning with, probabilistic risk information about software and its system interface, in *Proceedings of the 15th IEEE Int. Symp. on Software Software Reliability Engineering*, pp. 391–402.

Fenton, N. and Neil, M. (2012). *Risk Assessment and Decision Analysis with Bayesian Networks* (CRC Press).

Fung, R. and Chang, K. (1990). Weighing and integrating evidence for stochastic simulation in Bayesian networks, in M. Henrion (ed.), *Uncertainty in Artificial Intelligence*, Vol. 5 (North Holland), pp. 209–219.

Garribba, S., Guagnini, E. and Mussio, P. (1985). Multiple-valued logic trees: meaning and prime implicants, *IEEE Transactions on Reliability* **34**, pp. 436–472.

Geiger, D., Verma, T. and Pearl, J. (1989). d-separation: From theorems to algorithms, in *Proc. Annual Conference on Uncertainty in Artificial Intelligence (UAI-89)* (Windsor, ON), pp. 139–148.

Gilks, W., Richardson, S. and Spiegelhalter., D. (1996). *Markov Chain Monte Carlo in Practice* (Chapman and Hall).

Gimpel, K. (2006). Statistical inference in graphical models, http://ttic.uchicago.edu/~kgimpel/papers/da-02-draft.pdf.

Glover, W., Cross, J., Lucas, A., Stecki, C. and Stecki, J. (2010). The use of PHM for autonomous unmanned systems, in *Proc. Conf. PHM Society* (Portland, OR).

Gordon, N. (1993). Novel approach to nonlinear/non-Gaussian Bayesian state estimation, *IEE Proceedings (F)* **140**, 2, pp. 107–113.

Gribaudo, M., Sereno, M., Horvath, A. and Bobbio, A. (2001). Fluid Stochastic Petri Nets augmented with flush-out arcs: Modelling and analysis, *Discrete Event Dynamic Systems* **11(1/2)**, pp. 97–117.

Grzegorczyk, M. and Husmeier, D. (2009). Non-stationary continuous dynamic bayesian networks, in Y. Bengio, D. Schuurmans, J. Laftery, C. Williams and A. Culotta (eds.), *Advances in Neural Information Processing Systems. Series: Advances in neural information processing systems (22)*, pp. 682–690.

Gulati, R. and Dugan, J. B. (2003). A modular approach for analyzing static and dynamic fault-trees, in *Proceedings of the Annual Reliability and Maintainability Symposium*, pp. 57–63.

Heckerman, D., Mamdani, A. and Wellman, M. P. (1995). Real-world applications of Bayesian networks, **38**, 3, pp. 24–26.

Heckermann, D. and Breese, J. (1996). Causal independence for probability assessment and inference using Bayesian networks, *IEEE Transactions on System, Man and Cybernetics* **26**, 6, pp. 826–831.

Henley, E. and Kumamoto, H. (1981). *Reliability Engineering and Risk Assessment* (Englewood Cliffs).

Henrion, M. (1988). Propagating uncertainty in Bayesian networks by probabilistic logic sampling, in J. lemmer and L. Kanal (eds.), *Uncertainty in Artificial Intelligence*, Vol. 2 (North Holland), pp. 149–162.

Henrion, M. (1989). Some practical issues in constructing belief networks, in L. Kanal, T. Levitt and J. Lemmer (eds.), *Uncertainty in Artificial Intelligence*, Vol. 3 (Elsevier Science), pp. 161–173.

Howard, R. A. and Matheson, J. E. (1984). Influence diagrams, in R. A. Howard and J. E. Matheson (eds.), *Readings on the Principles and Applications of Decision Analysis*, Vol. II.

Hoyland, A. and Rausand, M. (1994). *System Reliability Theory* (John Wiley & Son).

Huang, C. and Darwiche, A. (1996). Inference in Belief Networks: A Procedural Guide, *International Journal of Approximate Reasoning* **15**, pp. 225–263.

J, J. S.-S. and Sucar, L. (2001). A methodology for reliable system design, in *Lecture Notes in Artificial Intelligence*, Vol. 2070 (Springer), pp. 734–745.

Jensen, F. and Jensen, F. (1994). Optimal junction trees, in *Proceedings of the 10th Conference on Uncertainty in Artificial Intelligence (UAI '94)* (Seattle, WA), pp. 360–366.

Jensen, F. V., Lauritzen, S. and Olesen, K. G. (1990). Bayesian updating in causal probabilistic networks by local computations, *Computational Statistics Quarterly* **4**, pp. 269–282.

Jensen, F. V. and Nielsen, T. D. (2007). *Bayesian Networks and Decision Graphs (2nd ed.)* (Springer).

Jones, B., Jenkinson, I., Yang, Z. and Wang, J. (2010). The use of Bayesian network modelling for maintenance planning in a manufacturing industry, *Reliability Engineering and System Safety* **95**, 3.

Jordan, M. I. (ed.) (1999). *Learning in Graphical Models* (MIT Press).

Jordan, M. I. (2004). Graphical models, *Statistical Science (special issue on Bayesian statistics)* **19**, pp. 140–155.

Kai, Y. (1990). Multistate fault-tree analysis, *Reliability Engineering and System Safety* **28**, 1, pp. 1–7.

Kim, D., Roy, A. and Trivedi, K. (2012). Scalable optimal countermeasure selection using implicit enmeration on attack countermeasure trees, in *Proc. 42nd Annual IEEE/IFIP Int. Conf. on Dependable Systems and Networks (DSN-12)*.

Kindermann, R. and Snell, J. (1980). *Markov Random Fields and their Applications* (American Mathematical Society), ISBN 0-8218-5001-6.

Kinney, R., Crucitti, P., Albert, R. and Latora, V. (2005). Modeling cascading failures in the north american power grid, *The European Physical Journal B* **46**, 1, pp. 101–107.

Kjaerulff, U. B. and Madsen, A. L. (2008). *Bayesian Networks and Inuence Diagrams: A Guide to Construction and Analysis* (Information Science and Statistics. Springer).

Koller, D. and Friedman, N. (2009). *Probabilistic Graphical Models: Principles and Techniques* (MIT Press).

Kordy, B., Mauw, S., Radomirovic, S. and Schweitzer, P. (2012). Attack defense trees, *The Journal of Logic and Computation* doi:10.1093/logcom/exs029.

Kovalenko, I. N., Kuznetsov, N. Y. and Pegg, P. A. (1997). Mathematical theory of Reliability of Time Dependent Systems with Practical Applications, *Wiley Series in Probability and Statistic* .

Kroeger, W. (2008). Critical infrastructures at risk: a need for a new conceptual approach and extended analytical tools, *Reliability Engineering and System Safety* **93**, pp. 1781–1787.

Kullback, S. and Leibler, R. (1951). On information and sufficiency, *Annals of Mathematical Statistics* **22**, 1, pp. 79–86.

Kwisthout, J. (2008). Complexity results for enumerating MPE and partial MAP, in *Proc. 4th European Workshop on Probabilistic Graphical Models (PGM '08)* (Hirtshals, Denmark), pp. 161–168.

Langseth, H., Nielsen, T., Rumí, R. and Salmerón, A. (2009). Inference in hybrid bayesian networks, *Reliability Engineering and System Safety* **94**, pp. 1499–1509.

Langseth, H. and Portinale, L. (2007). Bayesian networks in reliability, *Reliability Engineering and System Safety* **92**, 1, pp. 92–108.

Laprie, J. (1985). Dependable computing and fault tolerance: Concepts and terminology, in *Proc. 15th IEEE Int. Symp. on Fault-Tolerant Computing* (Ann Arbor, MI), pp. 2–11.

Lauritzen, S. and Jensen, F. (1997). Local computation with valuations from a commutative semigroup, *Annals of Mathematics and Artificial Intelligence* **21**, pp. 51–69.

Lauritzen, S. and Nilsson, D. (2001). Representing and solving decision problems with limited information, *Management Science* **47**, pp. 1235–1251.

Lauritzen, S. L. (2004). *Graphical Models* (Oxford University Press).

Lauritzen, S. L. and Spiegelhalter, D. (1988). Local computations with probabilities on graphical structures and their applications to expert systems (with discussion), *Journal of the Royal Statistical Society B* **50**, pp. 157–224.

Leveson, N. (1995). *Safeware: System safety and Computers* (Addison Wesley).

Li, Z. and D'Ambrosio, B. (1993). An efficient approach for finding the mpe in belief networks, in *Proceedings of the Ninth Conference Annual Conference on Uncertainty in Artificial Intelligence (UAI-93)* (San Francisco, CA), pp. 342–349.

Lininger, A., McMillin, B., Crow, M. and Chowdhury, B. (2007). Use of Max-

Flow on FACTS devices, in *Proceedings of the IEEE 39th North American Power Symposium* (Las Cruces, New Mexico, USA), pp. 288–294.

Malhotra, M. and Trivedi, K. (1995). Dependability modeling using Petri Nets, *IEEE Transactions on Reliability* **R-44**, pp. 428–440.

Manian, R., Coppit, D. W., Sullivan, K. J. and Dugan, J. B. (1999). Bridging the Gap Between Systems and Dynamic Fault Tree Models, in *Proceedings of the Annual Reliability and Maintainability Symposium*, pp. 105–111.

Marseguerra, M. and Zio, E. (1996). Monte Carlo Approach to PSA for dynamic process system, *Reliability Engineering and System Safety* **52**, pp. 227–241.

Martz, H. and Waller, R. (1990). Bayesian reliability analysis of complex series/ parallel systems of binomial subsystems and components, *Technometrics* **32**, 4, pp. 407–416.

Maua, D., de Campos, C. and Zaffalon, M. (2012). Solving limited memory influence diagrams, *Intern. Journal of Artificial Intelligence Research* **44**, pp. 97–140.

Meng, F. (2000). Relationships of Fussell–Vesely and Birnbaum importance to structural importance in coherent systems, *Reliability Engineering and System Safety* **67**, pp. 55–60.

Mengshoel, O. J., Darwiche, A., Cascio, K., M. Chavira, S. P. and Uckun, S. (2008). Diagnosing faults in electrical power systems of spacecraft and aircraft, in *Proceedings of Innovative Applications of Artificial Intelligence (IAAI-08)* (Chicago), pp. 1699–1705.

Montani, S., Portinale, L. and Bobbio, A. (2005). Dynamic Bayesian Networks for Modeling Advanced Fault Tree Features in Dependability Analysis, in *Advances in Safety and Reliability (ESREL 2005)*, Vol. 2 (Balkema), pp. 1415–1422.

Montani, S., Portinale, L., Bobbio, A. and Codetta-Raiteri, D. (2008). RADYBAN: a tool for reliability analysis of Dynamic Fault Trees through conversion into Dynamic Bayesian Networks, *Reliability Engineering and System Safety* **93**, 7, pp. 922–932.

Moral, S., Rumí, R. and Salmerón, A. (2001). Mixtures of truncated exponentials in hybrid bayesian networks, in *Proceedings of the 6th European Conference on Symbolic and Quantitative Approaches to Reasoning with Uncertainty (ECSQARU '01)* (Springer-Verlag, London, UK, UK), pp. 156–167.

Mosleh, A. (1988). Procedures for treating common cause failure in safety and reliability studies, Tech. Rep. CR-4780, NUREG.

Motter, A. and Lai, Y. (2002). Cascade based attacks on complex networks, *Physical Review E* **66**, pp. 065102/1–4.

Murphy, K. (2001). The Bayes Net Toolbox for Matlab, *Computing Science and Statistics* **33**.

Murphy, K., Weiss, Y. and Jordan, M. (1999). Loopy belief propagation for approximate inference: an empirical study, in *Proc. 15th Inter. Conference on Uncertainty in Artificial Intelligence (UAI 99)* (Stockholm, Sweden), pp. 467–476.

Murphy, K. P. (2002). *Dynamic Bayesian Networks: Representation, Inference and Learning*, Ph.D. thesis, UC Berkeley, Computer Science Division.

Neapolitan, R. (1990). *Probabilistic Reasoning In Expert Systems: Theory and Algorithms* (J. Wiley).

Nelson, W. (1980). Accelerated life testing - step-stress models and data analyses, *IEEE Transactions on Reliability* **29**, 2, pp. 103–108.

Newman, M. (2005). A measure of betweenness centrality based on random walks, *Social Networks* **27**, pp. 39–54.

Ou, Y. and Dugan, J. B. (2000). Sensitivity analysis of modular dynamic fault trees, in *IEEE International Computer Performance and Dependability Symposium*.

Pearl, J. (1987). Evidential reasoning using stochastic simulation of causal models, *Artifical Intelligence* **32**, pp. 245–257.

Pearl, J. (1988). *Probabilistic Reasoning in Intelligence Systems: Networks of Plausible Inference* (Morgan Kaufmann).

Poole, D. and Mackworth, A. (2010). Dynamic decision networks, in *Artificial Intelligence: Foundations of Computational Agents* (Cambridge Univ. Press).

Poole, D. and Zhang, N. (1996). Exploiting causal independence in Bayesian network inference, *Journal of Artificial Intelligence Research* **5**, p. 301–328.

Portinale, L. (1992). Modeling uncertain temporal evolutions, in *Proc. 8th International Conference on Uncertainty in Artificial Intelligence (UAI 92)* (Stanford, CA), pp. 244–251.

Portinale, L., Bobbio, A., Codetta-Raiteri, D. and Montani, S. (2007). Compiling dynamic fault trees into dynamic Bayesian nets for reliability analysis: the Radyban tool, in *Bayesian Modeling Applications Workshop* (Vancouver, Canada).

Portinale, L. and Codetta-Raiteri, D. (2009). Generalizing continuous time bayesian networks with immediate nodes, in *Proceedings of the Workshop on Graph Structures for Knowledge Representation and Reasoning* (Pasadena, USA), pp. 12–17.

Portinale, L. and Codetta-Raiteri, D. (2011a). ARPHA: an FDIR architecture for Autonomous Spacecrafts based on Dynamic Probabilistic Graphical Models, in *Proc. ESA Workshop on AI in Space @ IJCAI 2011* (Barcelona, Spain).

Portinale, L. and Codetta-Raiteri, D. (2011b). Using dynamic decision networks and extended fault trees for autonomous fdir, in *Proceedings of the International Conference on Tools with Artificial Intelligence* (IEEE Computer Society, Boca Raton, USA), pp. 480–484.

Portinale, L., Codetta-Raiteri, D. and Montani, S. (2010). Supporting Reliability Engineers in Exploiting the Power of Dynamic Bayesian Networks, *International Journal of Approximate Reasoning* **51**, 2, pp. 179 195.

Portinale, L. and Torasso, P. (1997). A comparative analysis of Horn models and Bayesian Networks for diagnosis, in *Proc. 5th Congress of the Italian Association for Artificial Intelligence (AI\*IA97), Lecture Notes in Artificial Intelligence 1321* (Rome, Italy), pp. 254–265.

Pourbeik, P., Kundur, P. S. and Taylor, C. W. (2006). The anatomy of a power grid blackout, *IEEE Power & Energy Magazine*, pp. 22–29.

Pourret, O., Naim, P. and Marcot, B. (2008). *Bayesian Networks: A Practical Guide to Applications* (J. Wiley).

Puterman, M. (1994). *Markov Decision Processes, Discrete Stochastic Dynamic Programming* (John Wiley & Sons).

Rabiner, L. (1989). A tutorial on hidden Markov models and selected applications in speech recognition, *Proceedings of the IEEE* **77**, 2, pp. 257–286.

Rauzy, A. (1993). New Algorithms for Fault Trees Analysis, *Reliability Engineering & System Safety* **05(59)**, pp. 203–211.

Rinaldi, S. M., Peerenboom, J. P. and Kelley, T. K. (2001). Identifying, understanding, and analyzing critical infrastructure interdependencies, *IEEE Control Systems Magazine* **21**, 6, pp. 11–25.

Rish, I. (2001). An empirical study of the naive bayes classifier, in *Proc. IJCAI 2001 Workshop on Empirical Methods in Artificial Intelligence* (Seattle, WA), pp. 41–46.

Robinson, P., Shirley, M., Fletcher, D., Alena, R., Duncavage, D. and Lee, C. (2003). Applying model-based reasoning to the FDIR of the command and data handling subsystem of the ISS, in *Proc. iSAIRAS 2003* (Nara, Japan).

Romessis, C. and Mathioudakis, K. (2006). Bayesian network approach for gas path fault diagnosis, *Journal of engineering for gas turbines and power* **128**, 1, pp. 64–72.

Roy, A., Kim, D. and Trivedi, K. (2011). Attack countermeasure trees (ACT): towards unifying the constructs of attack and defense trees, in *Security and Communication Networks* (J. Wiley).

Roy, A., Kim, D. and Trivedi, K. (2012). Scalable optimal countermeasure selection using implicit enmeration on attack countermeasure trees, in *Proc. 42nd Annual IEEE/IFIP International Conference on Dependable Systems and Networks (DSN 2012)* (Boston, MA).

Sahner, R., Trivedi, K. and Puliafito, A. (1996). *Performance and Reliability Analysis of Computer Systems; An Example-based Approach Using the SHARPE Software Package* (Kluwer Academic Publisher).

SalarKaleji, F. and Dayyani, A. (2013). A survey on Fault Detection, Isolation and Recovery (fdir) module in satellite onboard software, in *Proc. 6th International Conference on Recent Advances in Space Technologies (RAST), 2013* (IEEE Press, Instanbul), pp. 545–548.

Sanders, W. and Meyer, J. (2001). Stochastic activity networks: Formal definitions and concepts, *Lecture Notes in Computer Science* **2090**, pp. 315–343.

Scheyner, O. (2004). *Scenario Graphs and Attack Graphs*, Ph.D. thesis, Carnegie Mellon University, http://www.milena.org/thesis/sg-ag.pdf.

Schneeweiss, W. G. (1999). *The Fault Tree Method* (LiLoLe Verlag).

Schneier, B. (2000). *Secrets and Lies: digital security in a networked world* (J. Wiley).

Schwabacher, M., Feather, M. and Markosian, L. (2008). Verification and validation of advanced fault detection, isolation and recovery for a NASA space system, in *Proc. Int. Symp. on Software Reliability Engineering* (Seattle, WA).

Shachter, R. D. (1988). Probabilistic inference and inuence diagrams, *Operation Research* **36**, pp. 589–605.

Shafer, G. and Shenoy, P. (1990). Probability propagation, *Annals of Mathematics and Artificial Intelligence* **2**, pp. 327–352.

Shaw, W. (2012). SCADA system vulnerabilities to cyber attack, http://www.electricenergyonline.com/?page=show_article&mag=23&article=181.

Shenoy, P. (2006). Inference in hybrid bayesian networks using mixtures of gaussians, in *Proceedings of the Twenty-Second Conference Annual Conference on Uncertainty in Artificial Intelligence (UAI-06)* (AUAI Press, Arlington, Virginia), pp. 428–436.

Sommestad, T., Ekstedt, M. and Johnson, P. (2009). Cyber security risks assessment with bayesian defense graphs and architectural models, in *System Sciences, 2009. HICSS '09. 42nd Hawaii International Conference on*, pp. 1 –10, doi:10.1109/HICSS.2009.141.

Srinivas, S. (1993). A generalization of the noisy-or model, in *Proceedings of the Ninth Conference Annual Conference on Uncertainty in Artificial Intelligence (UAI-93)* (Seattle, WA), pp. 208–215.

Sullivan, K. J., Dugan, J. B. and Coppit, D. (1999). The Galileo fault tree analysis tool, in *Proc. of the Annual Int. Symposium on Fault-Tolerant Computing* (Madison, WI USA), pp. 232–235.

Tang, Z. and Dugan, J. B. (2004). Minimal Cut Set/Sequence Generation for Dynamic Fault Trees, in *Procedings of the Annual Reliability and Maintainability Symposium* (Los Angeles, CA USA), pp. 207–213.

Torres-Toledano, J. and Sucar, L. (1998). Bayesian networks for reliability analysis of complex systems, in *Lecture Notes in Artificial Intelligence*, Vol. 1484, pp. 195–206.

van Gerven, M. and Diez, F. (2006). Selecting strategies for infinite-horizon dynamic LIMID, in *proc. 3rd European Workshop on Probabilistic Graphical Models*, pp. 12–15.

von Neumann, J. and Morgenstern, O. (1953). *Theory of Games and Economic Behavior* (Princeton University Press).

Wang, C., Xing, L. and Levitin, G. (2012). Propagated failure analysis for non-repairable systems considering both global and selective effects, *Reliability Engineering & System Safety* **99**, pp. 96–104.

Weber, P. and Jouffe, L. (2003). Reliability modelling with dynamic Bayesian networks, in *Symposium on Fault Detection, Supervision and Safety of Technical Processes* (Washington DC, USA), pp. 57–62.

Wermuth, N. and Lauritzen, S. (1990). On substantive research hypotheses, conditional independence graphs and graphical chain models, *Journal of the Royal Statistical Society B* **52**, pp. 21–50.

Whittaker, J. (2009). *Graphical Models in Applied Multivariate Statistics* (J. Wiley).

Winsper, M. and Chli, M. (2013). Decentralized supply chain formation using max-sum loopy belief propagation, *Computational Intelligence* **29**, 2, pp. 281–309.

Wood, A. (1985). Multistate block diagrams and fault trees, *IEEE Transactions on Reliability* **34**, pp. 236–240.

Xing, L. and Amari, S. (2008). Fault tree analysis, in K. Misra (ed.), *Handbook of Performability Engineering* (Springer).

Xing, L. and Levitin, G. (2011). Combinatorial algorithm for reliability analysis of multistate systems with propagated failures and failure isolation effect, *IEEE Transactions on Systems, Man and Cybernetics, Part A: Systems and Humans* **41**, 6, pp. 1156–1165.

Xing, L. and Michel, H. E. (2006). Integrated modeling for wireless sensor networks reliability and security, in *Proceedings 52nd Annual Reliability and Maintainability Symposium (RAMS 2006)* (Newport Beach, CA), pp. 594–600.

Yongli, Z., Limin, H. and Jinling, L. (2006). Bayesian network-based approach for power system fault diagnosis, *IEEE Transactions on Power Delivery* **21**, pp. 634–639.

Zhang, H. (2004). The optimality of naive Bayes, in *Proc. of 17th FLAIRS Conference* (AAAI Press), pp. 562–567.

Zhang, N. and Poole, D. (1994). A simple approach to Bayesian network computation, in *Proc. 10th Canadian Conference on Artificial Intelligence*, pp. 171–178.

Zweig, G. (1996). *A forward-backward algorithm for inference in Bayesian networks and an empirical comparison with HMMs*, Master's thesis.

# Index

**Symbols**

1.5JT algorithm .. 62, 137, 161, 205, 227

2-TBN ................. 58, 67, 226

**A**

AgenaRisk ...................... 49

anomaly ...................... 168

Anomaly Resolution and Prognostic Health management for Autonomy (ARPHA) ............... 142, 158

approximate inference .... 47, 48, 66

artificial intelligence ............. 38

Attack Countermeasure Tree (ACT) 177, 180

Attack Defense Tree (ADT) ..... 177

Attack Graph .............. 175, 176

Attack Tree (AT) ............... 176

Autonomy Building Block (ABB) ... 167

availability .......... 6, 93, 108, 151

**B**

BayesiaLab ............... 49, 60, 67

Bayesian Network (BN) .. 38, 39, 69

belief propagation .......... 47, 224

belief updating ................. 224

benchmark .................... 192

Binary Decision Diagram (BDD) 19, 23, 33

Birnbaum Importance (BI) .. 18, 82, 184

BK algorithm ..... 62, 137, 168, 232

bk-cluster ............. 62, 142, 232

BNToolbox ..................... 49

Boolean gates .... 11, 33, 81, 88, 139

    AND ........ 11, 24, 88, 151, 162

    k out of n (k:n) ............ 11, 88

    NOT .......................... 12

    OR .......... 11, 26, 88, 151, 162

    XOR (eXclusive OR) .......... 12

**C**

C++ .......................... 142

canonical

    form ........................ 59

    variable ..................... 59

Cardiac Assist System (CAS) ... 105

cascading failures .............. 145

causal independence ......... 44, 97

Causal Independence (CI) interaction 98

Chain Graph .................... 38

chance node ................... 49

chord ......................... 220

clique ......................... 220

combinatorial analysis ........... 33

combinatorial models . 5, 10, 28, 147, 191

combined inference .............. 46

Common Cause Failure (CCF) ... 74

conditional independence 42, 88, 212

Conditional Probability Table (CPT) 40, 89, 109, 141, 151, 163, 197

confidentiality ..................... 1
conversion ......... 88, 115, 137, 166
Cooper's algorithm .............. 54
countermeasure ................. 187
coverage factor ................... 78
coverage set ................... 105
    basic coverage set ............ 107
critical infrastructures .......... 145
criticality ....................... 17
cumulative distribution function (cdf)
    6, 205
cut set ...................... 15, 69

**D**
d-separation .................... 42
Decision Network (DN) . 38, 49, 123,
    127, 176, 181, 182
decision node ................... 49
density function ................... 8
dependability 1, 28, 89, 139, 146, 157
diagnosis .............. 120, 158, 207
diagnostic inference .......... 46, 81
Directed Acyclic Graph (DAG) .. 10,
    38
discretization step ...... 89, 116, 140
divorcing ...................... 166
dormancy factor ......... 24, 88, 113
Draw-Net ...................... 138
DRPFTproc .................... 117
Dynamic Bayesian Network (DBN) .
    58, 87, 108, 137, 147, 159, 192
Dynamic Decision Network (DDN) ..
    67
Dynamic Fault Tree (DFT) .. 23, 29,
    33, 87, 105, 137, 146, 159, 191
    Extended Dynamic Fault Tree
        (EDFT) .............. 171
dynamic gates .. 23, 33, 87, 105, 139
    Cold Spare gate (CSP) .... 24, 87
    Functional Dependency gate
        (FDEP) .. 23, 87, 106, 163
    Hot Spare gate (HSP) ..... 24, 87
    Priority AND gate (PAND) 23, 87
    Probabilistic Dependency gate
        (PDEP) .............. 87
    one-shot PDEP ........... 93

    persistent PDEP ......... 93
    Sequence Enforcing gate (SEQ) ...
        24, 87
    Warm Spare gate (WSP) .. 24, 29,
        87, 105
dynamic reliability ............. 191

**E**
error ............................. 3
Event Handler ................. 167
events ......................... 10
    Basic Event (BE) .. 11, 24, 34, 97,
        105
    dependent events ....... 23, 29, 93
    Intermediate Event (IE) ....... 11
    Top Event (TE) ... 11, 26, 34, 69,
        116, 162
    trigger event .............. 23, 87
evidence .......... 46, 142, 206, 207
    soft evidence ............... 225
expected utility (EU) ........... 168
explaining away ................. 46

**F**
factor .......................... 38
factorization ......... 39, 42, 44, 212
failure .......................... 3
Failure Mode Effect Analysis
    (FMEA) .................... 157
failure on demand ............. 194
failure rate .... 8, 11, 24, 29, 88, 112,
    140, 147, 191
    Constant Failure Rate (CFR) ... 7
    Decreasing Failure Rate (DFR) . 7
    Increasing Failure Rate (IFR) ... 7
fault ............................. 3
Fault Detection, Identification and
    Recovery (FDIR) ......... 68, 157
fault forecasting .................. 3
fault prediction ................ 158
fault prevention .................. 3
fault removal ..................... 3
fault tolerance ................ 3, 15
Fault Tree (FT) .. 10, 23, 29, 33, 69,
    87, 119, 137, 149, 176, 191
    coherent Fault Tree ............ 12

Fault Tree Analysis (FTA) ... 15, 69, 158

Fault-Error-Failure chain .......... 3

filtering ... 61, 63, 116, 140, 205, 227

firing ...................... 30, 195

firing rate ....................... 31

formalism ................. 137, 159

forward interface algorithm ...... 62

frontier algorithm ............... 62

fully factorized ................. 142

Fussell-Vesely Importance (FVI) . 18, 82, 131, 184

**G**

Galileo ..................... 36, 115

Genie ........... 45, 49, 57, 61, 67

grace period ................... 194

Graphical User Interface (GUI) . 138

**H**

hazard ......................... 7

Hugin ................... 47, 49, 57

Hybrid Bayesian Network (HBN)  39

**I**

I-map ...................... 42, 44

IEEE 118 Bus Test Case ........ 148

impact ........................ 185

importance factors .............. 18

   Critical Importance Factor (CIF) . 18

   Diagnostic Impact Factor (DIF)  18

   Marginal Impact Factor (MIF)  18

   Risk Achievement Worth (RAW) . 19

   Risk Reduction Worth (RAW) . 19

in-clique ...................... 228

inference . 87, 119, 137, 153, 159, 199

Influence Diagram (ID) ..... 52, 188

informational arc ............... 50

integrity ........................ 1

interdependencies .............. 145

**J**

join tree ...................... 219

joint probability .......... 120, 140

junction tree ... 47, 61, 121, 159, 219

**L**

layer

   anterior .............. 59, 90, 140

   ulterior ......... 59, 89, 109, 140

leak probability ................ 45

LEON3 ........................ 169

level variation rate ............. 192

LIMID .................... 52, 188

**M**

main component ........ 24, 29, 105

maintainability ................ 1, 6

maintenance ............. 3, 69, 123

marking ............... 30, 154, 195

Markov Chain (MC) . 28, 30, 58, 191

   Continuous Time Markov Chain (CTMC) .. 29, 32, 88, 115, 146, 195

   Discrete Time Markov Chain (DTMC) .......... 28, 59

Markov Random Field (MRF) ... 38

Mars rover .................... 157

Maximum A Posteriori assignment (MAP) ................... 48, 85

Maximum Expected Utility (MEU) . 49, 124

Mean Time To Failure (MTTF)  7, 17

measurement-based method ....... 4

memory-less property ............ 8

Minimal Cut Sequence (MCSeq) . 36

Minimal Cut Set (MCS) . 15, 33, 195

   MCS order ................... 15

Minimal Path Set (MPS) ........ 15

Minimum Expected Cost (MEC)  124

mission step ................... 169

mission time . 34, 115, 140, 153, 167, 205

model-based method ............. 4

modules ................. 33, 97, 114

   Combinatorial Solution Module (CSM) ................. 33

   State space Solution Module (SSM) ................. 33

monitoring ................. 61, 63

Monte Carlo simulation ......... 192
moral graph ................... 220
Most Probable Explanation (MPE) . 48
Most Severe Prevailing (MSP) ... 98
MSBNx ........................ 49
multi-state components ..... 29, 161
multi-state variables ........ 78, 151
multiprocessor .................. 12

**N**
necessary evidence ............... 53
negative exponential distribution . 8, 14, 29, 105, 147, 192
Netica ......................... 49
no-forgetting .................... 52
node weight ................... 220
noisy gates ............. 44, 76, 182
   noisy-AND ............... 45, 77
   noisy-MAX .................. 45
   noisy-OR ................. 44, 77

**O**
observation stream ............. 116
observations ... 3, 119, 141, 154, 158, 205
off-board process .............. 159
on-board process .............. 158
order .......................... 193
out-clique ..................... 228
outage ......................... 147
outgoing interface .............. 226
overload ....................... 145

**P**
parallel module ................ 147
Petri Net (PN) .......... 28, 29, 191
   Fluid Stochastic Petri Net (FSPN) 195
   Generalized Stochastic Petri Net (GSPN) .. 31, 88, 154, 195
places ................. 29, 154, 195
   fluid places .................. 195
plan ........................... 160
policy ....................... 52, 53
potential ...................... 224

power grid ..................... 145
Power Supply Subsystem (PSS) . 159
prediction .... 61, 116, 140, 153, 227
predictive inference .......... 46, 81
Probabilistic Graphical Model (PGM) ...... 19, 38, 137, 158, 191
Probabilistic Networks Library (PNL) ....................... 142
probability density function (pdf) 7, 205
prognosis ................. 158, 206

**Q**
qualitative analysis ........... 15, 20
quantitative analysis . 22, 28, 88, 140

**R**
RADyBaN  59, 63, 64, 115, 137, 153, 162, 192
reachability graph .......... 32, 195
recovery ............... 28, 95, 158
   preventive recovery .......... 168
   reactive recovery ............ 168
recovery policy ............... 167
region ......................... 192
regularity assumption ........... 52
reliability .... 6, 10, 29, 36, 113, 137, 157, 191
Reliability Block Diagram (RBD) 10, 70, 151, 191
   Dynamic Reliability Block Diagrams (DRBD) .... 191
reliability function ............... 8
repair .......... 4, 29, 104, 151, 194
Repair Box (RB) .............. 105
repair policy ......... 105, 137, 151
   Component Repair (CR) 105, 151
   Subsystem Global Repair (SGR) .. 106
   Subsystem Local Repair (SLR) ... 106
repair rate ....... 105, 141, 151, 194
repairable system ........ 6, 124, 125
Return on Investment (ROI) ... 125, 133, 188
risk ................. 3, 18, 145, 185

rover simulator (ROSEX) ....... 169
RTEMS ....................... 169
running intersection property ... 220

**S**
safety ...................... 18, 157
safety critical systems ............. 1
SamIam ....................... 49
scenario ................... 146, 160
security ........................ 175
sensor ......................... 169
sepset ......................... 220
    cost ........................ 222
    mass ....................... 222
sequentially dependent failures ... 79
series module .................. 150
series/parallel diagram .......... 147
Shafer-Shenoy architecture ....... 47
Shannon's decomposition ........ 20
simulation ............ 5, 28, 32, 191
Single Policy Updating (SPU) .... 54
smoothing 61, 119, 140, 153, 206, 227
spacecraft ..................... 157
spare components . 4, 23, 24, 87, 113
    cold spare ................... 115
    warm spare .......... 24, 88, 106
state .......................... 28
    anomalous state ...... 28, 30, 166
    failed state ......... 28, 108, 166
    normal state ....... 2, 28, 30, 166
state dependent failure rates .... 193
state space analysis ....... 27, 28, 33
state space based models . 5, 28, 191
state transitions ...... 5, 28, 30, 192
stationary stochastic process ..... 58
statistical independence .......... 10
steady-state ................. 29, 32
Stochastic Activity Network (SAN) .
    195
strategy ............... 52, 53, 132
    expected cost ........... 124, 129
    expected utility .......... 54, 124
    optimal ..................... 54
System Context ............... 167

**T**
time step ..... 28, 115, 139, 167, 197
tokens .................... 29, 195
trail .......................... 42
transient ................... 29, 32
transition rate .................. 29
transitions ................. 29, 195
    immediate transitions ......... 31
    timed transitions ............. 31
translation ............. 88, 137, 149
triangulation ................... 220
TSIM ......................... 169

**U**
unavailability .................. 6, 93
Unified Modelling Language (UML) .
    167
unreliability . 5, 17, 81, 115, 129, 192
unreliability function ............. 8
utility function ................. 166

**V**
v-structure ..................... 42
value node ..................... 49
variable elimination ............. 47
Verification of Impact Failures by
    Model Checking (VeriFIM) ... 157

**X**
XML (eXtensible Markup Language)
    138

Printed in the United States
By Bookmasters